Love Is . . .

Love Is…

366 Meditations
on God's Heart of Love

Sarah Hornsby

Chosen Books

A Division of Baker Book House
Grand Rapids, Michigan 49516

© 1993 by Sarah Hornsby

Published by Chosen Books
a division of Baker Book House Company
P.O. Box 6287, Grand Rapids, MI 49516–6287

Library of Congress Cataloging-in-Publication Data

Hornsby, Sarah.
    Love is— : 366 meditations on God's heart of love / Sarah
Hornsby.
        p.   cm.
    ISBN 0-8007-9208-4
    1. God—Love—Meditations. 2. Love—Religious aspects—
Christianity. 3. Bible—Meditations. 4. Devotional calendars.
I. Title.
BT140.H65   1993
231'.6—dc20   93-4155

Unless otherwise noted, Scripture texts are from the Holy Bible, New
International Version®. NIV ®. Copyright 1973, 1978, 1984 by Interna-
tional Bible Society. Used by permission of Zondervan Publishing House.
All rights reserved.

Verses marked RSV are taken from the Revised Standard Version of the
Bible, copyright 1946, 1952, 1971, and 1973 by the Division of Christian
Education of the National Council of the Churches of Christ in the United
States of America.

Verses marked KJV are from the King James Version.

This book is dedicated to
James and Maria Hornsby-Tichy

Acknowledgments

Special thanks to **Jane Campbell,**
always encouraging editor and friend;
and my husband, **Jim**, for loving me
and my warts!

Contents

Introduction

Love Is . . . was written as I meditated on Scripture to discover what true love is. What is this love that is the basis of the universe, that God *is*? What is this love that Jesus exemplified by laying down His life? What is this love that He commanded us to live—loving God with all our heart, soul, mind and strength, our neighbors as ourselves?

As I discover all the things love is, I learn how full and rich and complete is God's love for me, for my loved ones, for the poor, for the enemy. I also discover my own inadequacy and inability to love that kind of love.

As I studied *Strong's Exhaustive Concordance* and *The New International Version Bible Concordance*, looking for Scriptures that describe love, I found 366 words that express qualities God has toward me or that I have toward God, my neighbor and myself when I am filled with God's love. Isaiah, the Psalms, the Gospels, the letters of Paul, Peter, James and John are rich with illustrations of what love is.

Writing Love Is . . . has been meaningful to me as I meditate on the ways my husband, Jim, has loved me through the years—32 of them!—and ponder how I can be more loving to him. What does it mean to be loving? How do you learn to fit into another's changing person, respecting the other's gifts, enabling the other, without losing yourself?

Love Is . . . was written as I watched the romance of our oldest son, James, and the lovely Austrian, Maria, blossom and mature for two years. As they worked together with youth in Matagalpa, getting to know each other through and through, I saw their indecision, their hesitation, their wondering if this was really "the one." I saw their devastation when one of them said that it was not really right, at least not yet.

The manuscript was completed on time—another marvel to me!—just before we flew to Salzburg, Austria, for James and Maria's wedding, a storybook affair, September 12, 1992. Though few Austrians would admit to having seen *The Sound of Music*, Maria's parents live only a block from the lake and mansion portrayed in that family favorite about Maria von Trapp.

In Austria I was confronted with an unexpected twist to the story, and to a deeper understanding of love. I learned that Maria's father had been in the German army during the second World War. Although he was an unwilling conscript—the Austrians having been taken over by Hitler's Third Reich early in the war—my mind could not help but race back to childhood memories of radio commentaries on the horrors being committed by the enemy, the Germans. Learning the German language was repugnant to me because subconsciously I still had not forgiven the Germans for that war. And now my son was marrying one associated with "the enemy."

"Love your enemy," Jesus said.

From Maria's family we learned that at the end of the war more than half the homes in Salzburg, including historic buildings like St. Peter's Church, were bombed by the Allies. More than 40,000 people were made homeless. Those people were victims of destruction from both sides, and our U.S. bombs caused them much anguish. The gracious hospitality we received from

13

Maria's family, therefore, was even more precious and poignant.

Maria is a Roman Catholic believer, and in Austria I learned that some of the prince-archbishops, in their efforts to rid their land of "undesirable" Protestants and Jews, committed several purges and made refugees of those non-Catholic citizens. It was gratifying for me, as the wife of a Protestant pastor, to learn that in recent years an archbishop had apologized publicly for those atrocities. "Let no debt remain outstanding, except the continuing debt to love one another, for he who loves his fellow man has fulfilled the law" (Romans 13:8).

My prayer for James and Maria as they begin their new life together, and for each reader of this book, is that the Holy Spirit will breathe through the Scriptures chosen and the meditations about those Scriptures and that God's love may become more real in everyday life.

As I wrote these words, I confess, they often convicted me of my own failure and lack of love, so I know this may not always be a comfortable book to read. Nevertheless, though I stumble and fall time and again, Jesus commissions me as God's love ambassador in a hurting world.

14

And God promises to enter my everyday circumstances with a surge of holy power to love. He promises to cleanse my faults and failures when I forgive others for theirs. He promises to *be in me* that love that I and others need.

"Words, words, words," said Eliza Doolittle disgustedly to her poetic admirer in *My Fair Lady*. Studying the words of love is obviously not enough, but they do give insights and reveal those areas that need to be warmed and fanned into the godly flame of compassionate, tender-and-tough love.

The good news is this: *We are not alone.* The Lord of love has come to us, as we are, and will be at home in us, making all things new.

"Let all that you do be done in love" (1 Corinthians 16:14, RSV).

Sarah Hornsby
Matagalpa, Nicaragua
September 28, 1992

January
Love Is New

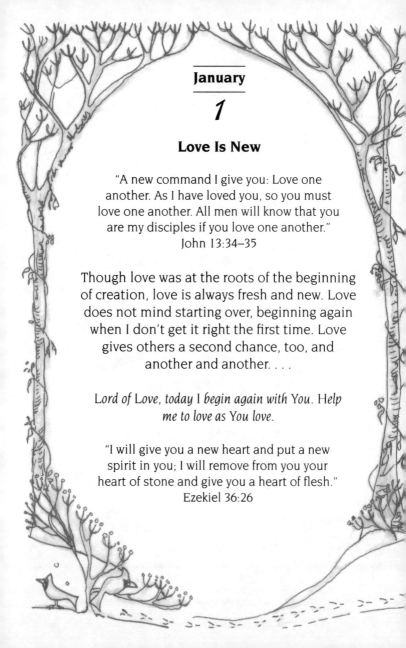

January

1

Love Is New

"A new command I give you: Love one another. As I have loved you, so you must love one another. All men will know that you are my disciples if you love one another."
John 13:34–35

Though love was at the roots of the beginning of creation, love is always fresh and new. Love does not mind starting over, beginning again when I don't get it right the first time. Love gives others a second chance, too, and another and another. . . .

Lord of Love, today I begin again with You. Help me to love as You love.

"I will give you a new heart and put a new spirit in you; I will remove from you your heart of stone and give you a heart of flesh."
Ezekiel 36:26

Love Is Now

And now these three remain: faith, hope and
love. But the greatest of these is love.
I Corinthians 13:13

Love is right now, here to stay. I can count on
love being for me now: yesterday, today and
forever. As I look back into my past, I can see
love's quiet work.

*Lord of Love, into all I am now, I ask You
to come.*

To him who is able to keep you from falling
and to present you before his glorious presence without fault and with great joy—to the
only God our Savior be glory, majesty, power
and authority, through Jesus Christ our Lord,
before all ages, now and forevermore! Amen.
Jude 24–25

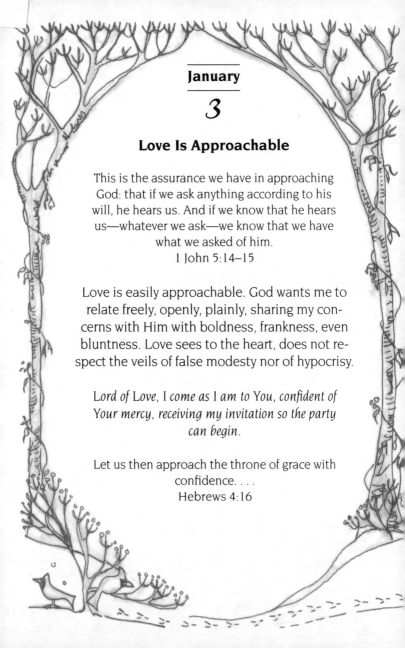

January

3

Love Is Approachable

This is the assurance we have in approaching
God: that if we ask anything according to his
will, he hears us. And if we know that he hears
us—whatever we ask—we know that we have
what we asked of him.
1 John 5:14–15

Love is easily approachable. God wants me to
relate freely, openly, plainly, sharing my concerns with Him with boldness, frankness, even
bluntness. Love sees to the heart, does not respect the veils of false modesty nor of hypocrisy.

*Lord of Love, I come as I am to You, confident of
Your mercy, receiving my invitation so the party
can begin.*

Let us then approach the throne of grace with
confidence. . . .
Hebrews 4:16

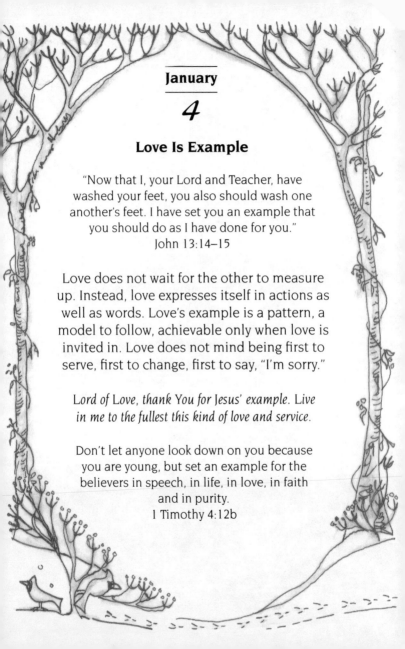

January

4

Love Is Example

"Now that I, your Lord and Teacher, have
washed your feet, you also should wash one
another's feet. I have set you an example that
you should do as I have done for you."
John 13:14–15

Love does not wait for the other to measure
up. Instead, love expresses itself in actions as
well as words. Love's example is a pattern, a
model to follow, achievable only when love is
invited in. Love does not mind being first to
serve, first to change, first to say, "I'm sorry."

*Lord of Love, thank You for Jesus' example. Live
in me to the fullest this kind of love and service.*

Don't let anyone look down on you because
you are young, but set an example for the
believers in speech, in life, in love, in faith
and in purity.
1 Timothy 4:12b

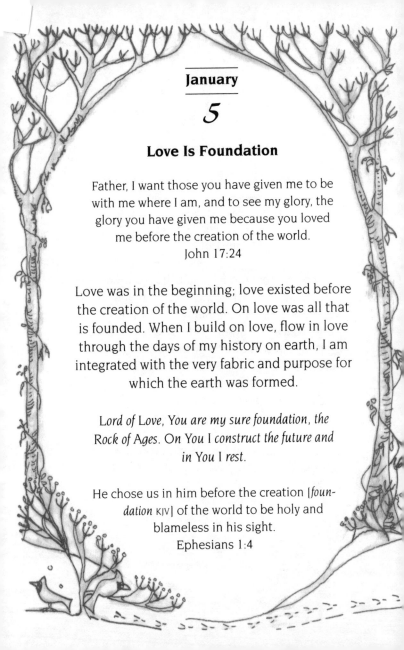

January

5

Love Is Foundation

Father, I want those you have given me to be
with me where I am, and to see my glory, the
glory you have given me because you loved
me before the creation of the world.
John 17:24

Love was in the beginning; love existed before
the creation of the world. On love was all that
is founded. When I build on love, flow in love
through the days of my history on earth, I am
integrated with the very fabric and purpose for
which the earth was formed.

*Lord of Love, You are my sure foundation, the
Rock of Ages. On You I construct the future and
in You I rest.*

He chose us in him before the creation [*foundation* KJV] of the world to be holy and
blameless in his sight.
Ephesians 1:4

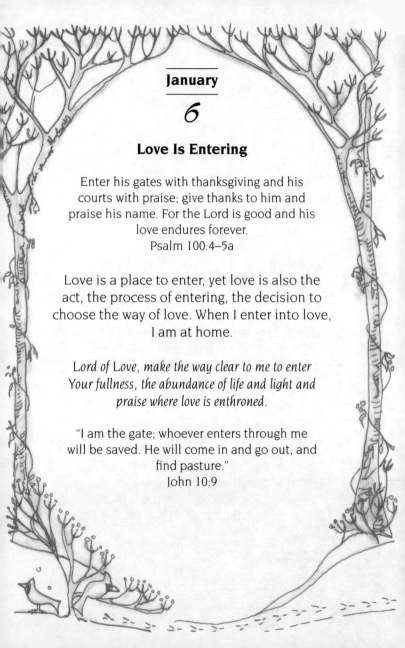

January

6

Love Is Entering

Enter his gates with thanksgiving and his
courts with praise; give thanks to him and
praise his name. For the Lord is good and his
love endures forever.
Psalm 100:4–5a

Love is a place to enter, yet love is also the
act, the process of entering, the decision to
choose the way of love. When I enter into love,
I am at home.

*Lord of Love, make the way clear to me to enter
Your fullness, the abundance of life and light and
praise where love is enthroned.*

"I am the gate; whoever enters through me
will be saved. He will come in and go out, and
find pasture."
John 10:9

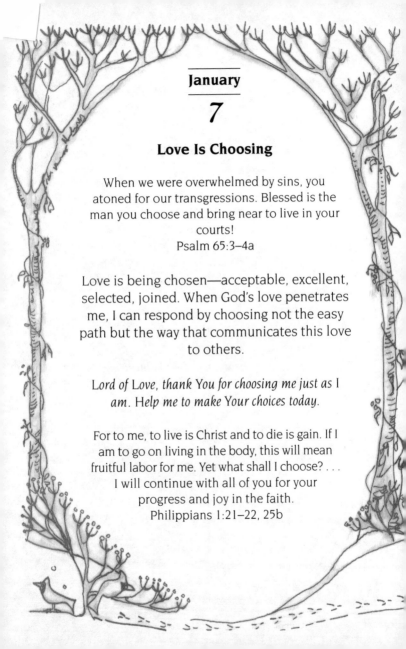

Love Is Choosing

When we were overwhelmed by sins, you
atoned for our transgressions. Blessed is the
man you choose and bring near to live in your
courts!
Psalm 65:3–4a

Love is being chosen—acceptable, excellent,
selected, joined. When God's love penetrates
me, I can respond by choosing not the easy
path but the way that communicates this love
to others.

*Lord of Love, thank You for choosing me just as I
am. Help me to make Your choices today.*

For to me, to live is Christ and to die is gain. If I
am to go on living in the body, this will mean
fruitful labor for me. Yet what shall I choose? . . .
I will continue with all of you for your
progress and joy in the faith.
Philippians 1:21–22, 25b

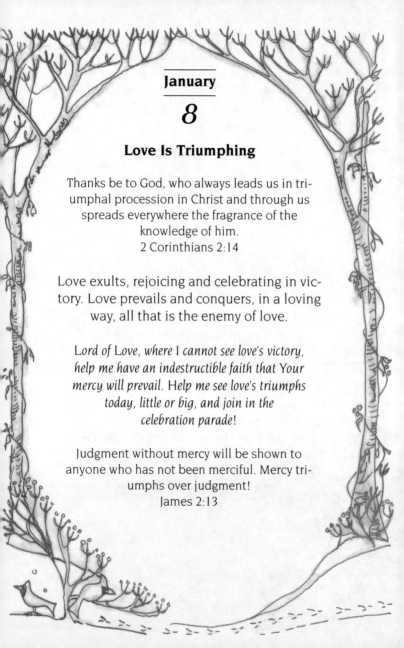

January

8

Love Is Triumphing

Thanks be to God, who always leads us in triumphal procession in Christ and through us spreads everywhere the fragrance of the knowledge of him.
2 Corinthians 2:14

Love exults, rejoicing and celebrating in victory. Love prevails and conquers, in a loving way, all that is the enemy of love.

Lord of Love, where I cannot see love's victory, help me have an indestructible faith that Your mercy will prevail. Help me see love's triumphs today, little or big, and join in the celebration parade!

Judgment without mercy will be shown to anyone who has not been merciful. Mercy triumphs over judgment!
James 2:13

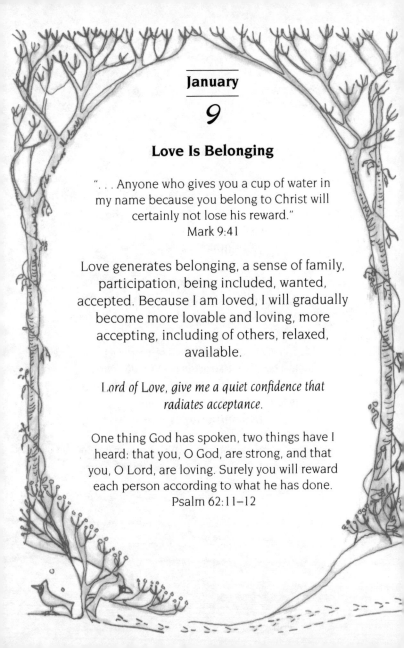

January

9

Love Is Belonging

". . . Anyone who gives you a cup of water in
my name because you belong to Christ will
certainly not lose his reward."
Mark 9:41

Love generates belonging, a sense of family,
participation, being included, wanted,
accepted. Because I am loved, I will gradually
become more lovable and loving, more
accepting, including of others, relaxed,
available.

*Lord of Love, give me a quiet confidence that
radiates acceptance.*

One thing God has spoken, two things have I
heard: that you, O God, are strong, and that
you, O Lord, are loving. Surely you will reward
each person according to what he has done.
Psalm 62:11–12

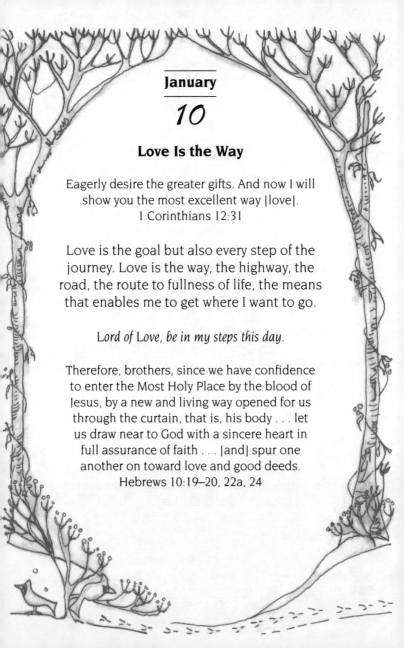

Love Is the Way

Eagerly desire the greater gifts. And now I will
show you the most excellent way [love].
1 Corinthians 12:31

Love is the goal but also every step of the
journey. Love is the way, the highway, the
road, the route to fullness of life, the means
that enables me to get where I want to go.

Lord of Love, be in my steps this day.

Therefore, brothers, since we have confidence
to enter the Most Holy Place by the blood of
Jesus, by a new and living way opened for us
through the curtain, that is, his body . . . let
us draw near to God with a sincere heart in
full assurance of faith . . . [and] spur one
another on toward love and good deeds.
Hebrews 10:19–20, 22a, 24

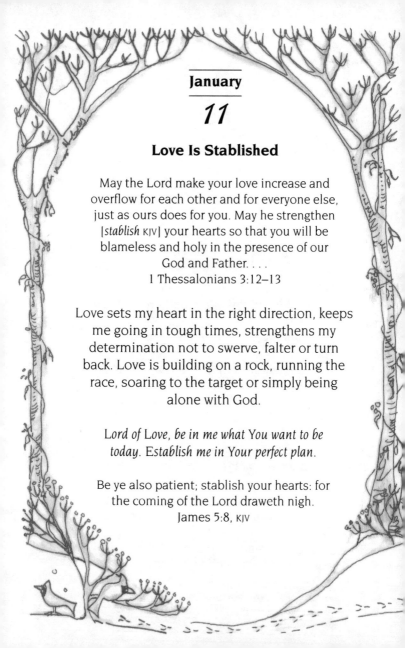

January

11

Love Is Stablished

May the Lord make your love increase and
overflow for each other and for everyone else,
just as ours does for you. May he strengthen
[*stablish* KJV] your hearts so that you will be
blameless and holy in the presence of our
God and Father. . . .
1 Thessalonians 3:12–13

Love sets my heart in the right direction, keeps
me going in tough times, strengthens my
determination not to swerve, falter or turn
back. Love is building on a rock, running the
race, soaring to the target or simply being
alone with God.

*Lord of Love, be in me what You want to be
today. Establish me in Your perfect plan.*

Be ye also patient; stablish your hearts: for
the coming of the Lord draweth nigh.
James 5:8, KJV

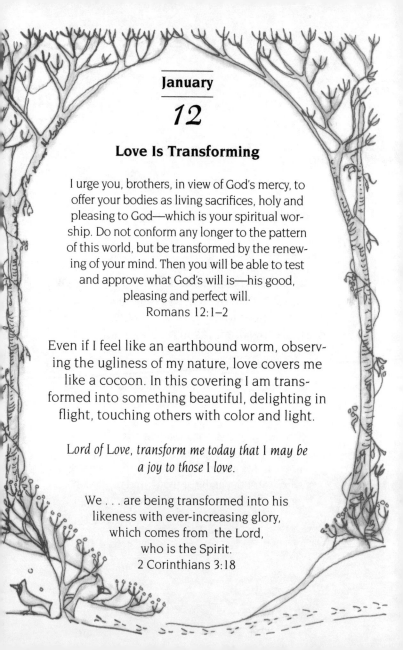

Love Is Transforming

I urge you, brothers, in view of God's mercy, to offer your bodies as living sacrifices, holy and pleasing to God—which is your spiritual worship. Do not conform any longer to the pattern of this world, but be transformed by the renewing of your mind. Then you will be able to test and approve what God's will is—his good, pleasing and perfect will.
Romans 12:1–2

Even if I feel like an earthbound worm, observing the ugliness of my nature, love covers me like a cocoon. In this covering I am transformed into something beautiful, delighting in flight, touching others with color and light.

Lord of Love, transform me today that I may be a joy to those I love.

We . . . are being transformed into his likeness with ever-increasing glory, which comes from the Lord, who is the Spirit.
2 Corinthians 3:18

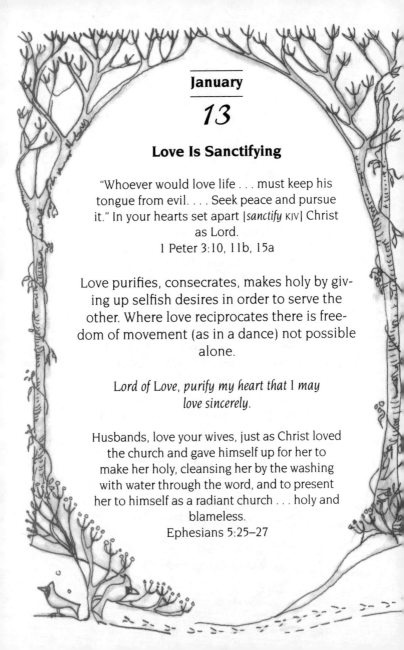

Love Is Sanctifying

"Whoever would love life . . . must keep his
tongue from evil. . . . Seek peace and pursue
it." In your hearts set apart [*sanctify* KJV] Christ
as Lord.
1 Peter 3:10, 11b, 15a

Love purifies, consecrates, makes holy by giving up selfish desires in order to serve the
other. Where love reciprocates there is freedom of movement (as in a dance) not possible
alone.

*Lord of Love, purify my heart that I may
love sincerely.*

Husbands, love your wives, just as Christ loved
the church and gave himself up for her to
make her holy, cleansing her by the washing
with water through the word, and to present
her to himself as a radiant church . . . holy and
blameless.
Ephesians 5:25–27

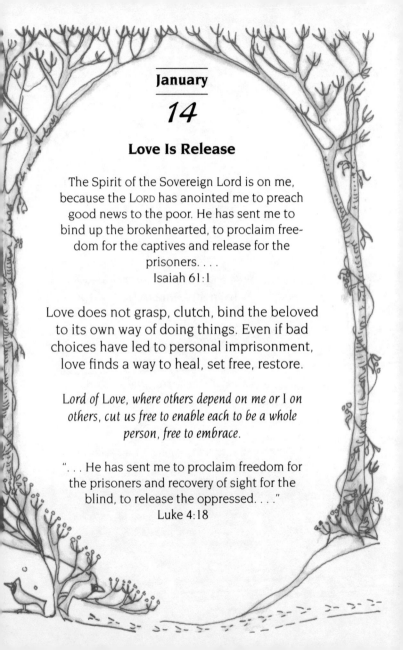

Love Is Release

The Spirit of the Sovereign Lord is on me,
because the LORD has anointed me to preach
good news to the poor. He has sent me to
bind up the brokenhearted, to proclaim freedom for the captives and release for the
prisoners. . . .
Isaiah 61:1

Love does not grasp, clutch, bind the beloved
to its own way of doing things. Even if bad
choices have led to personal imprisonment,
love finds a way to heal, set free, restore.

*Lord of Love, where others depend on me or I on
others, cut us free to enable each to be a whole
person, free to embrace.*

". . . He has sent me to proclaim freedom for
the prisoners and recovery of sight for the
blind, to release the oppressed. . . ."
Luke 4:18

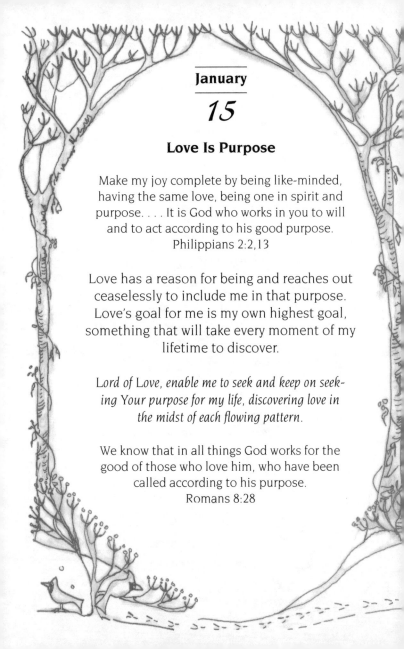

January

15

Love Is Purpose

Make my joy complete by being like-minded,
having the same love, being one in spirit and
purpose. . . . It is God who works in you to will
and to act according to his good purpose.
Philippians 2:2,13

Love has a reason for being and reaches out
ceaselessly to include me in that purpose.
Love's goal for me is my own highest goal,
something that will take every moment of my
lifetime to discover.

*Lord of Love, enable me to seek and keep on seek-
ing Your purpose for my life, discovering love in
the midst of each flowing pattern.*

We know that in all things God works for the
good of those who love him, who have been
called according to his purpose.
Romans 8:28

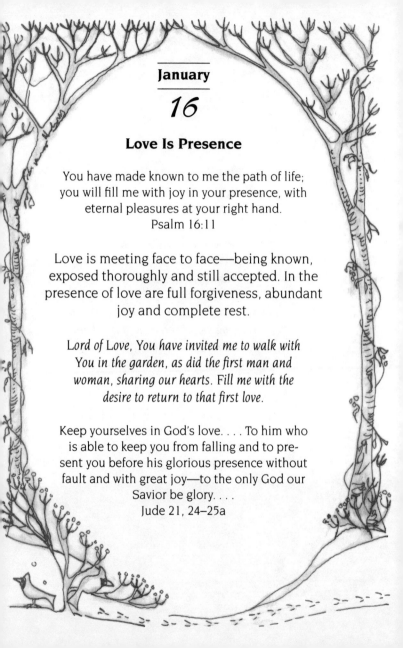

Love Is Presence

You have made known to me the path of life;
you will fill me with joy in your presence, with
eternal pleasures at your right hand.
Psalm 16:11

Love is meeting face to face—being known,
exposed thoroughly and still accepted. In the
presence of love are full forgiveness, abundant
joy and complete rest.

*Lord of Love, You have invited me to walk with
You in the garden, as did the first man and
woman, sharing our hearts. Fill me with the
desire to return to that first love.*

Keep yourselves in God's love. . . . To him who
is able to keep you from falling and to present you before his glorious presence without
fault and with great joy—to the only God our
Savior be glory. . . .
Jude 21, 24–25a

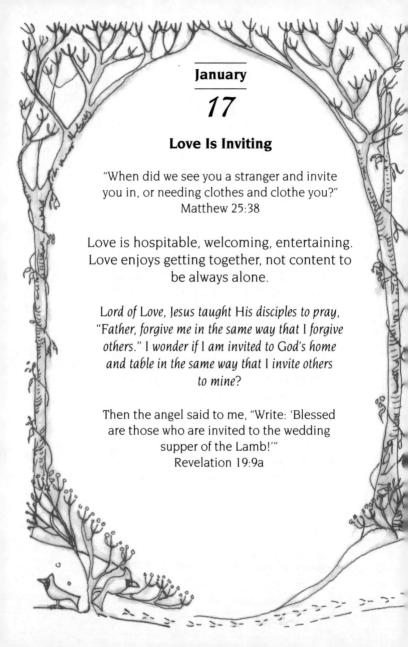

January

17

Love Is Inviting

"When did we see you a stranger and invite
you in, or needing clothes and clothe you?"
Matthew 25:38

Love is hospitable, welcoming, entertaining.
Love enjoys getting together, not content to
be always alone.

*Lord of Love, Jesus taught His disciples to pray,
"Father, forgive me in the same way that I forgive
others." I wonder if I am invited to God's home
and table in the same way that I invite others
to mine?*

Then the angel said to me, "Write: 'Blessed
are those who are invited to the wedding
supper of the Lamb!'"
Revelation 19:9a

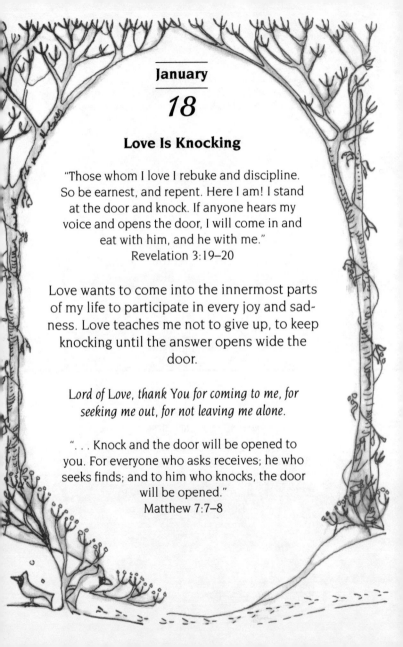

January

18

Love Is Knocking

"Those whom I love I rebuke and discipline.
So be earnest, and repent. Here I am! I stand
at the door and knock. If anyone hears my
voice and opens the door, I will come in and
eat with him, and he with me."
Revelation 3:19–20

Love wants to come into the innermost parts
of my life to participate in every joy and sad-
ness. Love teaches me not to give up, to keep
knocking until the answer opens wide the
door.

*Lord of Love, thank You for coming to me, for
seeking me out, for not leaving me alone.*

". . . Knock and the door will be opened to
you. For everyone who asks receives; he who
seeks finds; and to him who knocks, the door
will be opened."
Matthew 7:7–8

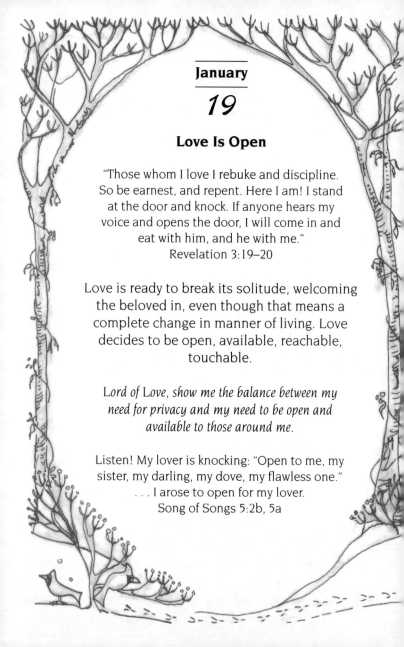

January

19

Love Is Open

"Those whom I love I rebuke and discipline.
So be earnest, and repent. Here I am! I stand
at the door and knock. If anyone hears my
voice and opens the door, I will come in and
eat with him, and he with me."
Revelation 3:19–20

Love is ready to break its solitude, welcoming
the beloved in, even though that means a
complete change in manner of living. Love
decides to be open, available, reachable,
touchable.

*Lord of Love, show me the balance between my
need for privacy and my need to be open and
available to those around me.*

Listen! My lover is knocking: "Open to me, my
sister, my darling, my dove, my flawless one."
. . . I arose to open for my lover.
Song of Songs 5:2b, 5a

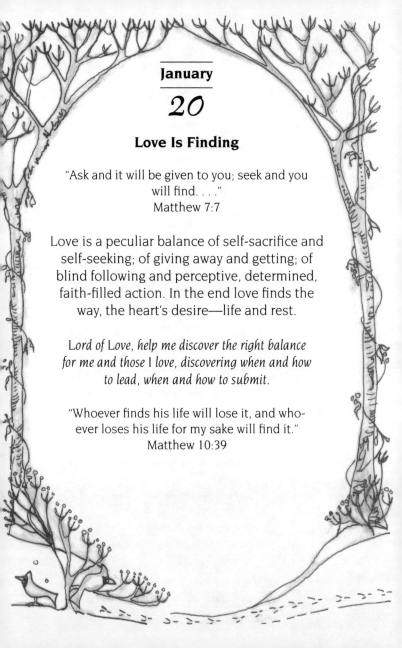

January

20

Love Is Finding

"Ask and it will be given to you; seek and you
will find. . . ."
Matthew 7:7

Love is a peculiar balance of self-sacrifice and
self-seeking; of giving away and getting; of
blind following and perceptive, determined,
faith-filled action. In the end love finds the
way, the heart's desire—life and rest.

*Lord of Love, help me discover the right balance
for me and those I love, discovering when and how
to lead, when and how to submit.*

"Whoever finds his life will lose it, and whoever loses his life for my sake will find it."
Matthew 10:39

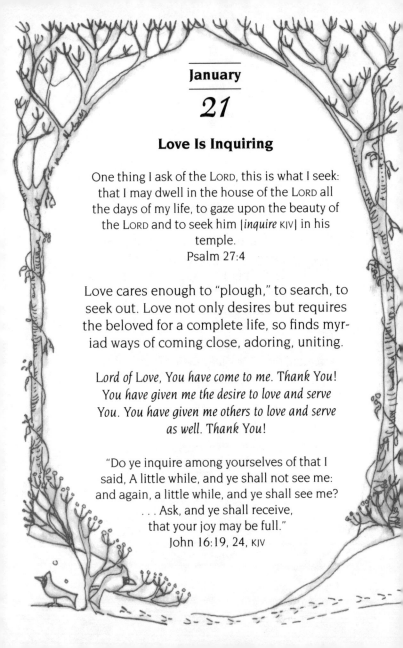

January

21

Love Is Inquiring

One thing I ask of the LORD, this is what I seek:
that I may dwell in the house of the LORD all
the days of my life, to gaze upon the beauty of
the LORD and to seek him [*inquire* KJV] in his
temple.
Psalm 27:4

Love cares enough to "plough," to search, to
seek out. Love not only desires but requires
the beloved for a complete life, so finds myriad ways of coming close, adoring, uniting.

Lord of Love, You have come to me. Thank You!
You have given me the desire to love and serve
You. You have given me others to love and serve
as well. Thank You!

"Do ye inquire among yourselves of that I
said, A little while, and ye shall not see me:
and again, a little while, and ye shall see me?
. . . Ask, and ye shall receive,
that your joy may be full."
John 16:19, 24, KJV

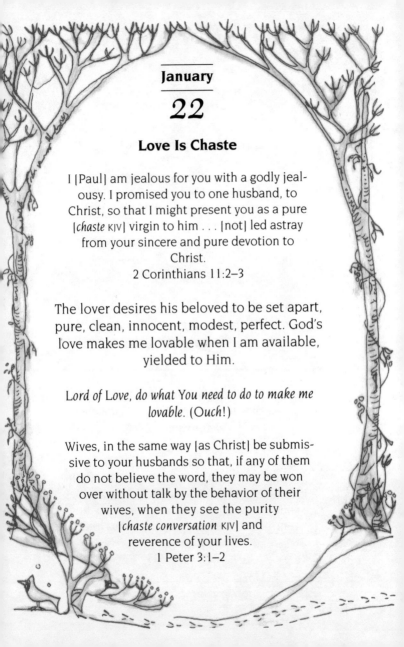

January

22

Love Is Chaste

I [Paul] am jealous for you with a godly jealousy. I promised you to one husband, to Christ, so that I might present you as a pure [*chaste* KJV] virgin to him . . . [not] led astray from your sincere and pure devotion to Christ.
2 Corinthians 11:2–3

The lover desires his beloved to be set apart, pure, clean, innocent, modest, perfect. God's love makes me lovable when I am available, yielded to Him.

Lord of Love, do what You need to do to make me lovable. (Ouch!)

Wives, in the same way [as Christ] be submissive to your husbands so that, if any of them do not believe the word, they may be won over without talk by the behavior of their wives, when they see the purity [*chaste conversation* KJV] and reverence of your lives.
1 Peter 3:1–2

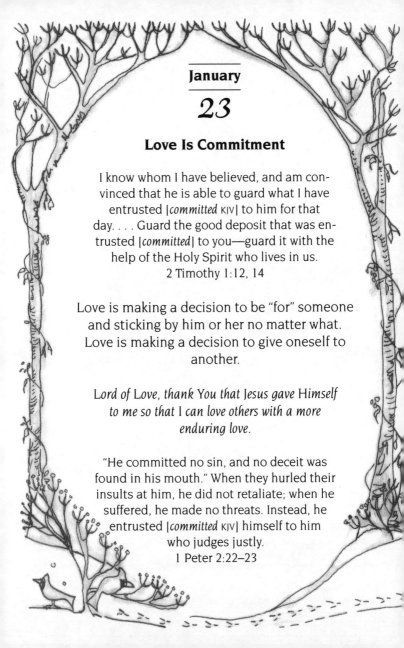

January

23

Love Is Commitment

I know whom I have believed, and am convinced that he is able to guard what I have entrusted [*committed* KJV] to him for that day. . . . Guard the good deposit that was entrusted [*committed*] to you—guard it with the help of the Holy Spirit who lives in us.
2 Timothy 1:12, 14

Love is making a decision to be "for" someone and sticking by him or her no matter what. Love is making a decision to give oneself to another.

Lord of Love, thank You that Jesus gave Himself to me so that I can love others with a more enduring love.

"He committed no sin, and no deceit was found in his mouth." When they hurled their insults at him, he did not retaliate; when he suffered, he made no threats. Instead, he entrusted [*committed* KJV] himself to him who judges justly.
1 Peter 2:22–23

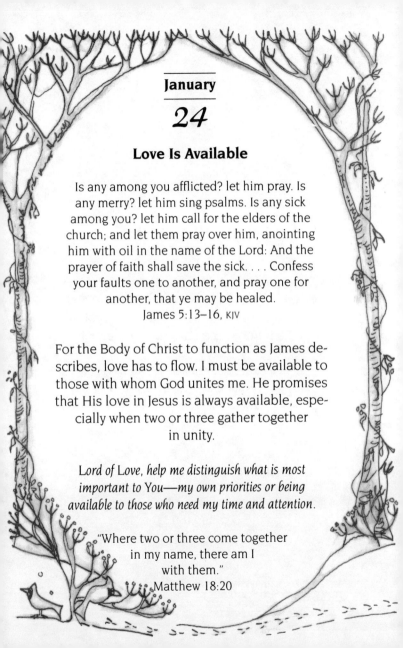

Love Is Available

Is any among you afflicted? let him pray. Is
any merry? let him sing psalms. Is any sick
among you? let him call for the elders of the
church; and let them pray over him, anointing
him with oil in the name of the Lord: And the
prayer of faith shall save the sick. . . . Confess
your faults one to another, and pray one for
another, that ye may be healed.
James 5:13–16, KJV

For the Body of Christ to function as James de-
scribes, love has to flow. I must be available to
those with whom God unites me. He promises
that His love in Jesus is always available, especially when two or three gather together
in unity.

*Lord of Love, help me distinguish what is most
important to You—my own priorities or being
available to those who need my time and attention.*

"Where two or three come together
in my name, there am I
with them."
Matthew 18:20

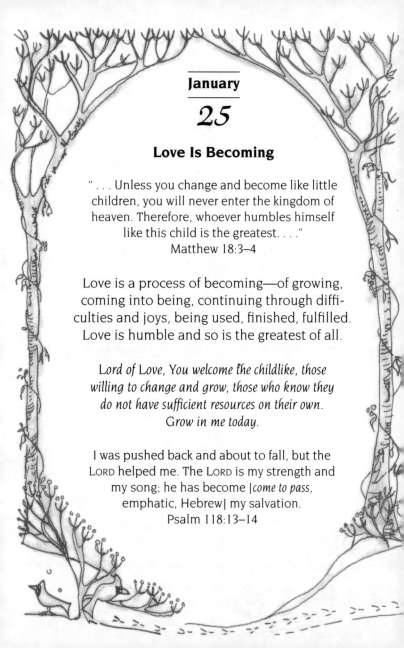

January

25

Love Is Becoming

" . . . Unless you change and become like little
children, you will never enter the kingdom of
heaven. Therefore, whoever humbles himself
like this child is the greatest. . . ."
Matthew 18:3–4

Love is a process of becoming—of growing,
coming into being, continuing through difficulties and joys, being used, finished, fulfilled.
Love is humble and so is the greatest of all.

*Lord of Love, You welcome the childlike, those
willing to change and grow, those who know they
do not have sufficient resources on their own.
Grow in me today.*

I was pushed back and about to fall, but the
LORD helped me. The LORD is my strength and
my song; he has become |*come to pass*,
emphatic, Hebrew| my salvation.
Psalm 118:13–14

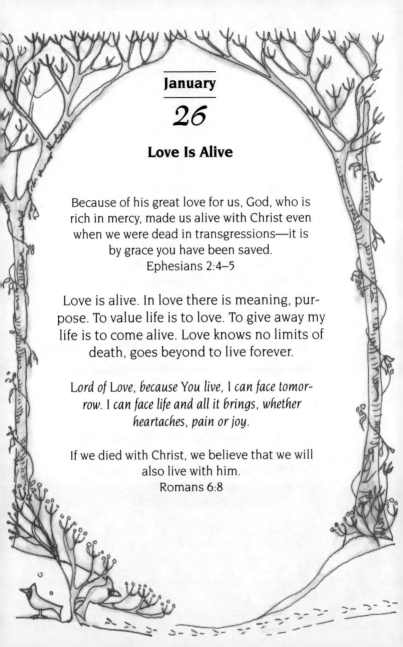

January

26

Love Is Alive

Because of his great love for us, God, who is rich in mercy, made us alive with Christ even when we were dead in transgressions—it is by grace you have been saved.
Ephesians 2:4–5

Love is alive. In love there is meaning, purpose. To value life is to love. To give away my life is to come alive. Love knows no limits of death, goes beyond to live forever.

Lord of Love, because You live, I can face tomorrow. I can face life and all it brings, whether heartaches, pain or joy.

If we died with Christ, we believe that we will also live with him.
Romans 6:8

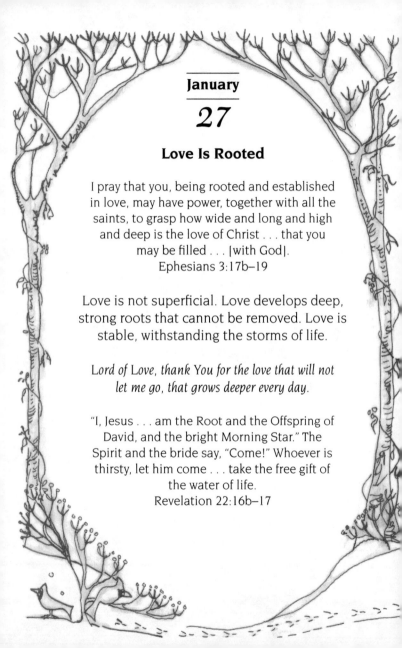

January

27

Love Is Rooted

I pray that you, being rooted and established in love, may have power, together with all the saints, to grasp how wide and long and high and deep is the love of Christ . . . that you may be filled . . . [with God].
Ephesians 3:17b–19

Love is not superficial. Love develops deep, strong roots that cannot be removed. Love is stable, withstanding the storms of life.

Lord of Love, thank You for the love that will not let me go, that grows deeper every day.

"I, Jesus . . . am the Root and the Offspring of David, and the bright Morning Star." The Spirit and the bride say, "Come!" Whoever is thirsty, let him come . . . take the free gift of the water of life.
Revelation 22:16b–17

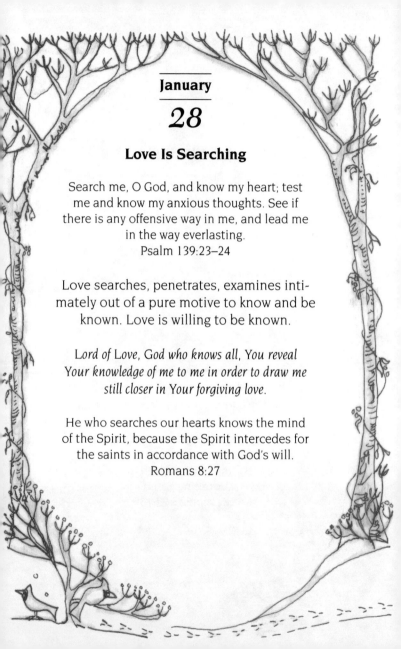

January

28

Love Is Searching

Search me, O God, and know my heart; test me and know my anxious thoughts. See if there is any offensive way in me, and lead me in the way everlasting.
Psalm 139:23–24

Love searches, penetrates, examines intimately out of a pure motive to know and be known. Love is willing to be known.

Lord of Love, God who knows all, You reveal Your knowledge of me to me in order to draw me still closer in Your forgiving love.

He who searches our hearts knows the mind of the Spirit, because the Spirit intercedes for the saints in accordance with God's will.
Romans 8:27

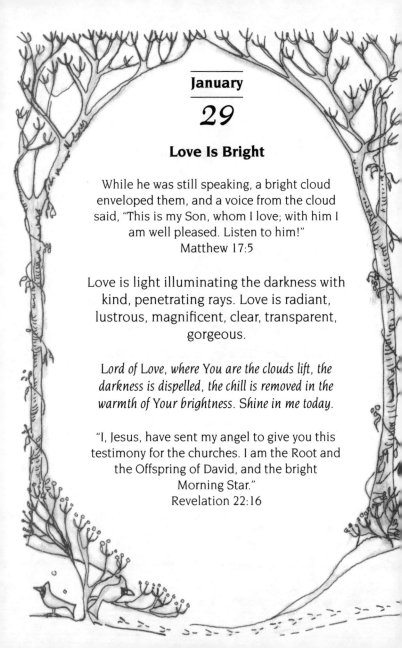

January

29

Love Is Bright

While he was still speaking, a bright cloud
enveloped them, and a voice from the cloud
said, "This is my Son, whom I love; with him I
am well pleased. Listen to him!"
Matthew 17:5

Love is light illuminating the darkness with
kind, penetrating rays. Love is radiant,
lustrous, magnificent, clear, transparent,
gorgeous.

*Lord of Love, where You are the clouds lift, the
darkness is dispelled, the chill is removed in the
warmth of Your brightness. Shine in me today.*

"I, Jesus, have sent my angel to give you this
testimony for the churches. I am the Root and
the Offspring of David, and the bright
Morning Star."
Revelation 22:16

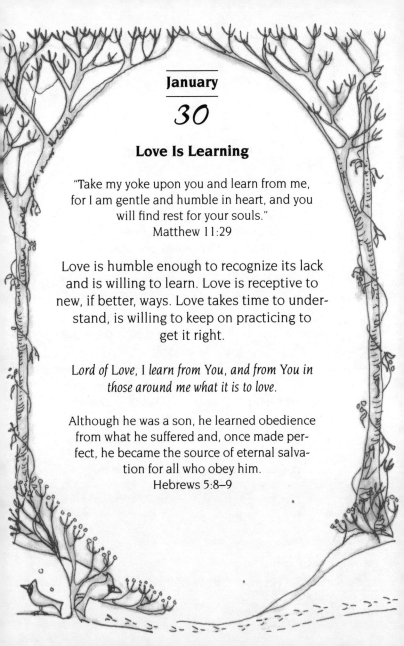

Love Is Learning

"Take my yoke upon you and learn from me,
for I am gentle and humble in heart, and you
will find rest for your souls."
Matthew 11:29

Love is humble enough to recognize its lack
and is willing to learn. Love is receptive to
new, if better, ways. Love takes time to understand, is willing to keep on practicing to
get it right.

*Lord of Love, I learn from You, and from You in
those around me what it is to love.*

Although he was a son, he learned obedience
from what he suffered and, once made perfect, he became the source of eternal salvation for all who obey him.
Hebrews 5:8–9

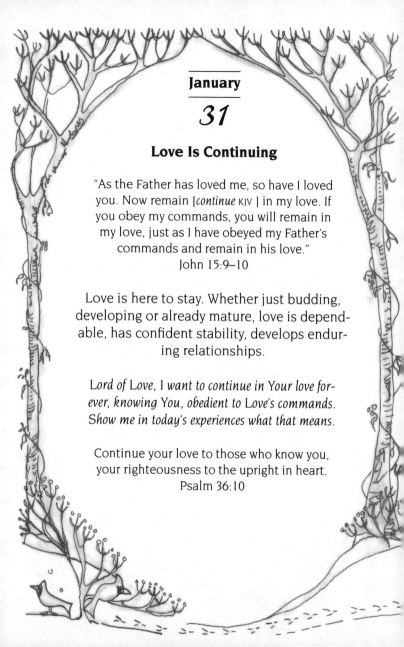

January

31

Love Is Continuing

"As the Father has loved me, so have I loved you. Now remain [*continue* KJV] in my love. If you obey my commands, you will remain in my love, just as I have obeyed my Father's commands and remain in his love."
John 15:9–10

Love is here to stay. Whether just budding, developing or already mature, love is dependable, has confident stability, develops enduring relationships.

Lord of Love, I want to continue in Your love forever, knowing You, obedient to Love's commands. Show me in today's experiences what that means.

Continue your love to those who know you, your righteousness to the upright in heart.
Psalm 36:10

February
Love Is Desire

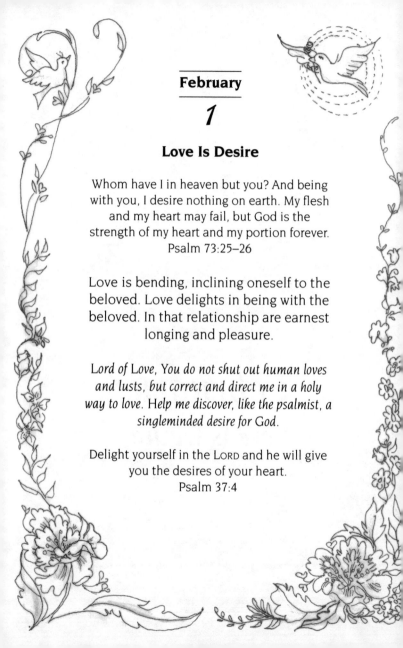

February

1

Love Is Desire

Whom have I in heaven but you? And being with you, I desire nothing on earth. My flesh and my heart may fail, but God is the strength of my heart and my portion forever.
Psalm 73:25–26

Love is bending, inclining oneself to the beloved. Love delights in being with the beloved. In that relationship are earnest longing and pleasure.

Lord of Love, You do not shut out human loves and lusts, but correct and direct me in a holy way to love. Help me discover, like the psalmist, a singleminded desire for God.

Delight yourself in the LORD and he will give you the desires of your heart.
Psalm 37:4

February

2

Love Is Enjoyment

Command those who are rich in this present world . . . to put their hope in God, who richly provides us with everything for our enjoyment. Command them to do good, to be rich in good deeds, and to be generous and willing to share . . . that they may take hold of the life that is truly life.
1 Timothy 6:17–19

Love enjoys the abundant blessings God gives and is generous and willing to share. Love is thankful, joyful at heart, even in the midst of difficulty.

Lord of Love, lift from me every cloud of discouragement and defeat so that Your clear sunlight reveals the many blessings You have given me today to enjoy.

. . . I pray that you may enjoy good health and that all may go well with you, even as your soul is getting along well.
3 John 2

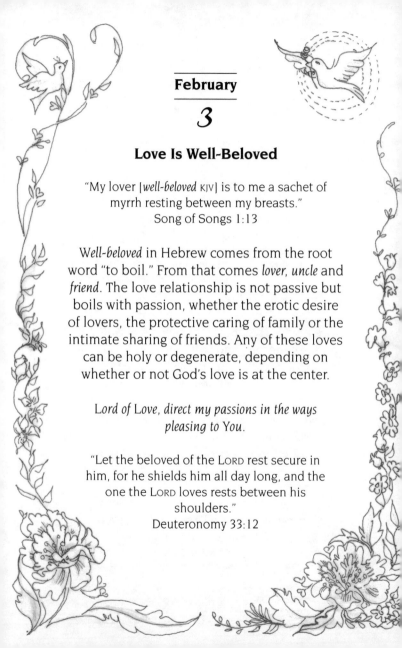

Love Is Well-Beloved

"My lover [*well-beloved* KJV] is to me a sachet of
myrrh resting between my breasts."
Song of Songs 1:13

Well-beloved in Hebrew comes from the root
word "to boil." From that comes *lover, uncle* and
friend. The love relationship is not passive but
boils with passion, whether the erotic desire
of lovers, the protective caring of family or the
intimate sharing of friends. Any of these loves
can be holy or degenerate, depending on
whether or not God's love is at the center.

*Lord of Love, direct my passions in the ways
pleasing to You.*

"Let the beloved of the LORD rest secure in
him, for he shields him all day long, and the
one the LORD loves rests between his
shoulders."
Deuteronomy 33:12

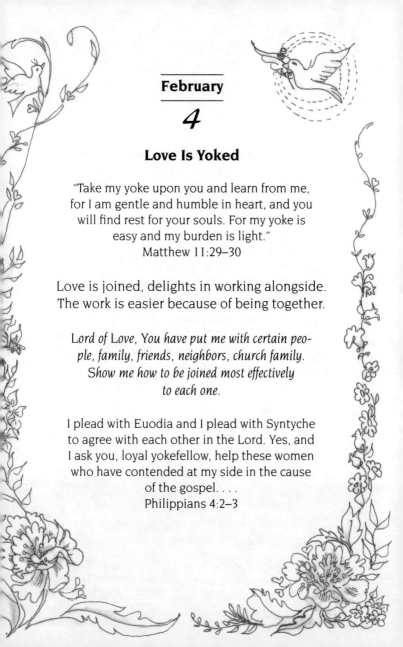

Love Is Yoked

"Take my yoke upon you and learn from me,
for I am gentle and humble in heart, and you
will find rest for your souls. For my yoke is
easy and my burden is light."
Matthew 11:29–30

Love is joined, delights in working alongside.
The work is easier because of being together.

*Lord of Love, You have put me with certain peo-
ple, family, friends, neighbors, church family.
Show me how to be joined most effectively
to each one.*

I plead with Euodia and I plead with Syntyche
to agree with each other in the Lord. Yes, and
I ask you, loyal yokefellow, help these women
who have contended at my side in the cause
of the gospel. . . .
Philippians 4:2–3

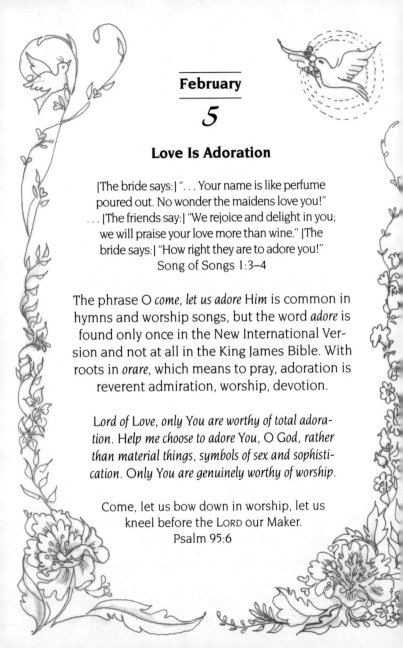

February

5

Love Is Adoration

[The bride says:] ". . . Your name is like perfume
poured out. No wonder the maidens love you!"
. . . [The friends say:] "We rejoice and delight in you;
we will praise your love more than wine." [The
bride says:] "How right they are to adore you!"
Song of Songs 1:3–4

The phrase O *come, let us adore* Him is common in
hymns and worship songs, but the word *adore* is
found only once in the New International Version and not at all in the King James Bible. With
roots in *orare*, which means to pray, adoration is
reverent admiration, worship, devotion.

Lord of Love, only You are worthy of total adora-
tion. Help me choose to adore You, O God, rather
than material things, symbols of sex and sophisti-
cation. Only You are genuinely worthy of worship.

Come, let us bow down in worship, let us
kneel before the Lord our Maker.
Psalm 95:6

Love Is Attentive

Out of the depths I cry to you, O LORD; O
Lord, hear my voice. Let your ears be attentive to my cry for mercy. . . . Put your hope in
the LORD, for with the LORD is unfailing love
and with him is full redemption.
Psalm 130:1–2, 7

Love hears me, listens, regards my concerns
and interests as important, is attentive.

*Lord of Love, I show my love for You by taking
time to listen to Your voice, hear Your heart. With
every other love relationship in my life today—
spouse, parent, child, friends, even enemy—I
want to notice to whom or to what I give my
attention and ask, "Why?"*

My son, pay attention to what I say; listen
closely to my words. . . . Keep them within
your heart; for they are life to those who find
them and health to a man's whole body.
Proverbs 4:20–22

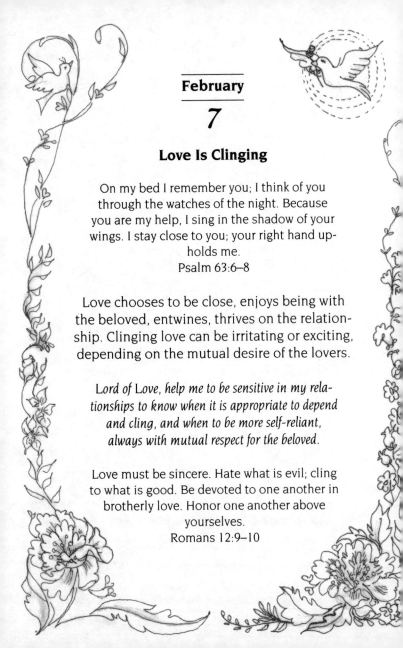

February

7

Love Is Clinging

On my bed I remember you; I think of you through the watches of the night. Because you are my help, I sing in the shadow of your wings. I stay close to you; your right hand upholds me.
Psalm 63:6–8

Love chooses to be close, enjoys being with the beloved, entwines, thrives on the relationship. Clinging love can be irritating or exciting, depending on the mutual desire of the lovers.

Lord of Love, help me to be sensitive in my relationships to know when it is appropriate to depend and cling, and when to be more self-reliant, always with mutual respect for the beloved.

Love must be sincere. Hate what is evil; cling to what is good. Be devoted to one another in brotherly love. Honor one another above yourselves.
Romans 12:9–10

February

8

Love Is Appealing

. . . Although in Christ I could be bold and
order you to do what you ought to do, yet I
appeal to you on the basis of love.
Philemon 8–9a

Love appeals, calls near, invites, implores, exhorts,
desires, consoles, prays. Although not based on
emotion, the love relationship runs the gamut of
emotions. Love shares its best with the beloved.
Not pushy or manipulative, love must share from
the heart, make its appeal and then rest.

*Lord of Love, I want the best for those I love. Help
me in my appeals to them to be wise and attractive, yet accept the choices they make, especially if
different from my own.*

To the elders among you, I appeal as a fellow
elder. . . . Be shepherds of God's flock that is
under your care . . . not because you must,
but because you are willing. . . .
1 Peter 5:1–2

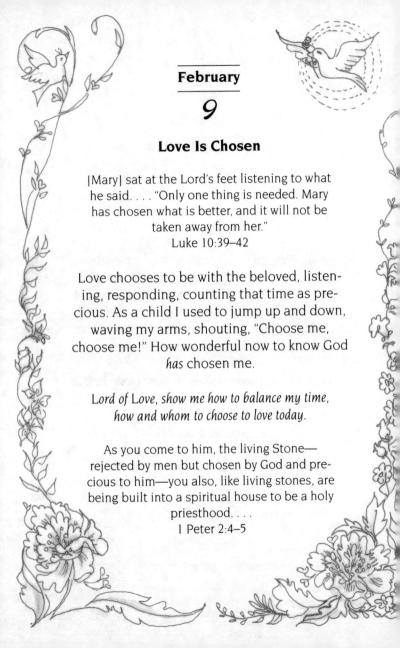

February

9

Love Is Chosen

[Mary] sat at the Lord's feet listening to what
he said. . . . "Only one thing is needed. Mary
has chosen what is better, and it will not be
taken away from her."
Luke 10:39–42

Love chooses to be with the beloved, listening, responding, counting that time as precious. As a child I used to jump up and down,
waving my arms, shouting, "Choose me,
choose me!" How wonderful now to know God
has chosen me.

*Lord of Love, show me how to balance my time,
how and whom to choose to love today.*

As you come to him, the living Stone—
rejected by men but chosen by God and precious to him—you also, like living stones, are
being built into a spiritual house to be a holy
priesthood. . . .
1 Peter 2:4–5

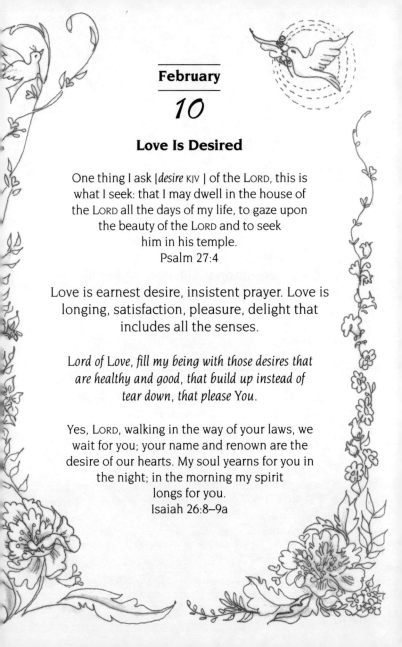

February

10

Love Is Desired

One thing I ask [*desire* KJV] of the LORD, this is
what I seek: that I may dwell in the house of
the LORD all the days of my life, to gaze upon
the beauty of the LORD and to seek
him in his temple.
Psalm 27:4

Love is earnest desire, insistent prayer. Love is
longing, satisfaction, pleasure, delight that
includes all the senses.

*Lord of Love, fill my being with those desires that
are healthy and good, that build up instead of
tear down, that please You.*

Yes, LORD, walking in the way of your laws, we
wait for you; your name and renown are the
desire of our hearts. My soul yearns for you in
the night; in the morning my spirit
longs for you.
Isaiah 26:8–9a

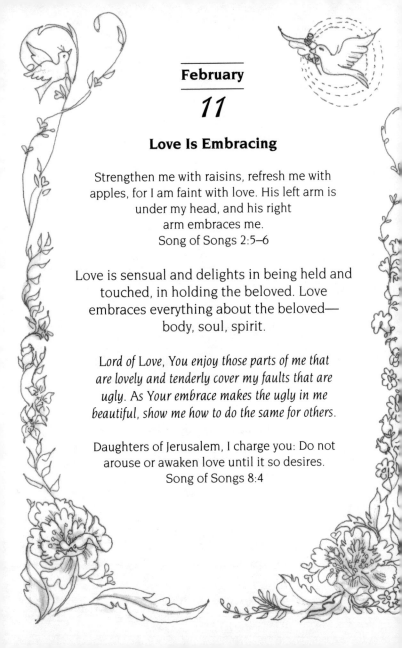

February

11

Love Is Embracing

Strengthen me with raisins, refresh me with
apples, for I am faint with love. His left arm is
under my head, and his right
arm embraces me.
Song of Songs 2:5–6

Love is sensual and delights in being held and
touched, in holding the beloved. Love
embraces everything about the beloved—
body, soul, spirit.

*Lord of Love, You enjoy those parts of me that
are lovely and tenderly cover my faults that are
ugly. As Your embrace makes the ugly in me
beautiful, show me how to do the same for others.*

Daughters of Jerusalem, I charge you: Do not
arouse or awaken love until it so desires.
Song of Songs 8:4

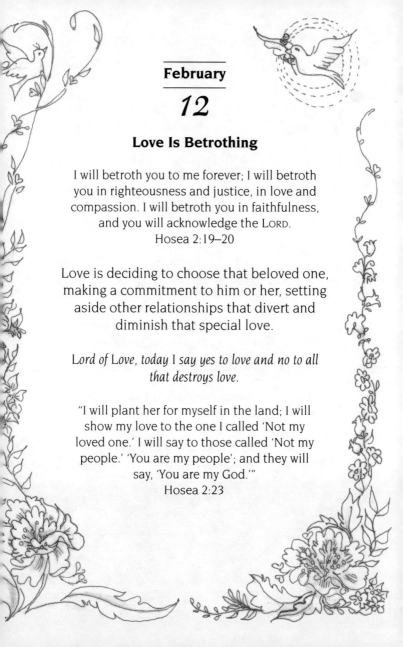

February

12

Love Is Betrothing

I will betroth you to me forever; I will betroth
you in righteousness and justice, in love and
compassion. I will betroth you in faithfulness,
and you will acknowledge the Lord.
Hosea 2:19–20

Love is deciding to choose that beloved one,
making a commitment to him or her, setting
aside other relationships that divert and
diminish that special love.

*Lord of Love, today I say yes to love and no to all
that destroys love.*

"I will plant her for myself in the land; I will
show my love to the one I called 'Not my
loved one.' I will say to those called 'Not my
people.' 'You are my people'; and they will
say, 'You are my God.'"
Hosea 2:23

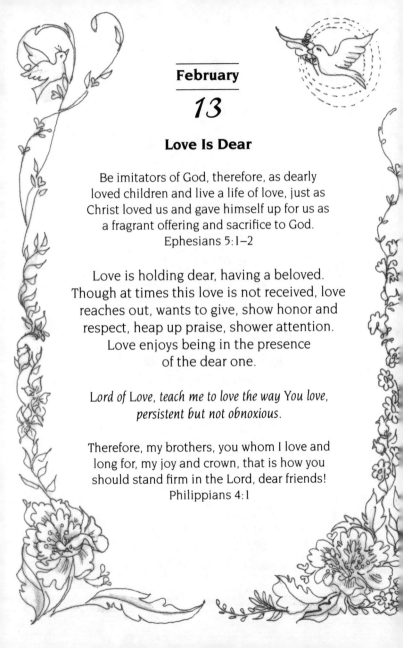

February

13

Love Is Dear

Be imitators of God, therefore, as dearly
loved children and live a life of love, just as
Christ loved us and gave himself up for us as
a fragrant offering and sacrifice to God.
Ephesians 5:1–2

Love is holding dear, having a beloved.
Though at times this love is not received, love
reaches out, wants to give, show honor and
respect, heap up praise, shower attention.
Love enjoys being in the presence
of the dear one.

*Lord of Love, teach me to love the way You love,
persistent but not obnoxious.*

Therefore, my brothers, you whom I love and
long for, my joy and crown, that is how you
should stand firm in the Lord, dear friends!
Philippians 4:1

February

14

Love Is Beloved

My lover [*beloved* KJV] is mine and I am his; he
browses among the lilies.
Song of Songs 2:16

Love attracts love without manipulating the
beloved. Love cherishes and holds the beloved
dear in an atmosphere of freedom
and creativity.

*Lord of Love, Jesus is Your Son, the Beloved in
whom You are well pleased. I know You love me,
too. I am beloved, adopted, chosen, wanted for
who I am and for what I will be when love has its
way in me.*

For he chose us in him before the creation of
the world to be holy and blameless in his
sight. In love he predestined us to be adopted
as his sons through Jesus Christ, in accordance with his pleasure and will—to the
praise of his glorious grace, which he has
freely given us in the One
he loves [*beloved* KJV].
Ephesians 1:4–6

Love Is Companionship

Sometimes you were publicly exposed to
insult and persecution; at other times you
stood side by side [*became companions* KJV] with
those who were so treated.
Hebrews 10:33

Love shares the good and the bad—in sickness and in health; for richer, for poorer; for
better, for worse. Love is a faithful partner who
stands beside, participating in the pains as
well as the joys in a way that encourages.

*Lord of Love, help me to keep being a faithful
companion even when times are rough.*

Pray for the peace of Jerusalem: "May those
who love you be secure. May there be peace
within your walls. . . ." For the sake of my
brothers and friends [*companions* KJV], I will say,
"Peace be within you."
Psalm 122:6–8

Love Is Affectionate

Be devoted to one another in brotherly love.
Honor one another above yourselves.
Romans 12:10

Love possesses the emotions of affectionate
desiring, longing, yearning for a deeper relationship, for the best for the beloved.

*Lord of Love, You have built into every human
heart the need for affection, intimacy, meaningful
relationship that goes beyond the physical and
mental. Immerse my spirit in the love for which
I was created.*

. . . We were gentle among you, like a mother
caring for her little children. We loved you so
much that we were delighted to share with you
not only the gospel of God but our lives as
well, because you had become so dear to us.
1 Thessalonians 2:7–8

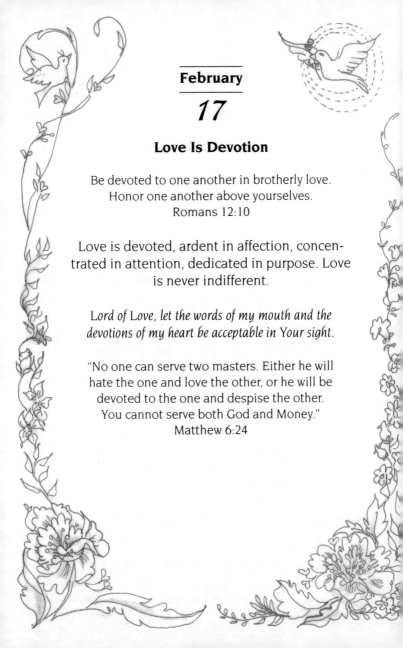

February

17

Love Is Devotion

Be devoted to one another in brotherly love.
Honor one another above yourselves.
Romans 12:10

Love is devoted, ardent in affection, concentrated in attention, dedicated in purpose. Love is never indifferent.

Lord of Love, let the words of my mouth and the devotions of my heart be acceptable in Your sight.

"No one can serve two masters. Either he will hate the one and love the other, or he will be devoted to the one and despise the other. You cannot serve both God and Money."
Matthew 6:24

February

18

Love Is Accepting

Let the words of my mouth, and the meditation of my heart, be acceptable in thy sight, O LORD, my strength, and my redeemer.
Psalm 19:14, KJV

Love is God delighting in my innermost being, desiring a relationship with me, bringing forth His favor and good pleasure. My earnest presenting of my body as a living sacrifice to God sets me in the place where His loving will, his "good, pleasing and perfect will" (Romans 12:2), can be established.

Lord of Love, in creating me You demonstrated loving desire for my life. In dying for me, You revealed determination to free me from all that holds me back from living freely in that love. Your Spirit is the seal of approval.

Accept one another, then, just as Christ accepted you, in order to bring praise to God.
Romans 15:7

February

19

Love Is Cherishing

. . . Husbands ought to love their wives as
their own bodies. He who loves his wife loves
himself. After all, no one ever hated his own
body, but he feeds and cares for it [*nourisheth
and cherisheth it* KJV], just as Christ does the
church—for we are members of his body.
Ephesians 5:28–30

Love broods like a mother hen over her chicks
when there is need, but releases the beloved
to be all God has planned. The hen pecks the
ground to show her little ones where food is,
but they have to scamper to get it. Then at
night they snuggle under her comforting
wings.

*Lord of Love, thank You for Your cherishing nur-
ture. Enable me to cherish those You have given
me to love in Your liberating way.*

We were gentle among you, like a mother
caring for [*cherishing* KJV] her
little children.
1 Thessalonians 2:7

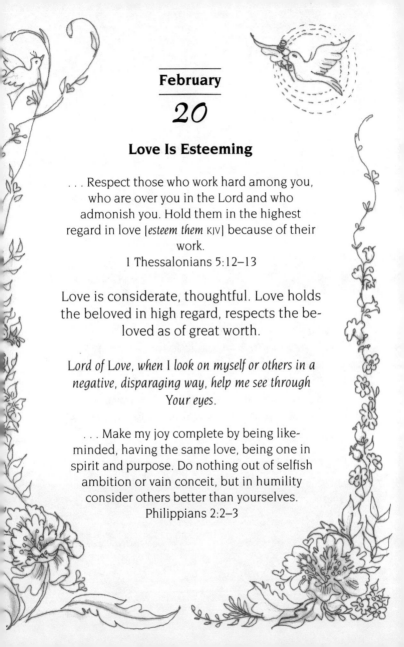

February

20

Love Is Esteeming

. . . Respect those who work hard among you,
who are over you in the Lord and who
admonish you. Hold them in the highest
regard in love [*esteem them* KJV] because of their
work.
1 Thessalonians 5:12–13

Love is considerate, thoughtful. Love holds
the beloved in high regard, respects the beloved as of great worth.

Lord of Love, when I look on myself or others in a
negative, disparaging way, help me see through
Your eyes.

. . . Make my joy complete by being like-
minded, having the same love, being one in
spirit and purpose. Do nothing out of selfish
ambition or vain conceit, but in humility
consider others better than yourselves.
Philippians 2:2–3

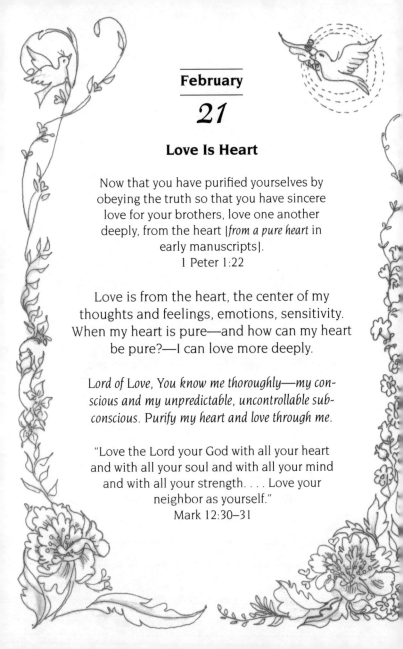

February

21

Love Is Heart

Now that you have purified yourselves by obeying the truth so that you have sincere love for your brothers, love one another deeply, from the heart [*from a pure heart* in early manuscripts].
1 Peter 1:22

Love is from the heart, the center of my thoughts and feelings, emotions, sensitivity. When my heart is pure—and how can my heart be pure?—I can love more deeply.

Lord of Love, You know me thoroughly—my conscious and my unpredictable, uncontrollable subconscious. Purify my heart and love through me.

"Love the Lord your God with all your heart and with all your soul and with all your mind and with all your strength. . . . Love your neighbor as yourself."
Mark 12:30–31

February

22

Love Is Trusting

[Love] always protects, always trusts, always
hopes, always perseveres.
1 Corinthians 13:7

Love is childlike, trusting, expecting that the
best is yet to come. Only God is totally trustworthy, so only love for God and from God can
totally fulfill the definition of love as trusting
and trustworthy.

*Lord of Love, fill my heart with Your trust, Your
hope, Your consistent trustworthiness toward
those I love. Your love is my security,
my confidence.*

Trust in the LORD with all your heart and lean
not on your own understanding; in all your
ways acknowledge him, and he will make your
paths straight.
Proverbs 3:5

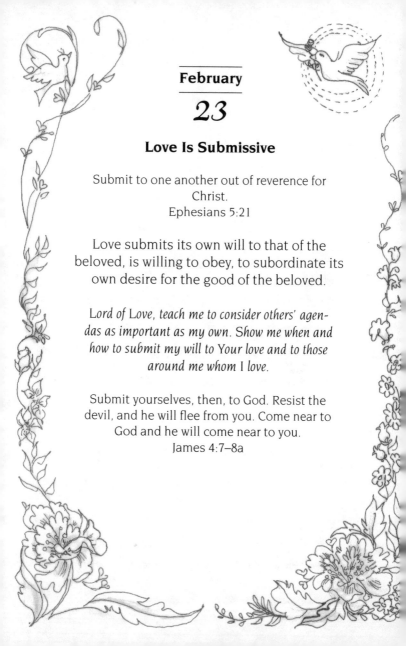

February

23

Love Is Submissive

Submit to one another out of reverence for
Christ.
Ephesians 5:21

Love submits its own will to that of the
beloved, is willing to obey, to subordinate its
own desire for the good of the beloved.

*Lord of Love, teach me to consider others' agendas as important as my own. Show me when and
how to submit my will to Your love and to those
around me whom I love.*

Submit yourselves, then, to God. Resist the
devil, and he will flee from you. Come near to
God and he will come near to you.
James 4:7–8a

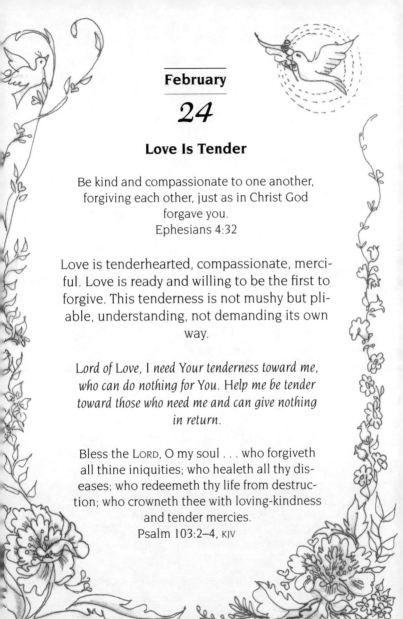

February

24

Love Is Tender

Be kind and compassionate to one another,
forgiving each other, just as in Christ God
forgave you.
Ephesians 4:32

Love is tenderhearted, compassionate, merciful. Love is ready and willing to be the first to
forgive. This tenderness is not mushy but pliable, understanding, not demanding its own
way.

Lord of Love, I need Your tenderness toward me,
who can do nothing for You. Help me be tender
toward those who need me and can give nothing
in return.

Bless the LORD, O my soul . . . who forgiveth
all thine iniquities; who healeth all thy diseases; who redeemeth thy life from destruction; who crowneth thee with loving-kindness
and tender mercies.
Psalm 103:2–4, KJV

February

25

Love Is Sweet

[God's commands] are more precious than
gold, than much pure gold; they are sweeter
than honey, than honey from the comb.
Psalm 19:10

Love is sweet, desirable, enjoyable, good to
the taste, something to savor. Scripture asso-
ciates sweetness with God's Word, which is
love directed toward me—in written form in
the holy Scriptures, and in Jesus, the living,
incarnate Word.

*Lord of Love, write Your love in my heart so that
I become a love letter to those around me.*

Your lips drop sweetness as the honeycomb,
my bride; milk and honey are under your
tongue. . . . His mouth is sweetness itself; he
is altogether lovely. This is my lover, this is
my friend.
Song of Songs 4:11; 5:16

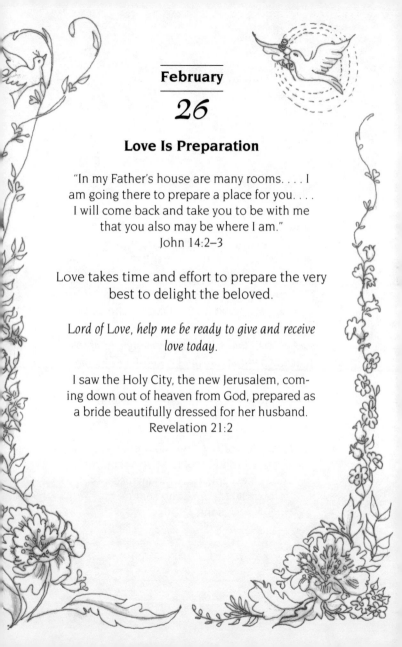

Love Is Preparation

"In my Father's house are many rooms. . . . I
am going there to prepare a place for you. . . .
I will come back and take you to be with me
that you also may be where I am."
John 14:2–3

Love takes time and effort to prepare the very
best to delight the beloved.

*Lord of Love, help me be ready to give and receive
love today.*

I saw the Holy City, the new Jerusalem, coming down out of heaven from God, prepared as
a bride beautifully dressed for her husband.
Revelation 21:2

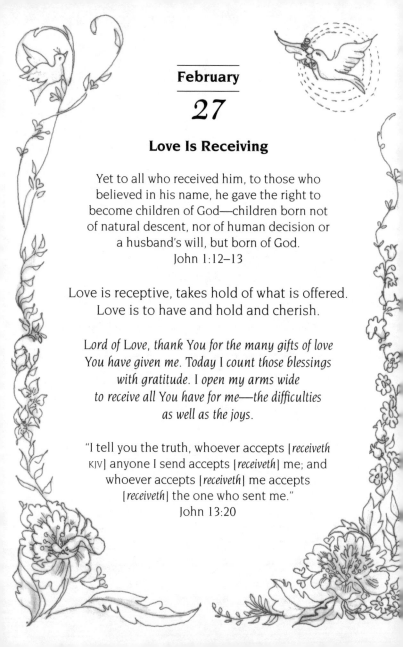

Love Is Receiving

Yet to all who received him, to those who
believed in his name, he gave the right to
become children of God—children born not
of natural descent, nor of human decision or
a husband's will, but born of God.
John 1:12–13

Love is receptive, takes hold of what is offered.
Love is to have and hold and cherish.

Lord of Love, thank You for the many gifts of love
You have given me. Today I count those blessings
with gratitude. I open my arms wide
to receive all You have for me—the difficulties
as well as the joys.

"I tell you the truth, whoever accepts [*receiveth*
KJV] anyone I send accepts [*receiveth*] me; and
whoever accepts [*receiveth*] me accepts
[*receiveth*] the one who sent me."
John 13:20

Love Is Friendship

"Greater love has no one than this, that one
lay down his life for his friends. You are my
friends if you do what I command. . . . Everything that I learned from my Father I have
made known to you."
John 15:13–15

Love is the kind of friendship that is forever
faithful, giving its life for the beloved.

*Lord of Love, I stand in awe of Your example of
self-giving friendship. Be in me all I need to be a
friend, too.*

A friend loves at all times, and a brother is
born for adversity.
Proverbs 17:17

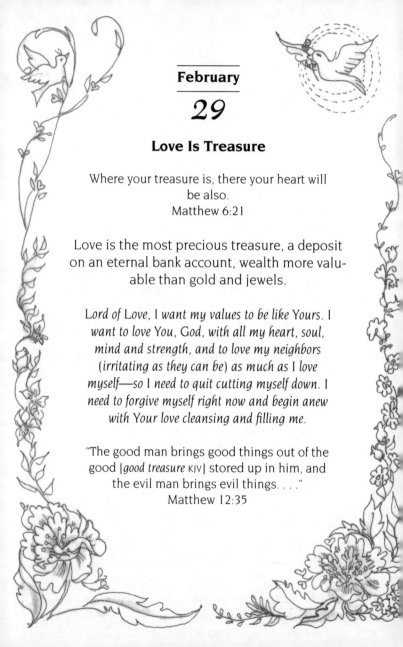

February

29

Love Is Treasure

Where your treasure is, there your heart will
be also.
Matthew 6:21

Love is the most precious treasure, a deposit
on an eternal bank account, wealth more valuable than gold and jewels.

*Lord of Love, I want my values to be like Yours. I
want to love You, God, with all my heart, soul,
mind and strength, and to love my neighbors
(irritating as they can be) as much as I love
myself—so I need to quit cutting myself down. I
need to forgive myself right now and begin anew
with Your love cleansing and filling me.*

"The good man brings good things out of the
good [*good treasure* KJV] stored up in him, and
the evil man brings evil things. . . ."
Matthew 12:35

March
Love Is Yielding

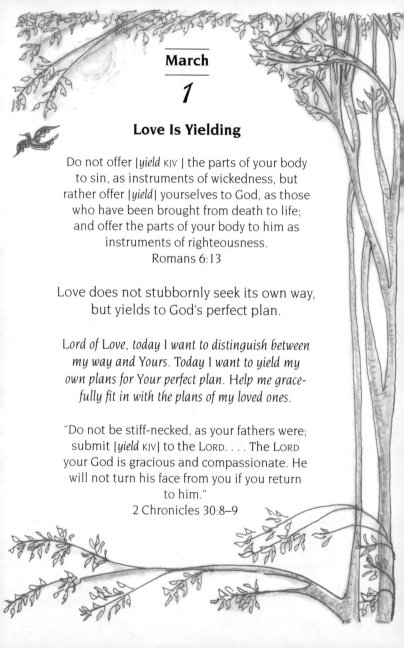

Love Is Yielding

Do not offer [*yield* KJV] the parts of your body
to sin, as instruments of wickedness, but
rather offer [*yield*] yourselves to God, as those
who have been brought from death to life;
and offer the parts of your body to him as
instruments of righteousness.
Romans 6:13

Love does not stubbornly seek its own way,
but yields to God's perfect plan.

*Lord of Love, today I want to distinguish between
my way and Yours. Today I want to yield my
own plans for Your perfect plan. Help me grace-
fully fit in with the plans of my loved ones.*

"Do not be stiff-necked, as your fathers were;
submit [*yield* KJV] to the LORD. . . . The LORD
your God is gracious and compassionate. He
will not turn his face from you if you return
to him."
2 Chronicles 30:8–9

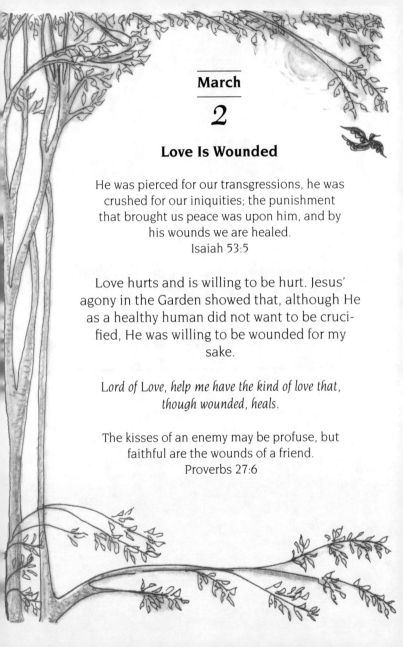

March

2

Love Is Wounded

He was pierced for our transgressions, he was
crushed for our iniquities; the punishment
that brought us peace was upon him, and by
his wounds we are healed.
Isaiah 53:5

Love hurts and is willing to be hurt. Jesus'
agony in the Garden showed that, although He
as a healthy human did not want to be crucified, He was willing to be wounded for my
sake.

*Lord of Love, help me have the kind of love that,
though wounded, heals.*

The kisses of an enemy may be profuse, but
faithful are the wounds of a friend.
Proverbs 27:6

March

3

Love Is Travail

He shall see of the travail of his soul, and
shall be satisfied: by his knowledge shall my
righteous servant justify many; for he shall
bear their iniquities.
Isaiah 53:11, KJV

Sometimes love is travail, toil, wearing effort
of body or mind. Travail is like the experience
of birth pangs. The one who loves does not
find it pleasant or smooth or easy, but when
the new life has successfully come forth, what
joy!

*Lord of Love, You are with me in the travail, in
the struggle and pain. You bring me into joy.
Thank You!*

My little children, of whom I travail in birth
again until Christ be formed in you, I desire
to be present with you now. . . .
Galatians 4:19–20, KJV

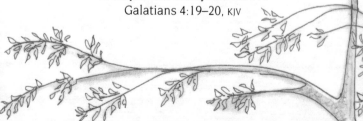

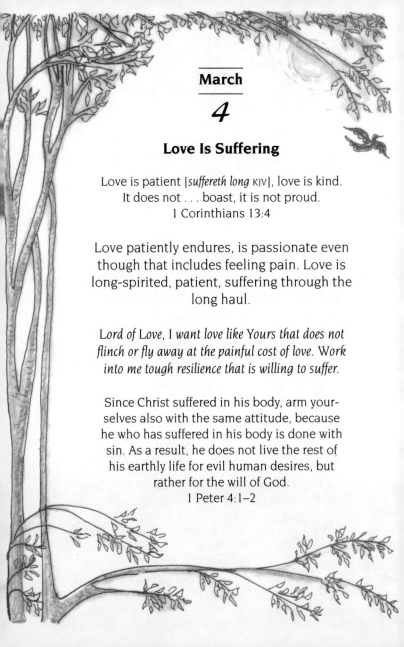

March

4

Love Is Suffering

Love is patient [*suffereth long* KJV], love is kind.
It does not . . . boast, it is not proud.
1 Corinthians 13:4

Love patiently endures, is passionate even
though that includes feeling pain. Love is
long-spirited, patient, suffering through the
long haul.

*Lord of Love, I want love like Yours that does not
flinch or fly away at the painful cost of love. Work
into me tough resilience that is willing to suffer.*

Since Christ suffered in his body, arm yourselves also with the same attitude, because
he who has suffered in his body is done with
sin. As a result, he does not live the rest of
his earthly life for evil human desires, but
rather for the will of God.
1 Peter 4:1–2

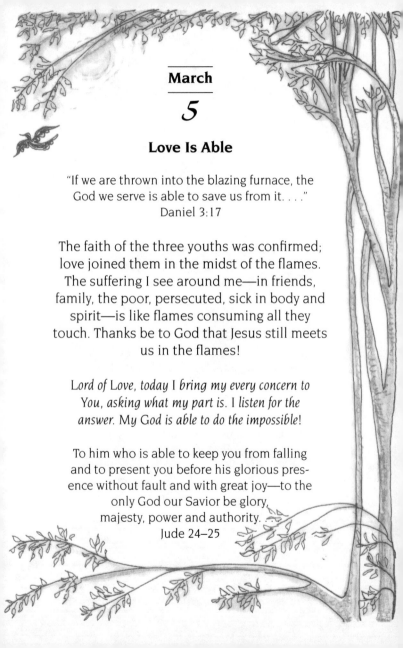

March

5

Love Is Able

"If we are thrown into the blazing furnace, the
God we serve is able to save us from it. . . ."
Daniel 3:17

The faith of the three youths was confirmed;
love joined them in the midst of the flames.
The suffering I see around me—in friends,
family, the poor, persecuted, sick in body and
spirit—is like flames consuming all they
touch. Thanks be to God that Jesus still meets
us in the flames!

*Lord of Love, today I bring my every concern to
You, asking what my part is. I listen for the
answer. My God is able to do the impossible!*

To him who is able to keep you from falling
and to present you before his glorious presence without fault and with great joy—to the
only God our Savior be glory,
majesty, power and authority.
Jude 24–25

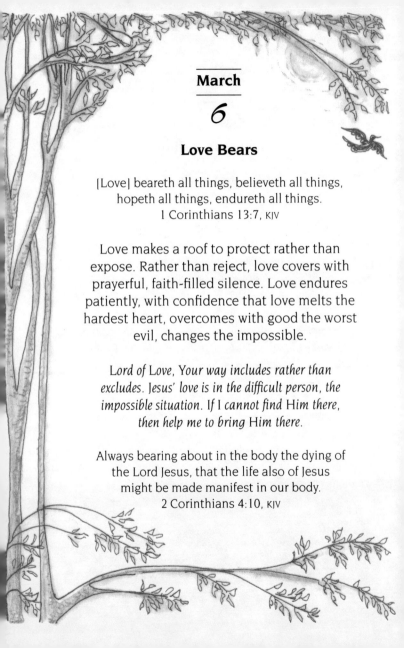

March

6

Love Bears

[Love] beareth all things, believeth all things,
hopeth all things, endureth all things.
1 Corinthians 13:7, KJV

Love makes a roof to protect rather than
expose. Rather than reject, love covers with
prayerful, faith-filled silence. Love endures
patiently, with confidence that love melts the
hardest heart, overcomes with good the worst
evil, changes the impossible.

*Lord of Love, Your way includes rather than
excludes. Jesus' love is in the difficult person, the
impossible situation. If I cannot find Him there,
then help me to bring Him there.*

Always bearing about in the body the dying of
the Lord Jesus, that the life also of Jesus
might be made manifest in our body.
2 Corinthians 4:10, KJV

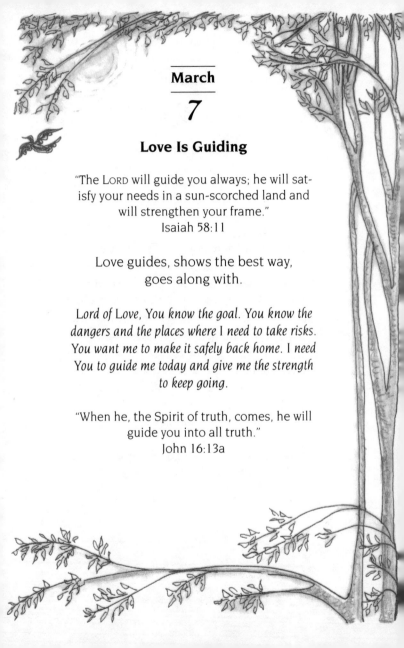

March

7

Love Is Guiding

"The LORD will guide you always; he will satisfy your needs in a sun-scorched land and
will strengthen your frame."
Isaiah 58:11

Love guides, shows the best way,
goes along with.

Lord of Love, You know the goal. You know the
dangers and the places where I need to take risks.
You want me to make it safely back home. I need
You to guide me today and give me the strength
to keep going.

"When he, the Spirit of truth, comes, he will
guide you into all truth."
John 16:13a

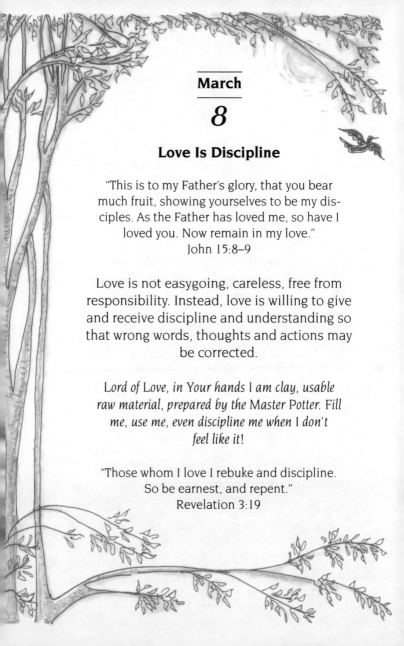

March

8

Love Is Discipline

"This is to my Father's glory, that you bear much fruit, showing yourselves to be my disciples. As the Father has loved me, so have I loved you. Now remain in my love."
John 15:8–9

Love is not easygoing, careless, free from responsibility. Instead, love is willing to give and receive discipline and understanding so that wrong words, thoughts and actions may be corrected.

Lord of Love, in Your hands I am clay, usable raw material, prepared by the Master Potter. Fill me, use me, even discipline me when I don't feel like it!

"Those whom I love I rebuke and discipline. So be earnest, and repent."
Revelation 3:19

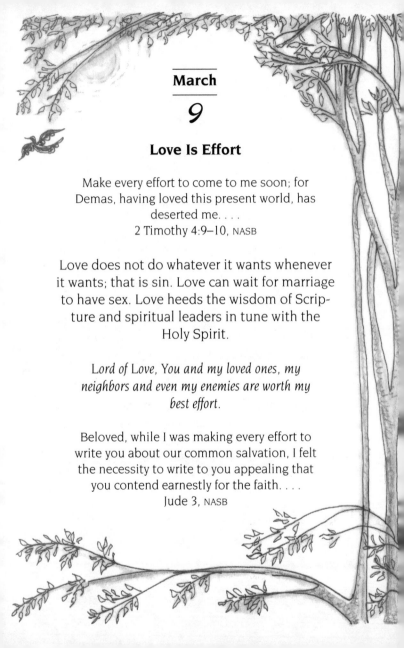

Love Is Effort

Make every effort to come to me soon; for
Demas, having loved this present world, has
deserted me. . . .
2 Timothy 4:9–10, NASB

Love does not do whatever it wants whenever
it wants; that is sin. Love can wait for marriage
to have sex. Love heeds the wisdom of Scripture and spiritual leaders in tune with the
Holy Spirit.

*Lord of Love, You and my loved ones, my
neighbors and even my enemies are worth my
best effort.*

Beloved, while I was making every effort to
write you about our common salvation, I felt
the necessity to write to you appealing that
you contend earnestly for the faith. . . .
Jude 3, NASB

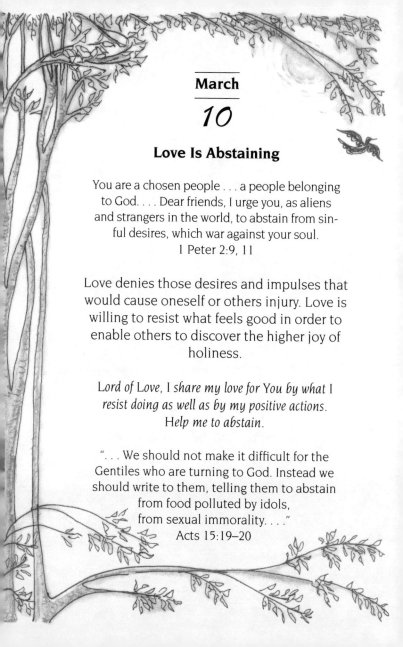

Love Is Abstaining

You are a chosen people . . . a people belonging
to God. . . . Dear friends, I urge you, as aliens
and strangers in the world, to abstain from sinful desires, which war against your soul.
1 Peter 2:9, 11

Love denies those desires and impulses that
would cause oneself or others injury. Love is
willing to resist what feels good in order to
enable others to discover the higher joy of
holiness.

Lord of Love, I share my love for You by what I
resist doing as well as by my positive actions.
Help me to abstain.

". . . We should not make it difficult for the
Gentiles who are turning to God. Instead we
should write to them, telling them to abstain
from food polluted by idols,
from sexual immorality. . . ."
Acts 15:19–20

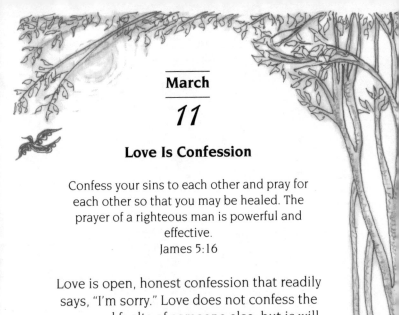

March

11

Love Is Confession

Confess your sins to each other and pray for each other so that you may be healed. The prayer of a righteous man is powerful and effective.
James 5:16

Love is open, honest confession that readily says, "I'm sorry." Love does not confess the errors and faults of someone else, but is willing to examine itself and make the necessary changes.

Lord of Love, help me see my own faults and get the log out!

If we confess our sins, he is faithful and just and will forgive us our sins and purify us from all unrighteousness.
1 John 1:9

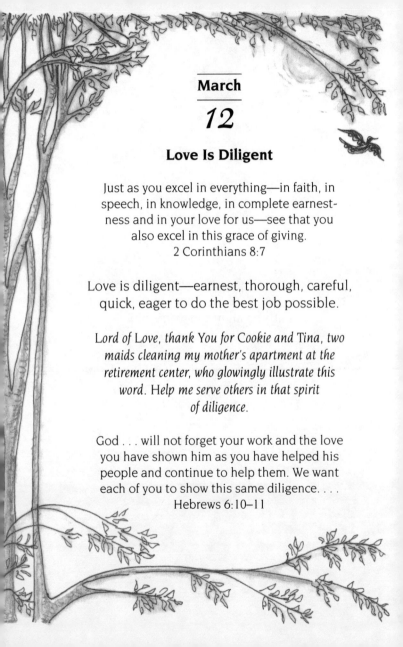

March

12

Love Is Diligent

Just as you excel in everything—in faith, in speech, in knowledge, in complete earnestness and in your love for us—see that you also excel in this grace of giving.
2 Corinthians 8:7

Love is diligent—earnest, thorough, careful, quick, eager to do the best job possible.

Lord of Love, thank You for Cookie and Tina, two maids cleaning my mother's apartment at the retirement center, who glowingly illustrate this word. Help me serve others in that spirit of diligence.

God . . . will not forget your work and the love you have shown him as you have helped his people and continue to help them. We want each of you to show this same diligence. . . .
Hebrews 6:10–11

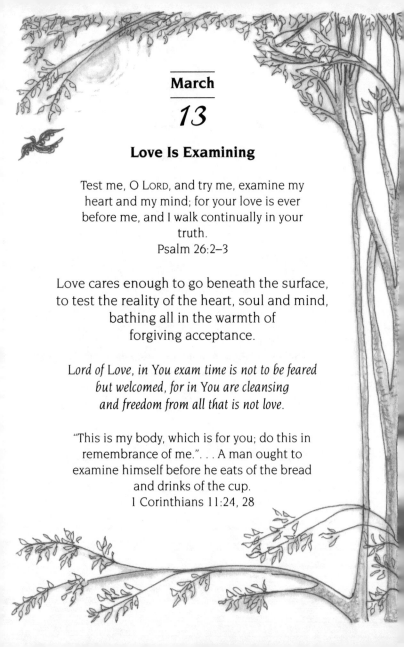

March

13

Love Is Examining

Test me, O Lᴏʀᴅ, and try me, examine my
heart and my mind; for your love is ever
before me, and I walk continually in your
truth.
Psalm 26:2–3

Love cares enough to go beneath the surface,
to test the reality of the heart, soul and mind,
bathing all in the warmth of
forgiving acceptance.

*Lord of Love, in You exam time is not to be feared
but welcomed, for in You are cleansing
and freedom from all that is not love.*

"This is my body, which is for you; do this in
remembrance of me.". . . A man ought to
examine himself before he eats of the bread
and drinks of the cup.
1 Corinthians 11:24, 28

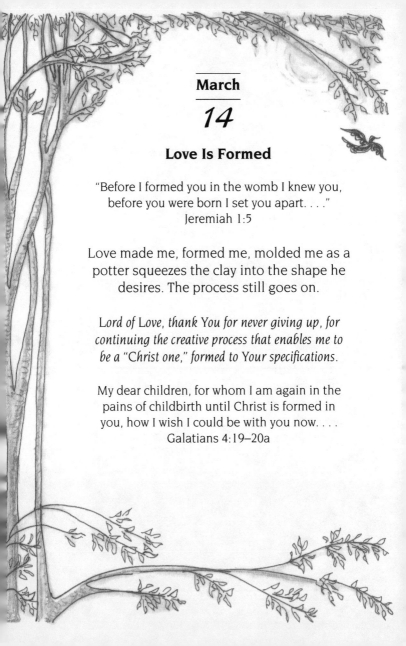

March

14

Love Is Formed

"Before I formed you in the womb I knew you,
before you were born I set you apart. . . ."
Jeremiah 1:5

Love made me, formed me, molded me as a
potter squeezes the clay into the shape he
desires. The process still goes on.

*Lord of Love, thank You for never giving up, for
continuing the creative process that enables me to
be a "Christ one," formed to Your specifications.*

My dear children, for whom I am again in the
pains of childbirth until Christ is formed in
you, how I wish I could be with you now. . . .
Galatians 4:19–20a

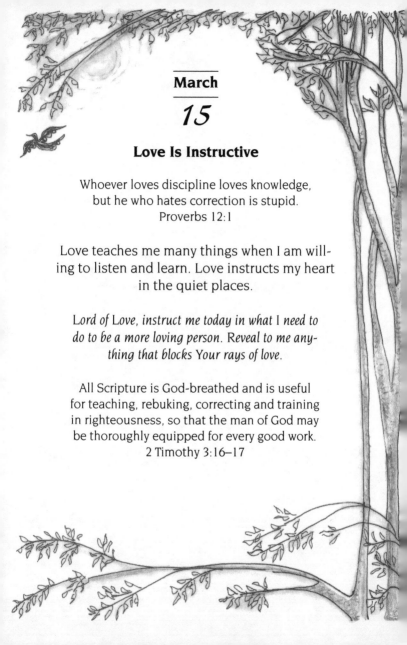

Love Is Instructive

Whoever loves discipline loves knowledge,
but he who hates correction is stupid.
Proverbs 12:1

Love teaches me many things when I am willing to listen and learn. Love instructs my heart
in the quiet places.

*Lord of Love, instruct me today in what I need to
do to be a more loving person. Reveal to me anything that blocks Your rays of love.*

All Scripture is God-breathed and is useful
for teaching, rebuking, correcting and training
in righteousness, so that the man of God may
be thoroughly equipped for every good work.
2 Timothy 3:16–17

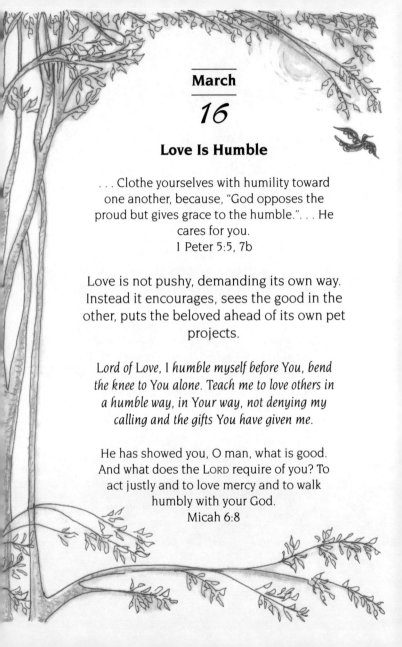

Love Is Humble

. . . Clothe yourselves with humility toward
one another, because, "God opposes the
proud but gives grace to the humble.". . . He
cares for you.
1 Peter 5:5, 7b

Love is not pushy, demanding its own way.
Instead it encourages, sees the good in the
other, puts the beloved ahead of its own pet
projects.

*Lord of Love, I humble myself before You, bend
the knee to You alone. Teach me to love others in
a humble way, in Your way, not denying my
calling and the gifts You have given me.*

He has showed you, O man, what is good.
And what does the LORD require of you? To
act justly and to love mercy and to walk
humbly with your God.
Micah 6:8

Love Is Meek

What do you prefer? Shall I come to you with a
whip, or in love and with a gentle [*meek* KJV]
Spirit?
1 Corinthians 4:21

Love is gentle, humble, meek. Love chooses to
give others another chance. Love waits for anger
to subside so that it can speak and act reasonably,
gently, from a heart that sees first its own faults.

*Lord of Love, thank You for the example of Jesus,
and also of Moses, the "meekest man on earth."
In my struggles to live like You, amid distressing
and sometimes crushing circumstances, give me
Your meek spirit.*

Remind the people to be subject to rulers
and authorities, to be obedient, to be ready
to do whatever is good, to slander no one, to
be peaceable and considerate, and
to show true humility [*all meekness* KJV]
toward all men.
Titus 3:1–2

18

Love Is Integrity

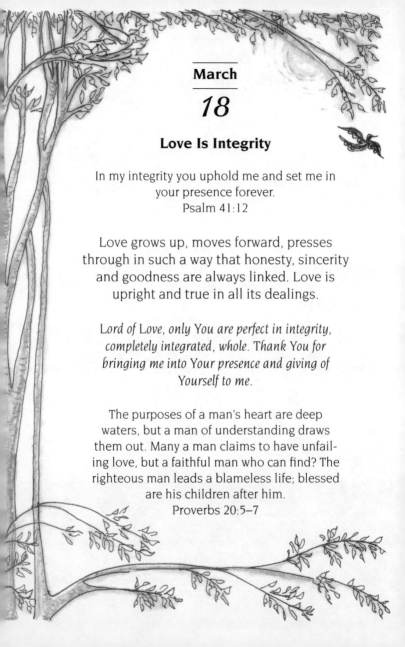

In my integrity you uphold me and set me in
your presence forever.
Psalm 41:12

Love grows up, moves forward, presses
through in such a way that honesty, sincerity
and goodness are always linked. Love is
upright and true in all its dealings.

*Lord of Love, only You are perfect in integrity,
completely integrated, whole. Thank You for
bringing me into Your presence and giving of
Yourself to me.*

The purposes of a man's heart are deep
waters, but a man of understanding draws
them out. Many a man claims to have unfailing love, but a faithful man who can find? The
righteous man leads a blameless life; blessed
are his children after him.
Proverbs 20:5–7

March

19

Love Is Renewal

Create in me a pure heart, O God, and renew
a steadfast spirit within me.
Psalm 51:10

Love is always new and renewing. Love
rebuilds the broken, repairs the ruins, makes
better than before.

*Lord of Love, I give You my broken heart, my
crushed spirit, my failing energy and hopes. As I
come into Your presence I find all I need to be
renewed, refreshed and to begin again holding
tightly onto Your hand.*

Those who hope in the LORD will renew their
strength. They will soar on wings like eagles;
they will run and not grow weary, they will
walk and not be faint.
Isaiah 40:31

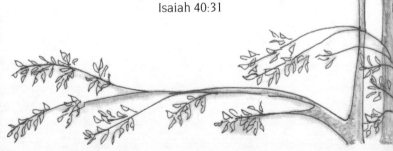

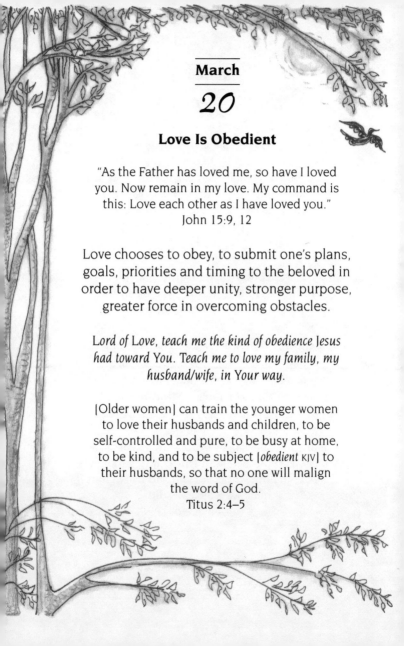

March

20

Love Is Obedient

"As the Father has loved me, so have I loved
you. Now remain in my love. My command is
this: Love each other as I have loved you."
John 15:9, 12

Love chooses to obey, to submit one's plans,
goals, priorities and timing to the beloved in
order to have deeper unity, stronger purpose,
greater force in overcoming obstacles.

*Lord of Love, teach me the kind of obedience Jesus
had toward You. Teach me to love my family, my
husband/wife, in Your way.*

[Older women] can train the younger women
to love their husbands and children, to be
self-controlled and pure, to be busy at home,
to be kind, and to be subject [*obedient* KJV] to
their husbands, so that no one will malign
the word of God.
Titus 2:4–5

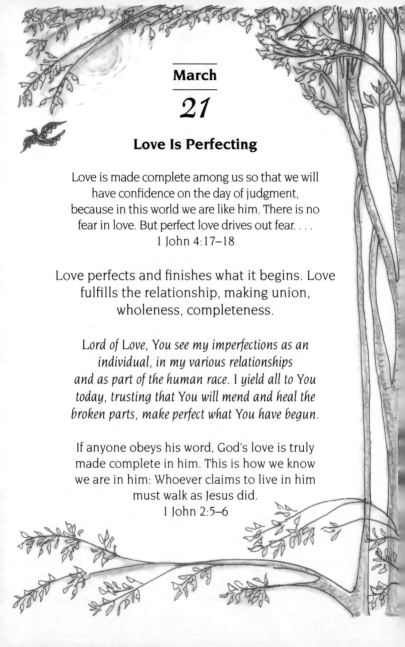

March

21

Love Is Perfecting

Love is made complete among us so that we will
have confidence on the day of judgment,
because in this world we are like him. There is no
fear in love. But perfect love drives out fear. . . .
1 John 4:17–18

Love perfects and finishes what it begins. Love
fulfills the relationship, making union,
wholeness, completeness.

Lord of Love, You see my imperfections as an
individual, in my various relationships
and as part of the human race. I yield all to You
today, trusting that You will mend and heal the
broken parts, make perfect what You have begun.

If anyone obeys his word, God's love is truly
made complete in him. This is how we know
we are in him: Whoever claims to live in him
must walk as Jesus did.
1 John 2:5–6

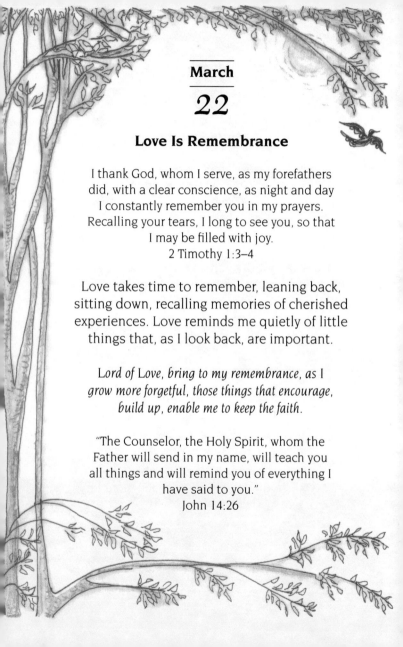

Love Is Remembrance

I thank God, whom I serve, as my forefathers
did, with a clear conscience, as night and day
I constantly remember you in my prayers.
Recalling your tears, I long to see you, so that
I may be filled with joy.
2 Timothy 1:3–4

Love takes time to remember, leaning back,
sitting down, recalling memories of cherished
experiences. Love reminds me quietly of little
things that, as I look back, are important.

*Lord of Love, bring to my remembrance, as I
grow more forgetful, those things that encourage,
build up, enable me to keep the faith.*

"The Counselor, the Holy Spirit, whom the
Father will send in my name, will teach you
all things and will remind you of everything I
have said to you."
John 14:26

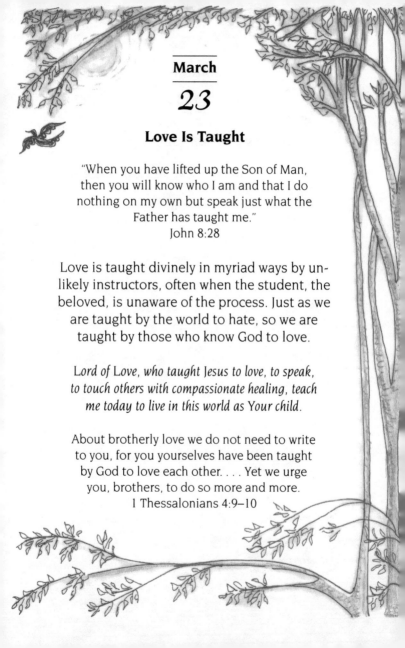

March

23

Love Is Taught

"When you have lifted up the Son of Man, then you will know who I am and that I do nothing on my own but speak just what the Father has taught me."
John 8:28

Love is taught divinely in myriad ways by un-likely instructors, often when the student, the beloved, is unaware of the process. Just as we are taught by the world to hate, so we are taught by those who know God to love.

Lord of Love, who taught Jesus to love, to speak, to touch others with compassionate healing, teach me today to live in this world as Your child.

About brotherly love we do not need to write to you, for you yourselves have been taught by God to love each other. . . . Yet we urge you, brothers, to do so more and more.
1 Thessalonians 4:9–10

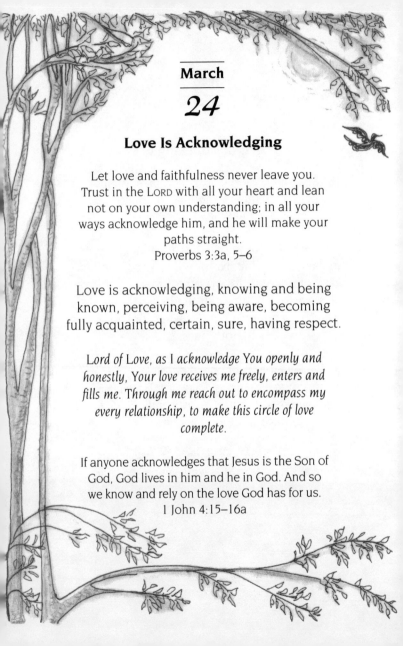

Love Is Acknowledging

Let love and faithfulness never leave you.
Trust in the Lord with all your heart and lean
not on your own understanding; in all your
ways acknowledge him, and he will make your
paths straight.
Proverbs 3:3a, 5–6

Love is acknowledging, knowing and being
known, perceiving, being aware, becoming
fully acquainted, certain, sure, having respect.

*Lord of Love, as I acknowledge You openly and
honestly, Your love receives me freely, enters and
fills me. Through me reach out to encompass my
every relationship, to make this circle of love
complete.*

If anyone acknowledges that Jesus is the Son of
God, God lives in him and he in God. And so
we know and rely on the love God has for us.
1 John 4:15–16a

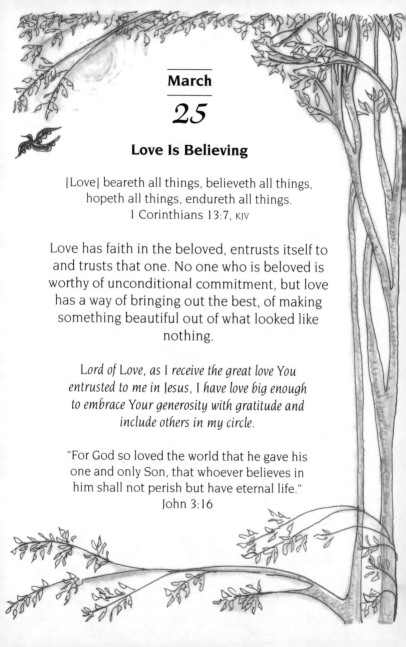

March

25

Love Is Believing

[Love] beareth all things, believeth all things,
hopeth all things, endureth all things.
1 Corinthians 13:7, KJV

Love has faith in the beloved, entrusts itself to
and trusts that one. No one who is beloved is
worthy of unconditional commitment, but love
has a way of bringing out the best, of making
something beautiful out of what looked like
nothing.

*Lord of Love, as I receive the great love You
entrusted to me in Jesus, I have love big enough
to embrace Your generosity with gratitude and
include others in my circle.*

"For God so loved the world that he gave his
one and only Son, that whoever believes in
him shall not perish but have eternal life."
John 3:16

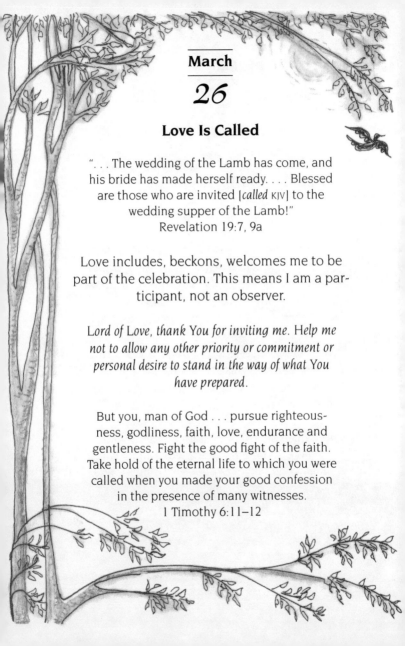

Love Is Called

". . . The wedding of the Lamb has come, and
his bride has made herself ready. . . . Blessed
are those who are invited [*called* KJV] to the
wedding supper of the Lamb!"
Revelation 19:7, 9a

Love includes, beckons, welcomes me to be
part of the celebration. This means I am a par-
ticipant, not an observer.

*Lord of Love, thank You for inviting me. Help me
not to allow any other priority or commitment or
personal desire to stand in the way of what You
have prepared.*

But you, man of God . . . pursue righteousness, godliness, faith, love, endurance and
gentleness. Fight the good fight of the faith.
Take hold of the eternal life to which you were
called when you made your good confession
in the presence of many witnesses.
1 Timothy 6:11–12

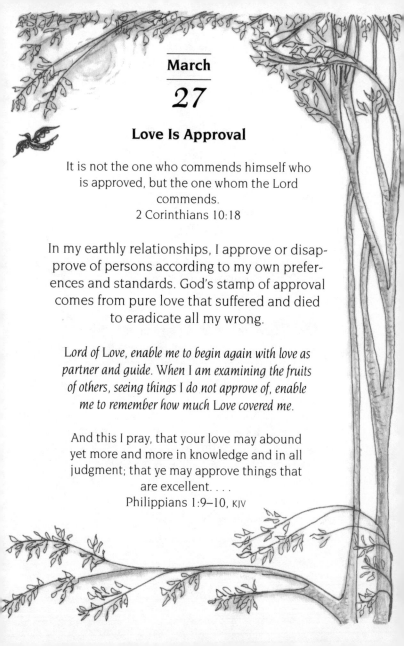

March

27

Love Is Approval

It is not the one who commends himself who
is approved, but the one whom the Lord
commends.
2 Corinthians 10:18

In my earthly relationships, I approve or disap-
prove of persons according to my own prefer-
ences and standards. God's stamp of approval
comes from pure love that suffered and died
to eradicate all my wrong.

Lord of Love, enable me to begin again with love as
partner and guide. When I am examining the fruits
of others, seeing things I do not approve of, enable
me to remember how much Love covered me.

And this I pray, that your love may abound
yet more and more in knowledge and in all
judgment; that ye may approve things that
are excellent. . . .
Philippians 1:9–10, KJV

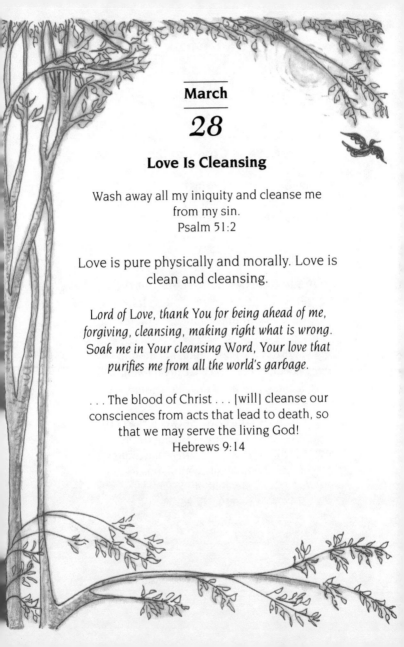

March

28

Love Is Cleansing

Wash away all my iniquity and cleanse me
from my sin.
Psalm 51:2

Love is pure physically and morally. Love is
clean and cleansing.

*Lord of Love, thank You for being ahead of me,
forgiving, cleansing, making right what is wrong.
Soak me in Your cleansing Word, Your love that
purifies me from all the world's garbage.*

. . . The blood of Christ . . . [will] cleanse our
consciences from acts that lead to death, so
that we may serve the living God!
Hebrews 9:14

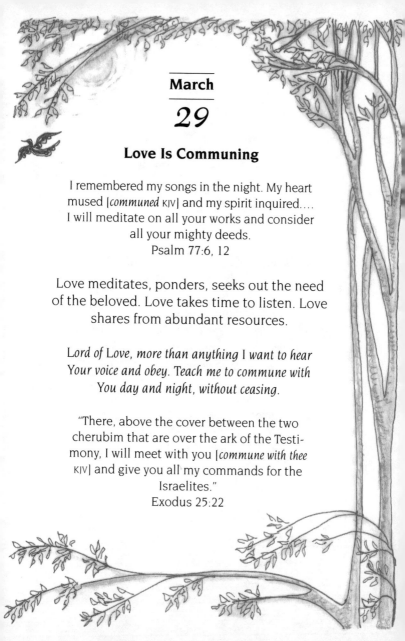

March

29

Love Is Communing

I remembered my songs in the night. My heart
mused [*communed* KJV] and my spirit inquired....
I will meditate on all your works and consider
all your mighty deeds.
Psalm 77:6, 12

Love meditates, ponders, seeks out the need
of the beloved. Love takes time to listen. Love
shares from abundant resources.

*Lord of Love, more than anything I want to hear
Your voice and obey. Teach me to commune with
You day and night, without ceasing.*

"There, above the cover between the two
cherubim that are over the ark of the Testi-
mony, I will meet with you [*commune with thee*
KJV] and give you all my commands for the
Israelites."
Exodus 25:22

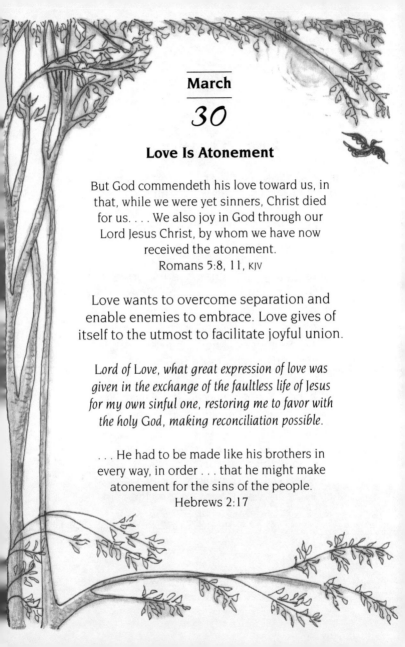

Love Is Atonement

But God commendeth his love toward us, in that, while we were yet sinners, Christ died for us. . . . We also joy in God through our Lord Jesus Christ, by whom we have now received the atonement.
Romans 5:8, 11, KJV

Love wants to overcome separation and enable enemies to embrace. Love gives of itself to the utmost to facilitate joyful union.

Lord of Love, what great expression of love was given in the exchange of the faultless life of Jesus for my own sinful one, restoring me to favor with the holy God, making reconciliation possible.

. . . He had to be made like his brothers in every way, in order . . . that he might make atonement for the sins of the people.
Hebrews 2:17

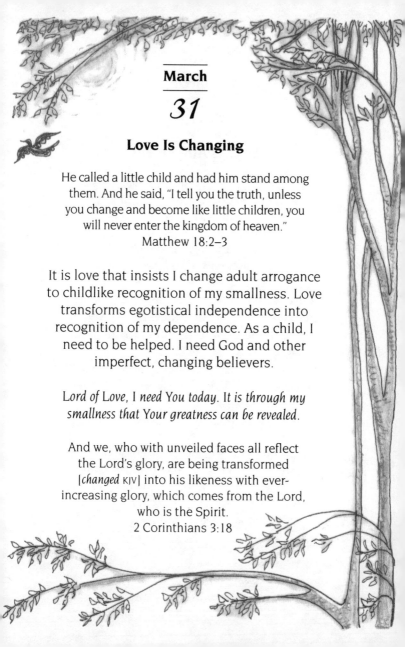

March

31

Love Is Changing

He called a little child and had him stand among
them. And he said, "I tell you the truth, unless
you change and become like little children, you
will never enter the kingdom of heaven."
Matthew 18:2–3

It is love that insists I change adult arrogance
to childlike recognition of my smallness. Love
transforms egotistical independence into
recognition of my dependence. As a child, I
need to be helped. I need God and other
imperfect, changing believers.

*Lord of Love, I need You today. It is through my
smallness that Your greatness can be revealed.*

And we, who with unveiled faces all reflect
the Lord's glory, are being transformed
[*changed* KJV] into his likeness with ever-
increasing glory, which comes from the Lord,
who is the Spirit.
2 Corinthians 3:18

April
Love Is Enduring

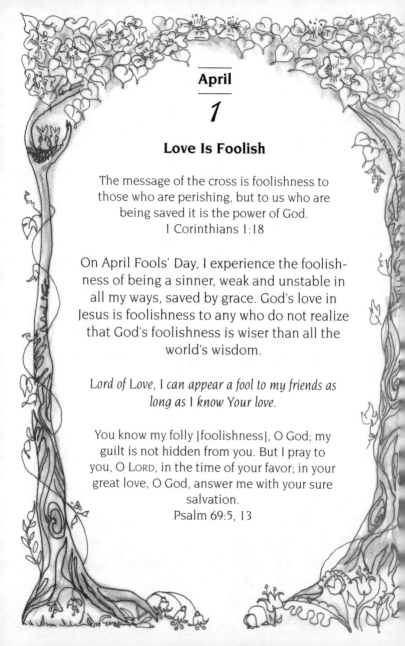

April

1

Love Is Foolish

The message of the cross is foolishness to
those who are perishing, but to us who are
being saved it is the power of God.
1 Corinthians 1:18

On April Fools' Day, I experience the foolishness of being a sinner, weak and unstable in
all my ways, saved by grace. God's love in
Jesus is foolishness to any who do not realize
that God's foolishness is wiser than all the
world's wisdom.

*Lord of Love, I can appear a fool to my friends as
long as I know Your love.*

You know my folly [foolishness], O God; my
guilt is not hidden from you. But I pray to
you, O Lord, in the time of your favor; in your
great love, O God, answer me with your sure
salvation.
Psalm 69:5, 13

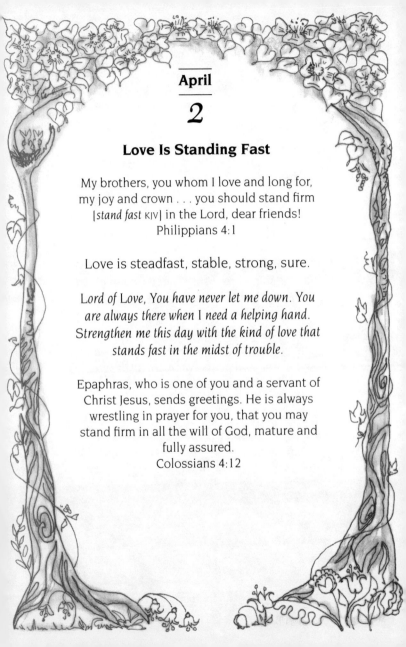

April

2

Love Is Standing Fast

My brothers, you whom I love and long for,
my joy and crown . . . you should stand firm
[*stand fast* KJV] in the Lord, dear friends!
Philippians 4:1

Love is steadfast, stable, strong, sure.

*Lord of Love, You have never let me down. You
are always there when I need a helping hand.
Strengthen me this day with the kind of love that
stands fast in the midst of trouble.*

Epaphras, who is one of you and a servant of
Christ Jesus, sends greetings. He is always
wrestling in prayer for you, that you may
stand firm in all the will of God, mature and
fully assured.
Colossians 4:12

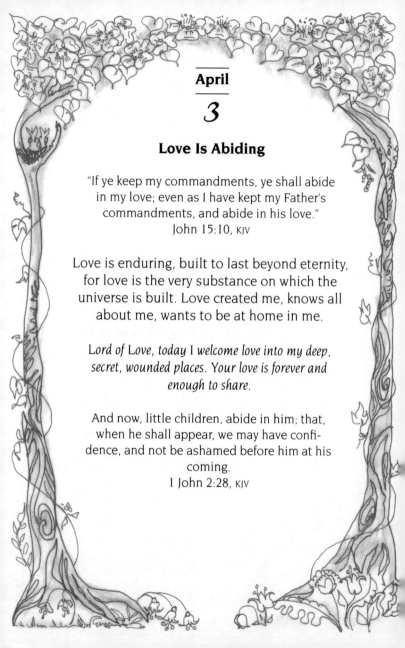

April

3

Love Is Abiding

"If ye keep my commandments, ye shall abide
in my love; even as I have kept my Father's
commandments, and abide in his love."
John 15:10, KJV

Love is enduring, built to last beyond eternity,
for love is the very substance on which the
universe is built. Love created me, knows all
about me, wants to be at home in me.

*Lord of Love, today I welcome love into my deep,
secret, wounded places. Your love is forever and
enough to share.*

And now, little children, abide in him; that,
when he shall appear, we may have confidence, and not be ashamed before him at his
coming.
1 John 2:28, KJV

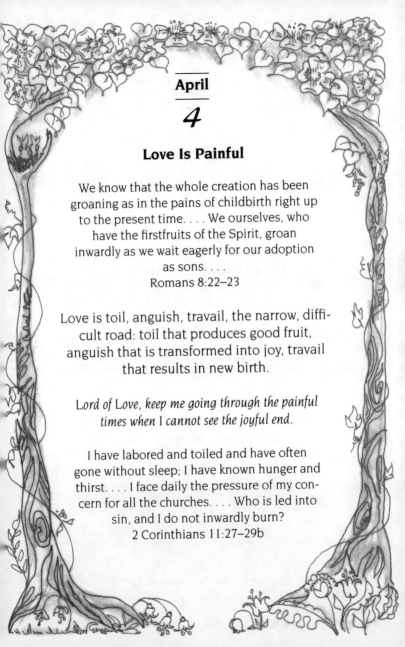

Love Is Painful

We know that the whole creation has been groaning as in the pains of childbirth right up to the present time. . . . We ourselves, who have the firstfruits of the Spirit, groan inwardly as we wait eagerly for our adoption as sons. . . .
Romans 8:22–23

Love is toil, anguish, travail, the narrow, difficult road: toil that produces good fruit, anguish that is transformed into joy, travail that results in new birth.

Lord of Love, keep me going through the painful times when I cannot see the joyful end.

I have labored and toiled and have often gone without sleep; I have known hunger and thirst. . . . I face daily the pressure of my concern for all the churches. . . . Who is led into sin, and I do not inwardly burn?
2 Corinthians 11:27–29b

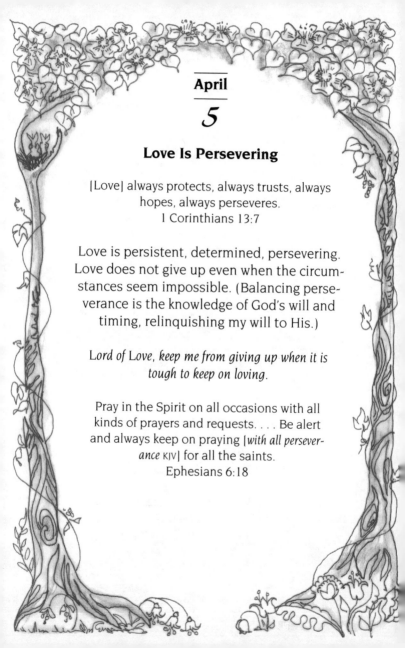

April

5

Love Is Persevering

[Love] always protects, always trusts, always
hopes, always perseveres.
1 Corinthians 13:7

Love is persistent, determined, persevering.
Love does not give up even when the circumstances seem impossible. (Balancing perseverance is the knowledge of God's will and
timing, relinquishing my will to His.)

*Lord of Love, keep me from giving up when it is
tough to keep on loving.*

Pray in the Spirit on all occasions with all
kinds of prayers and requests. . . . Be alert
and always keep on praying [*with all perseverance* KJV] for all the saints.
Ephesians 6:18

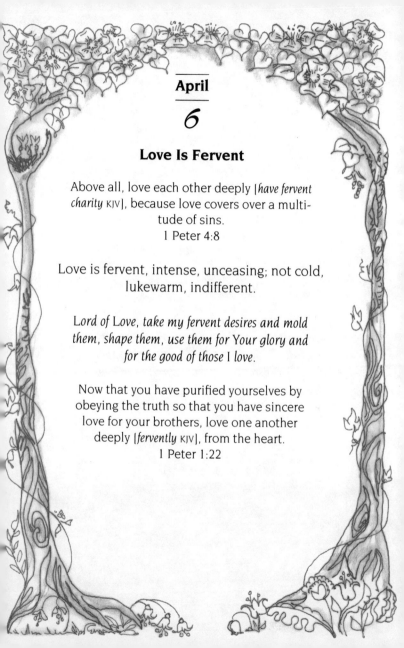

Love Is Fervent

Above all, love each other deeply [*have fervent charity* KJV], because love covers over a multitude of sins.
1 Peter 4:8

Love is fervent, intense, unceasing; not cold, lukewarm, indifferent.

Lord of Love, take my fervent desires and mold them, shape them, use them for Your glory and for the good of those I love.

Now that you have purified yourselves by obeying the truth so that you have sincere love for your brothers, love one another deeply [*fervently* KJV], from the heart.
1 Peter 1:22

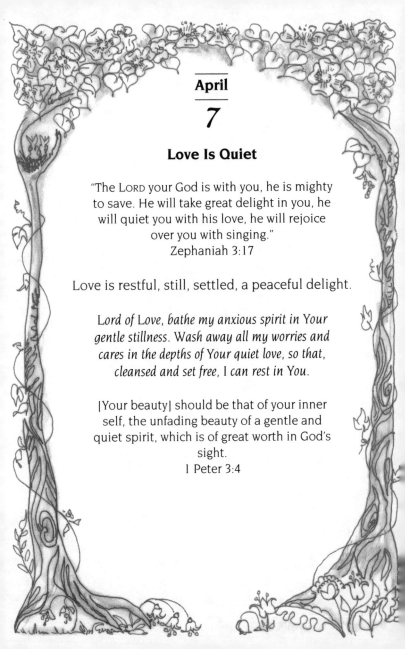

April

7

Love Is Quiet

"The LORD your God is with you, he is mighty
to save. He will take great delight in you, he
will quiet you with his love, he will rejoice
over you with singing."
Zephaniah 3:17

Love is restful, still, settled, a peaceful delight.

*Lord of Love, bathe my anxious spirit in Your
gentle stillness. Wash away all my worries and
cares in the depths of Your quiet love, so that,
cleansed and set free, I can rest in You.*

[Your beauty] should be that of your inner
self, the unfading beauty of a gentle and
quiet spirit, which is of great worth in God's
sight.
1 Peter 3:4

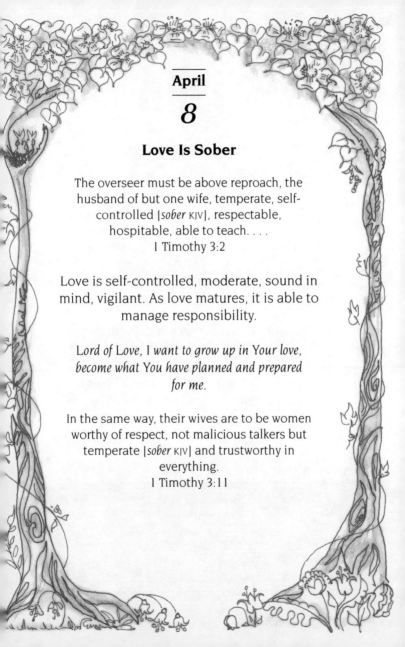

April

8

Love Is Sober

The overseer must be above reproach, the
husband of but one wife, temperate, self-
controlled [*sober* KJV], respectable,
hospitable, able to teach. . . .
1 Timothy 3:2

Love is self-controlled, moderate, sound in
mind, vigilant. As love matures, it is able to
manage responsibility.

Lord of Love, I want to grow up in Your love,
become what You have planned and prepared
for me.

In the same way, their wives are to be women
worthy of respect, not malicious talkers but
temperate [*sober* KJV] and trustworthy in
everything.
1 Timothy 3:11

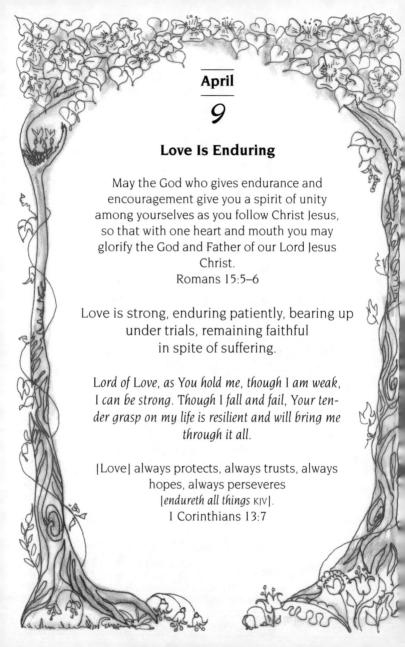

April

9

Love Is Enduring

May the God who gives endurance and
encouragement give you a spirit of unity
among yourselves as you follow Christ Jesus,
so that with one heart and mouth you may
glorify the God and Father of our Lord Jesus
Christ.
Romans 15:5–6

Love is strong, enduring patiently, bearing up
under trials, remaining faithful
in spite of suffering.

*Lord of Love, as You hold me, though I am weak,
I can be strong. Though I fall and fail, Your tender grasp on my life is resilient and will bring me
through it all.*

[Love] always protects, always trusts, always
hopes, always perseveres
[*endureth all things* KJV].
1 Corinthians 13:7

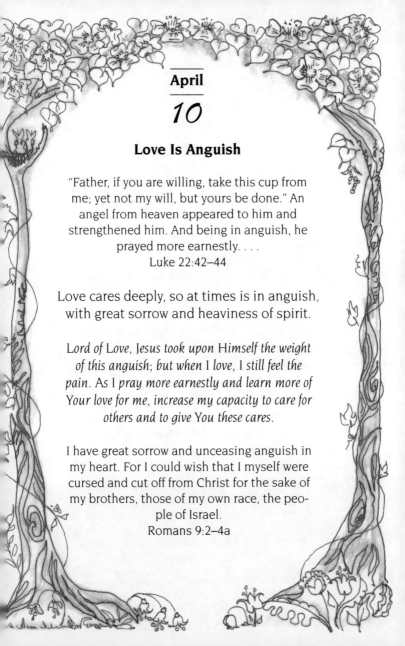

April

10

Love Is Anguish

"Father, if you are willing, take this cup from me; yet not my will, but yours be done." An angel from heaven appeared to him and strengthened him. And being in anguish, he prayed more earnestly. . . .
Luke 22:42–44

Love cares deeply, so at times is in anguish, with great sorrow and heaviness of spirit.

Lord of Love, Jesus took upon Himself the weight of this anguish; but when I love, I still feel the pain. As I pray more earnestly and learn more of Your love for me, increase my capacity to care for others and to give You these cares.

I have great sorrow and unceasing anguish in my heart. For I could wish that I myself were cursed and cut off from Christ for the sake of my brothers, those of my own race, the people of Israel.
Romans 9:2–4a

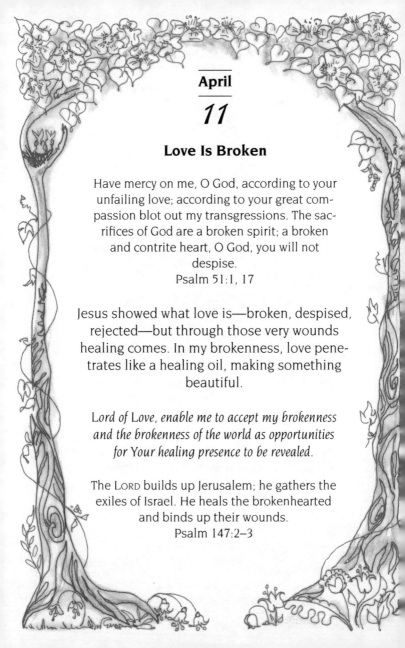

April

11

Love Is Broken

Have mercy on me, O God, according to your unfailing love; according to your great compassion blot out my transgressions. The sacrifices of God are a broken spirit; a broken and contrite heart, O God, you will not despise.
Psalm 51:1, 17

Jesus showed what love is—broken, despised, rejected—but through those very wounds healing comes. In my brokenness, love penetrates like a healing oil, making something beautiful.

Lord of Love, enable me to accept my brokenness and the brokenness of the world as opportunities for Your healing presence to be revealed.

The LORD builds up Jerusalem; he gathers the exiles of Israel. He heals the brokenhearted and binds up their wounds.
Psalm 147:2–3

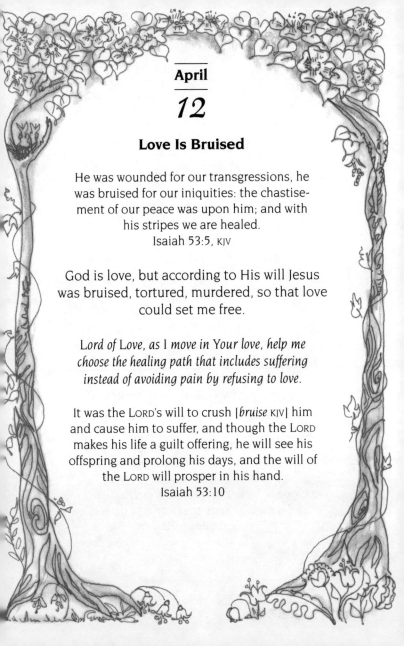

April

12

Love Is Bruised

He was wounded for our transgressions, he was bruised for our iniquities: the chastisement of our peace was upon him; and with his stripes we are healed.
Isaiah 53:5, KJV

God is love, but according to His will Jesus was bruised, tortured, murdered, so that love could set me free.

Lord of Love, as I move in Your love, help me choose the healing path that includes suffering instead of avoiding pain by refusing to love.

It was the LORD's will to crush [*bruise* KJV] him and cause him to suffer, and though the LORD makes his life a guilt offering, he will see his offspring and prolong his days, and the will of the LORD will prosper in his hand.
Isaiah 53:10

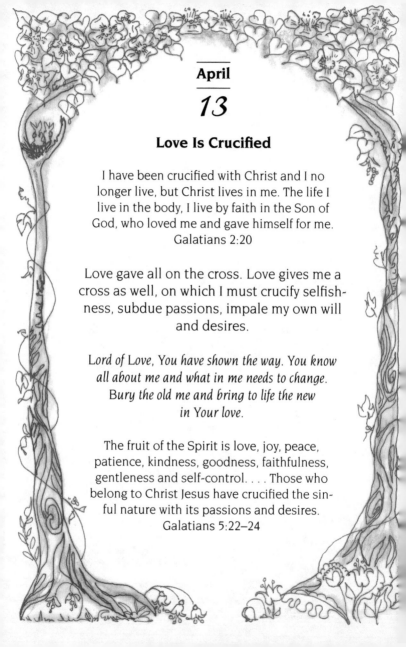

April

13

Love Is Crucified

I have been crucified with Christ and I no longer live, but Christ lives in me. The life I live in the body, I live by faith in the Son of God, who loved me and gave himself for me.
Galatians 2:20

Love gave all on the cross. Love gives me a cross as well, on which I must crucify selfishness, subdue passions, impale my own will and desires.

Lord of Love, You have shown the way. You know all about me and what in me needs to change. Bury the old me and bring to life the new in Your love.

The fruit of the Spirit is love, joy, peace, patience, kindness, goodness, faithfulness, gentleness and self-control. . . . Those who belong to Christ Jesus have crucified the sinful nature with its passions and desires.
Galatians 5:22–24

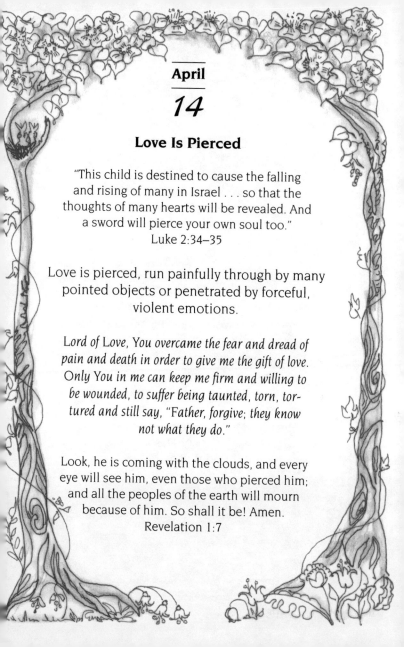

April

14

Love Is Pierced

"This child is destined to cause the falling
and rising of many in Israel . . . so that the
thoughts of many hearts will be revealed. And
a sword will pierce your own soul too."
Luke 2:34–35

Love is pierced, run painfully through by many
pointed objects or penetrated by forceful,
violent emotions.

*Lord of Love, You overcame the fear and dread of
pain and death in order to give me the gift of love.
Only You in me can keep me firm and willing to
be wounded, to suffer being taunted, torn, tortured and still say, "Father, forgive; they know
not what they do."*

Look, he is coming with the clouds, and every
eye will see him, even those who pierced him;
and all the peoples of the earth will mourn
because of him. So shall it be! Amen.
Revelation 1:7

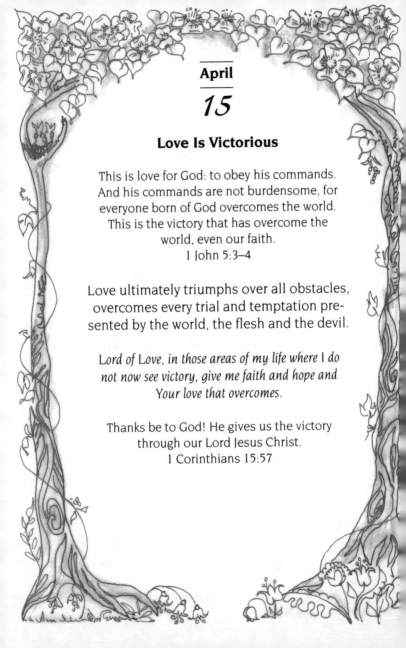

April

15

Love Is Victorious

This is love for God: to obey his commands.
And his commands are not burdensome, for
everyone born of God overcomes the world.
This is the victory that has overcome the
world, even our faith.
1 John 5:3–4

Love ultimately triumphs over all obstacles,
overcomes every trial and temptation pre-
sented by the world, the flesh and the devil.

*Lord of Love, in those areas of my life where I do
not now see victory, give me faith and hope and
Your love that overcomes.*

Thanks be to God! He gives us the victory
through our Lord Jesus Christ.
1 Corinthians 15:57

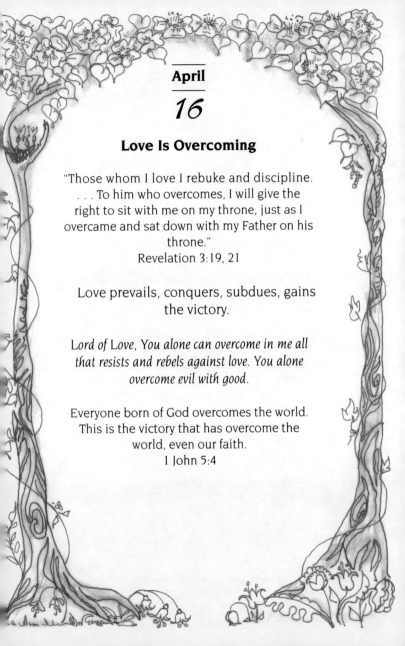

April

16

Love Is Overcoming

"Those whom I love I rebuke and discipline.
. . . To him who overcomes, I will give the
right to sit with me on my throne, just as I
overcame and sat down with my Father on his
throne."
Revelation 3:19, 21

Love prevails, conquers, subdues, gains
the victory.

*Lord of Love, You alone can overcome in me all
that resists and rebels against love. You alone
overcome evil with good.*

Everyone born of God overcomes the world.
This is the victory that has overcome the
world, even our faith.
1 John 5:4

Love Is Rejoicing

Love does not delight in evil but rejoices with
the truth.
1 Corinthians 13:6

Love is cheerful, calmly happy, glad, joyful.

Lord of Love, as You reign in me, clouds of sad-
ness and grief and angry depression lift so that
the sunshine of Your joy, full of glory, can shine
brighter and brighter.

Though you have not seen him, you love him;
and even though you do not see him now,
you believe in him and are filled with an inex-
pressible and glorious joy.
1 Peter 1:8

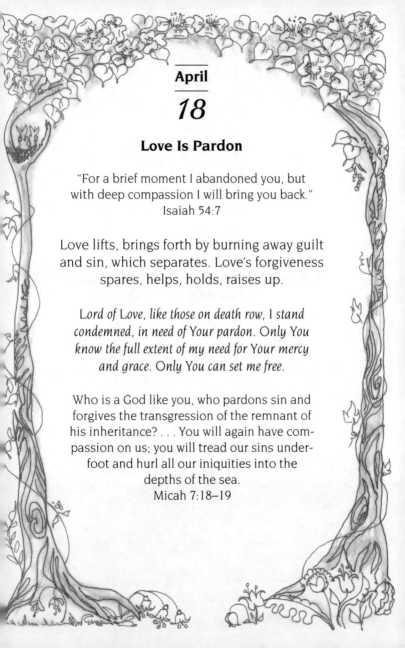

April

18

Love Is Pardon

"For a brief moment I abandoned you, but
with deep compassion I will bring you back."
Isaiah 54:7

Love lifts, brings forth by burning away guilt
and sin, which separates. Love's forgiveness
spares, helps, holds, raises up.

*Lord of Love, like those on death row, I stand
condemned, in need of Your pardon. Only You
know the full extent of my need for Your mercy
and grace. Only You can set me free.*

Who is a God like you, who pardons sin and
forgives the transgression of the remnant of
his inheritance? . . . You will again have compassion on us; you will tread our sins under-
foot and hurl all our iniquities into the
depths of the sea.
Micah 7:18–19

April

19

Love Is Longsuffering

The fruit of the Spirit is love, joy, peace, patience [*long-suffering* KJV], kindness, goodness, faithfulness, gentleness and self-control. . . .
Galatians 5:22–23

Love suffers long with patience and forbearance and fortitude.

Lord of Love, I do not want to suffer or persist in patience for a long time when those I love are not doing things my way. Grow in me all the fruit of Your Spirit, even longsuffering.

You, however, know all about my teaching, my way of life, my purpose, faith, patience [*long-suffering* KJV], love, endurance, persecutions, sufferings. . . . Yet the Lord rescued me from all of them.
2 Timothy 3:10–11

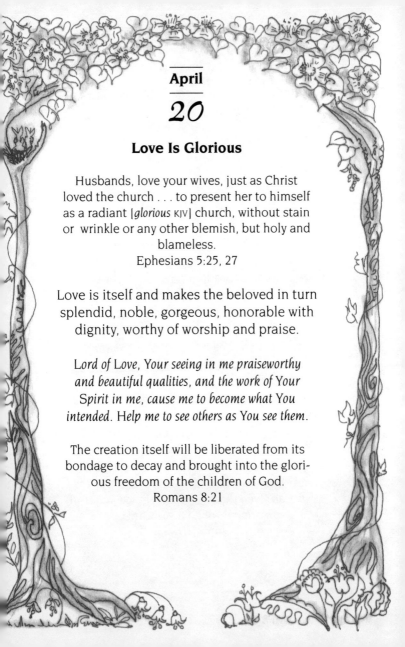

April

20

Love Is Glorious

Husbands, love your wives, just as Christ
loved the church . . . to present her to himself
as a radiant [*glorious* KJV] church, without stain
or wrinkle or any other blemish, but holy and
blameless.
Ephesians 5:25, 27

Love is itself and makes the beloved in turn
splendid, noble, gorgeous, honorable with
dignity, worthy of worship and praise.

*Lord of Love, Your seeing in me praiseworthy
and beautiful qualities, and the work of Your
Spirit in me, cause me to become what You
intended. Help me to see others as You see them.*

The creation itself will be liberated from its
bondage to decay and brought into the glorious freedom of the children of God.
Romans 8:21

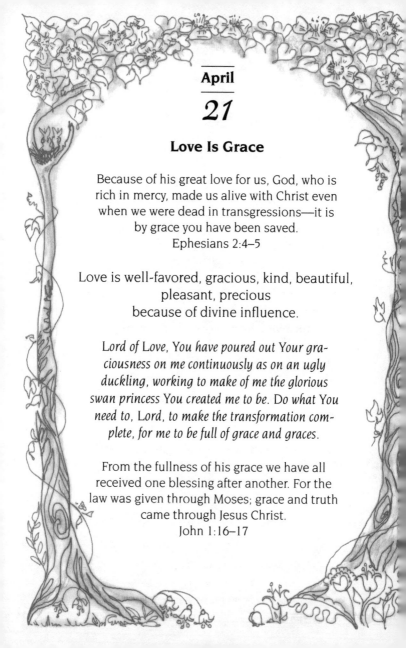

April

21

Love Is Grace

Because of his great love for us, God, who is
rich in mercy, made us alive with Christ even
when we were dead in transgressions—it is
by grace you have been saved.
Ephesians 2:4–5

Love is well-favored, gracious, kind, beautiful,
pleasant, precious
because of divine influence.

*Lord of Love, You have poured out Your gra-
ciousness on me continuously as on an ugly
duckling, working to make of me the glorious
swan princess You created me to be. Do what You
need to, Lord, to make the transformation complete, for me to be full of grace and graces.*

From the fullness of his grace we have all
received one blessing after another. For the
law was given through Moses; grace and truth
came through Jesus Christ.
John 1:16–17

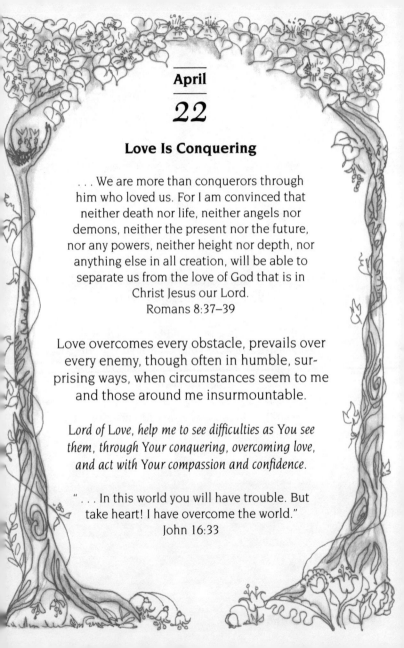

April

22

Love Is Conquering

. . . We are more than conquerors through
him who loved us. For I am convinced that
neither death nor life, neither angels nor
demons, neither the present nor the future,
nor any powers, neither height nor depth, nor
anything else in all creation, will be able to
separate us from the love of God that is in
Christ Jesus our Lord.
Romans 8:37–39

Love overcomes every obstacle, prevails over
every enemy, though often in humble, surprising ways, when circumstances seem to me
and those around me insurmountable.

*Lord of Love, help me to see difficulties as You see
them, through Your conquering, overcoming love,
and act with Your compassion and confidence.*

" . . . In this world you will have trouble. But
take heart! I have overcome the world."
John 16:33

April

23

Love Is Kind

Love is patient, love is kind. It does not envy,
it does not boast, it is not proud. It is not
rude, it is not self-seeking, it is not easily
angered, it keeps no record of wrongs.
1 Corinthians 13:4–5

Love acts benevolently, makes itself useful, is
easy, good, gracious, kind.

*Lord of Love, forgive the many times I have not
demonstrated Your kindness to others. Thank
You for Your many kindnesses to me. Help me
today to share.*

Be kind and compassionate to one another,
forgiving each other, just as in Christ God
forgave you.
Ephesians 4:32

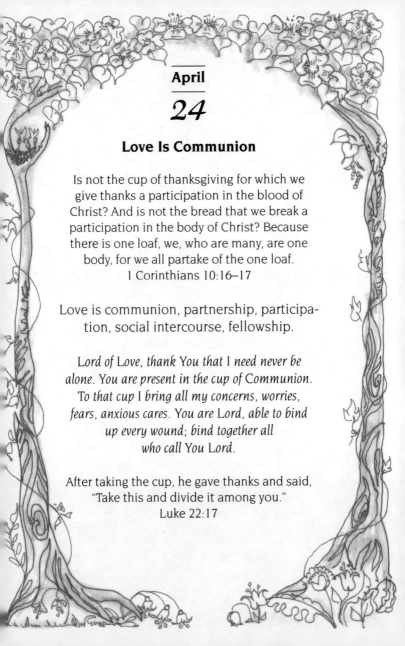

Love Is Communion

Is not the cup of thanksgiving for which we give thanks a participation in the blood of Christ? And is not the bread that we break a participation in the body of Christ? Because there is one loaf, we, who are many, are one body, for we all partake of the one loaf.
1 Corinthians 10:16–17

Love is communion, partnership, participation, social intercourse, fellowship.

Lord of Love, thank You that I need never be alone. You are present in the cup of Communion. To that cup I bring all my concerns, worries, fears, anxious cares. You are Lord, able to bind up every wound; bind together all who call You Lord.

After taking the cup, he gave thanks and said, "Take this and divide it among you."
Luke 22:17

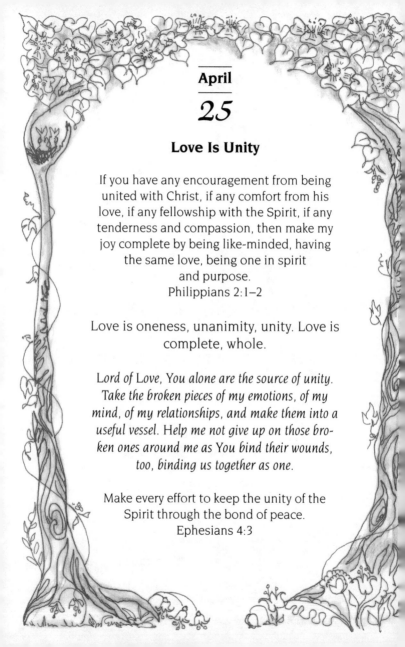

April

25

Love Is Unity

If you have any encouragement from being
united with Christ, if any comfort from his
love, if any fellowship with the Spirit, if any
tenderness and compassion, then make my
joy complete by being like-minded, having
the same love, being one in spirit
and purpose.
Philippians 2:1–2

Love is oneness, unanimity, unity. Love is
complete, whole.

Lord of Love, You alone are the source of unity.
Take the broken pieces of my emotions, of my
mind, of my relationships, and make them into a
useful vessel. Help me not give up on those bro-
ken ones around me as You bind their wounds,
too, binding us together as one.

Make every effort to keep the unity of the
Spirit through the bond of peace.
Ephesians 4:3

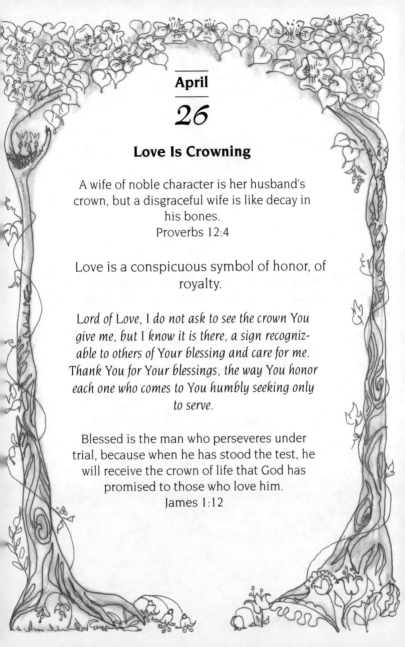

Love Is Crowning

A wife of noble character is her husband's
crown, but a disgraceful wife is like decay in
his bones.
Proverbs 12:4

Love is a conspicuous symbol of honor, of
royalty.

*Lord of Love, I do not ask to see the crown You
give me, but I know it is there, a sign recogniz-
able to others of Your blessing and care for me.
Thank You for Your blessings, the way You honor
each one who comes to You humbly seeking only
to serve.*

Blessed is the man who perseveres under
trial, because when he has stood the test, he
will receive the crown of life that God has
promised to those who love him.
James 1:12

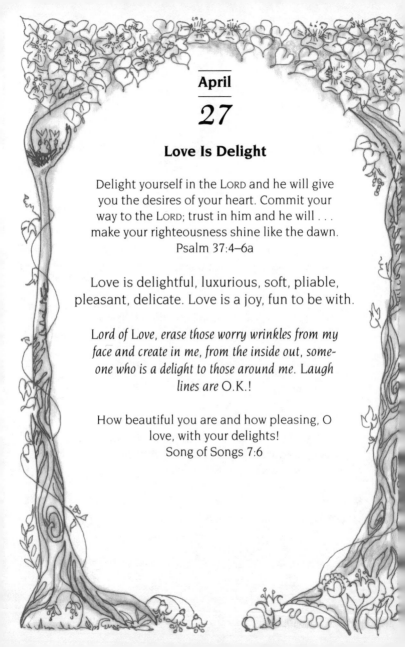

Love Is Delight

Delight yourself in the Lord and he will give
you the desires of your heart. Commit your
way to the Lord; trust in him and he will . . .
make your righteousness shine like the dawn.
Psalm 37:4–6a

Love is delightful, luxurious, soft, pliable,
pleasant, delicate. Love is a joy, fun to be with.

*Lord of Love, erase those worry wrinkles from my
face and create in me, from the inside out, someone who is a delight to those around me. Laugh
lines are O.K.!*

How beautiful you are and how pleasing, O
love, with your delights!
Song of Songs 7:6

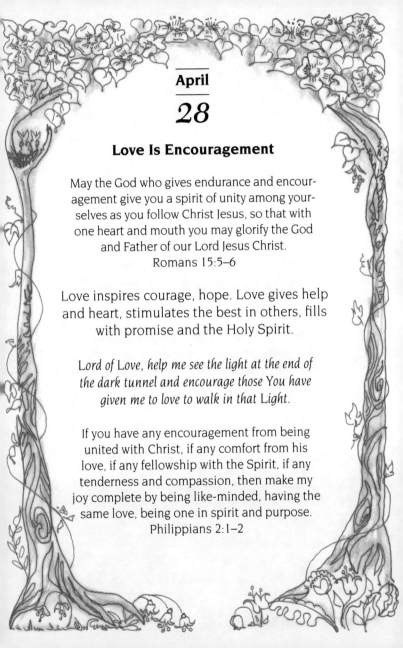

Love Is Encouragement

May the God who gives endurance and encouragement give you a spirit of unity among yourselves as you follow Christ Jesus, so that with
one heart and mouth you may glorify the God
and Father of our Lord Jesus Christ.
Romans 15:5–6

Love inspires courage, hope. Love gives help
and heart, stimulates the best in others, fills
with promise and the Holy Spirit.

Lord of Love, help me see the light at the end of
the dark tunnel and encourage those You have
given me to love to walk in that Light.

If you have any encouragement from being
united with Christ, if any comfort from his
love, if any fellowship with the Spirit, if any
tenderness and compassion, then make my
joy complete by being like-minded, having the
same love, being one in spirit and purpose.
Philippians 2:1–2

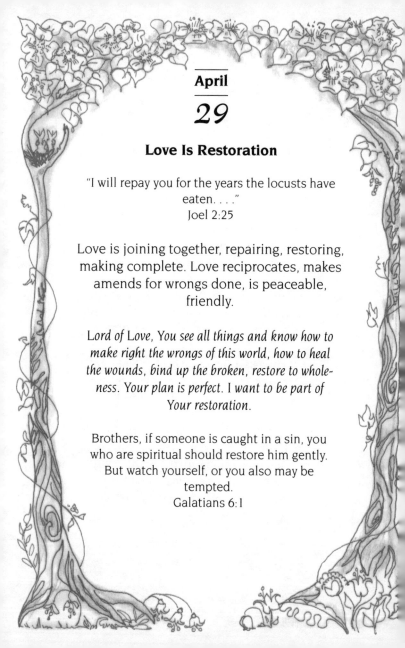

Love Is Restoration

"I will repay you for the years the locusts have
eaten. . . ."
Joel 2:25

Love is joining together, repairing, restoring,
making complete. Love reciprocates, makes
amends for wrongs done, is peaceable,
friendly.

*Lord of Love, You see all things and know how to
make right the wrongs of this world, how to heal
the wounds, bind up the broken, restore to wholeness. Your plan is perfect. I want to be part of
Your restoration.*

Brothers, if someone is caught in a sin, you
who are spiritual should restore him gently.
But watch yourself, or you also may be
tempted.
Galatians 6:1

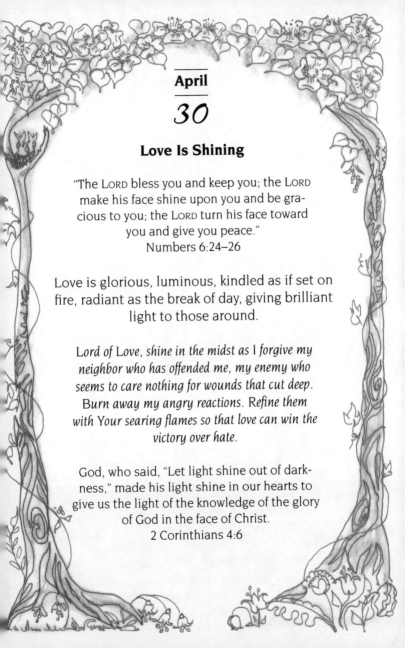

Love Is Shining

"The LORD bless you and keep you; the LORD make his face shine upon you and be gracious to you; the LORD turn his face toward you and give you peace."
Numbers 6:24–26

Love is glorious, luminous, kindled as if set on fire, radiant as the break of day, giving brilliant light to those around.

Lord of Love, shine in the midst as I forgive my neighbor who has offended me, my enemy who seems to care nothing for wounds that cut deep. Burn away my angry reactions. Refine them with Your searing flames so that love can win the victory over hate.

God, who said, "Let light shine out of darkness," made his light shine in our hearts to give us the light of the knowledge of the glory of God in the face of Christ.
2 Corinthians 4:6

May
Love Is Being

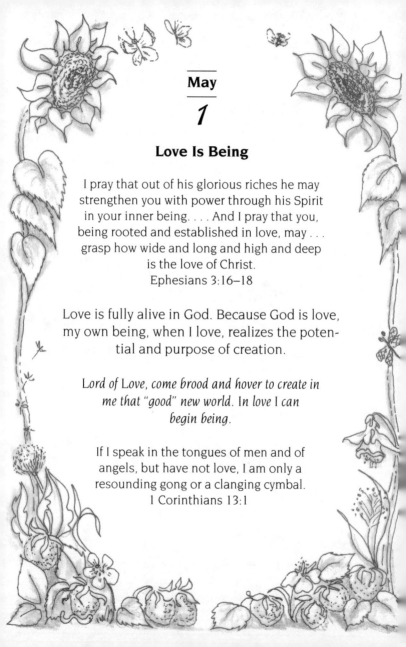

Love Is Being

I pray that out of his glorious riches he may
strengthen you with power through his Spirit
in your inner being. . . . And I pray that you,
being rooted and established in love, may . . .
grasp how wide and long and high and deep
is the love of Christ.
Ephesians 3:16–18

Love is fully alive in God. Because God is love,
my own being, when I love, realizes the potential and purpose of creation.

*Lord of Love, come brood and hover to create in
me that "good" new world. In love I can
begin being.*

If I speak in the tongues of men and of
angels, but have not love, I am only a
resounding gong or a clanging cymbal.
I Corinthians 13:1

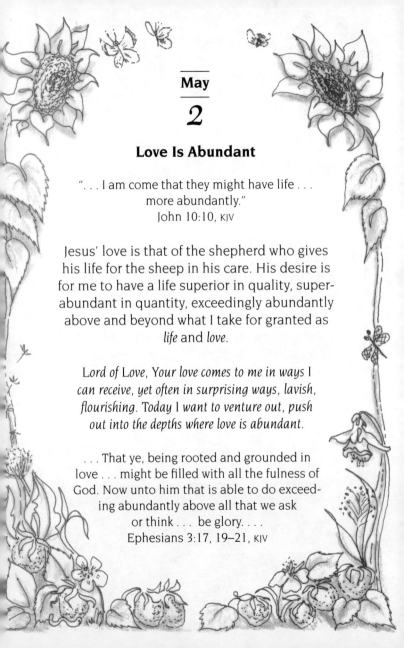

May

2

Love Is Abundant

"... I am come that they might have life ...
more abundantly."
John 10:10, KJV

Jesus' love is that of the shepherd who gives
his life for the sheep in his care. His desire is
for me to have a life superior in quality, super-
abundant in quantity, exceedingly abundantly
above and beyond what I take for granted as
life and *love.*

*Lord of Love, Your love comes to me in ways I
can receive, yet often in surprising ways, lavish,
flourishing. Today I want to venture out, push
out into the depths where love is abundant.*

... That ye, being rooted and grounded in
love ... might be filled with all the fulness of
God. Now unto him that is able to do exceeding abundantly above all that we ask
or think ... be glory. ...
Ephesians 3:17, 19–21, KJV

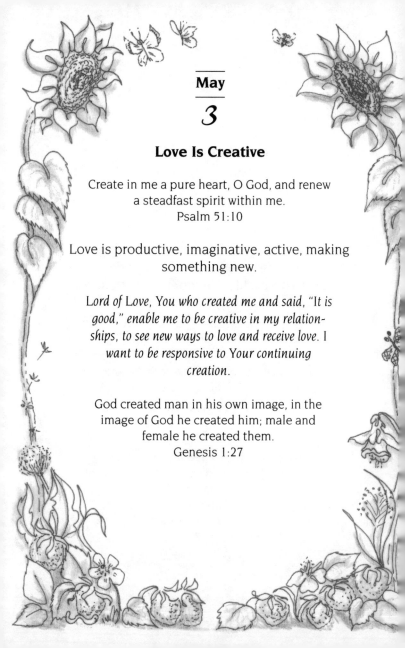

May

3

Love Is Creative

Create in me a pure heart, O God, and renew
a steadfast spirit within me.
Psalm 51:10

Love is productive, imaginative, active, making
something new.

*Lord of Love, You who created me and said, "It is
good," enable me to be creative in my relationships, to see new ways to love and receive love. I
want to be responsive to Your continuing
creation.*

God created man in his own image, in the
image of God he created him; male and
female he created them.
Genesis 1:27

Love Is Childlike

Jesus said, "Let the little children come to
me, and do not hinder them, for the kingdom
of heaven belongs to such as these."
Matthew 19:14

Love is childlike, innocent, trusting, straight-
forward, ingenuous, hopeful, growing—not
cynical, bitter.

*Lord of Love, wash me today of those sophisti-
cated crusts that living in the world has formed. I
want to look on what You are doing in me and in
others with a child's delighted smile, knowing that
You are not finished with us yet.*

How great is the love the Father has lavished
on us, that we should be called children of
God! And that is what we are! . . .
1 John 3:1

Love Is Eager

. . . We wait for the blessed hope—the glorious appearing of our great God and Savior, Jesus Christ, who gave himself . . . to purify for himself a people that are his very own, eager to do what is good.
Titus 2:13–14

Love is ready and willing, eager to be involved, to give of itself for the beloved. Love is marked by enthusiastic interest and desire.

Lord of Love, where I have become dull or boring, excite in me the eagerness of my first love for You.

Be shepherds of God's flock . . . not because you must, but because you are willing, as God wants you to be; not greedy for money, but eager to serve; not lording it over those entrusted to you, but being examples to the flock.
1 Peter 5:2–3

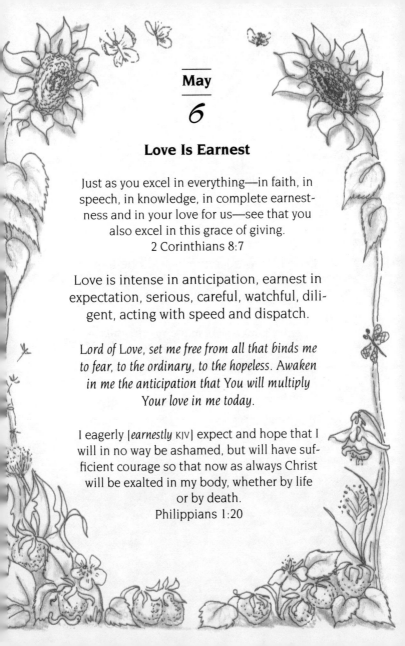

Love Is Earnest

Just as you excel in everything—in faith, in speech, in knowledge, in complete earnestness and in your love for us—see that you also excel in this grace of giving.
2 Corinthians 8:7

Love is intense in anticipation, earnest in expectation, serious, careful, watchful, diligent, acting with speed and dispatch.

Lord of Love, set me free from all that binds me to fear, to the ordinary, to the hopeless. Awaken in me the anticipation that You will multiply Your love in me today.

I eagerly [*earnestly* KJV] expect and hope that I will in no way be ashamed, but will have sufficient courage so that now as always Christ will be exalted in my body, whether by life or by death.
Philippians 1:20

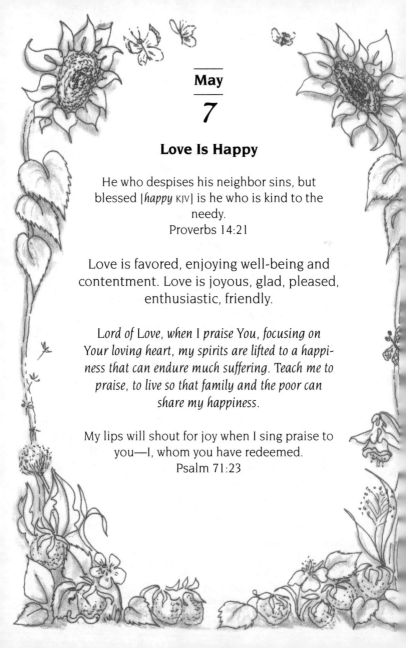

Love Is Happy

He who despises his neighbor sins, but
blessed [*happy* KJV] is he who is kind to the
needy.
Proverbs 14:21

Love is favored, enjoying well-being and
contentment. Love is joyous, glad, pleased,
enthusiastic, friendly.

*Lord of Love, when I praise You, focusing on
Your loving heart, my spirits are lifted to a happiness that can endure much suffering. Teach me to
praise, to live so that family and the poor can
share my happiness.*

My lips will shout for joy when I sing praise to
you—I, whom you have redeemed.
Psalm 71:23

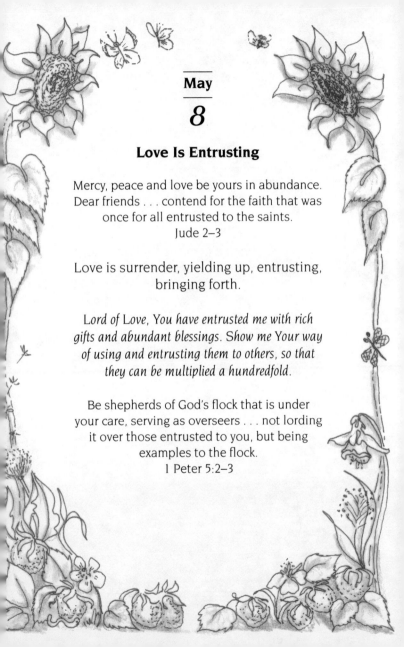

May

8

Love Is Entrusting

Mercy, peace and love be yours in abundance.
Dear friends . . . contend for the faith that was
once for all entrusted to the saints.
Jude 2–3

Love is surrender, yielding up, entrusting,
bringing forth.

*Lord of Love, You have entrusted me with rich
gifts and abundant blessings. Show me Your way
of using and entrusting them to others, so that
they can be multiplied a hundredfold.*

Be shepherds of God's flock that is under
your care, serving as overseers . . . not lording
it over those entrusted to you, but being
examples to the flock.
1 Peter 5:2–3

May

9

Love Is Good News

A cheerful look brings joy to the heart, and
good news gives health to the bones.
Proverbs 15:30

Love is announcing good news. Love is evan-
gelizing, declaring, preaching, bringing glad
tidings.

*Lord of Love, You have shown me the reality of
the Good News of Jesus Christ. I know He is
alive; He is risen! Let my whole life be an attractive witness to this eternal message of love.*

The angel said to them, "Do not be afraid. I
bring you good news of great joy that will be
for all the people."
Luke 2:10

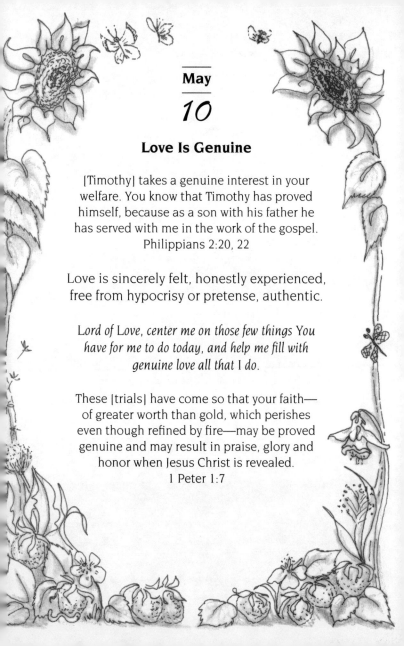

Love Is Genuine

[Timothy] takes a genuine interest in your welfare. You know that Timothy has proved himself, because as a son with his father he has served with me in the work of the gospel.
Philippians 2:20, 22

Love is sincerely felt, honestly experienced, free from hypocrisy or pretense, authentic.

Lord of Love, center me on those few things You have for me to do today, and help me fill with genuine love all that I do.

These [trials] have come so that your faith—of greater worth than gold, which perishes even though refined by fire—may be proved genuine and may result in praise, glory and honor when Jesus Christ is revealed.
1 Peter 1:7

May
11

Love Is Honest

. . . Whatever is true, whatever is noble, whatever is right, whatever is pure, whatever is lovely, whatever is admirable—if anything is excellent or praiseworthy—think about such things.
Philippians 4:8

Love is honorable, praiseworthy, free from fraud or deception. Love is marked by integrity, sincerity; is genuine, real, humble, plain.

Lord of Love, You know all about me and yet still love me. I want to be honest with myself and others, and with You, so that no walls separate me from Your love.

Speaking the truth in love, we will in all things grow up into him who is the Head, that is, Christ.
Ephesians 4:15

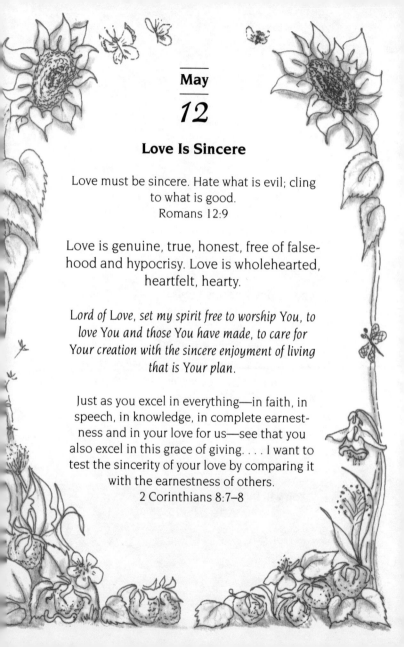

Love Is Sincere

Love must be sincere. Hate what is evil; cling
to what is good.
Romans 12:9

Love is genuine, true, honest, free of false-
hood and hypocrisy. Love is wholehearted,
heartfelt, hearty.

*Lord of Love, set my spirit free to worship You, to
love You and those You have made, to care for
Your creation with the sincere enjoyment of living
that is Your plan.*

Just as you excel in everything—in faith, in
speech, in knowledge, in complete earnestness and in your love for us—see that you
also excel in this grace of giving. . . . I want to
test the sincerity of your love by comparing it
with the earnestness of others.
2 Corinthians 8:7–8

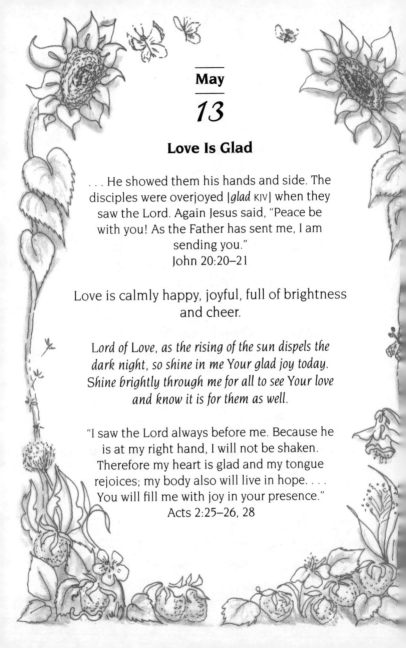

May

13

Love Is Glad

. . . He showed them his hands and side. The disciples were overjoyed [*glad* KJV] when they saw the Lord. Again Jesus said, "Peace be with you! As the Father has sent me, I am sending you."
John 20:20–21

Love is calmly happy, joyful, full of brightness and cheer.

Lord of Love, as the rising of the sun dispels the dark night, so shine in me Your glad joy today. Shine brightly through me for all to see Your love and know it is for them as well.

"I saw the Lord always before me. Because he is at my right hand, I will not be shaken. Therefore my heart is glad and my tongue rejoices; my body also will live in hope. . . . You will fill me with joy in your presence."
Acts 2:25–26, 28

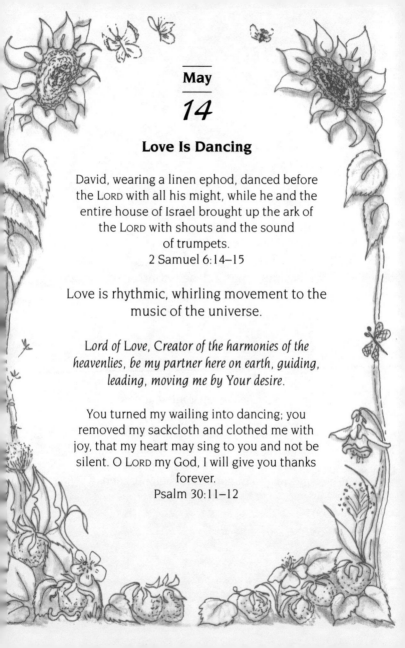

May

14

Love Is Dancing

David, wearing a linen ephod, danced before the LORD with all his might, while he and the entire house of Israel brought up the ark of the LORD with shouts and the sound of trumpets.
2 Samuel 6:14–15

Love is rhythmic, whirling movement to the music of the universe.

Lord of Love, Creator of the harmonies of the heavenlies, be my partner here on earth, guiding, leading, moving me by Your desire.

You turned my wailing into dancing; you removed my sackcloth and clothed me with joy, that my heart may sing to you and not be silent. O LORD my God, I will give you thanks forever.
Psalm 30:11–12

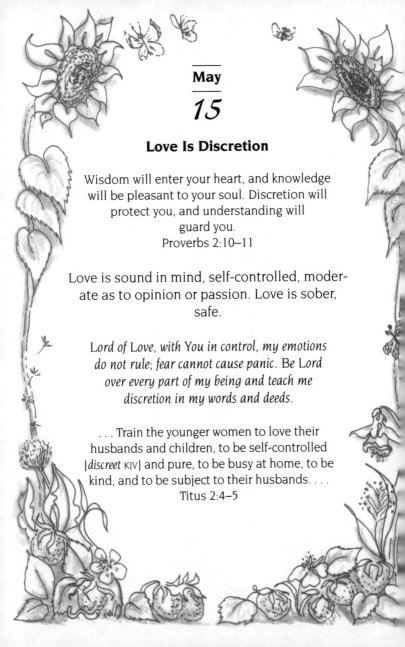

May

15

Love Is Discretion

Wisdom will enter your heart, and knowledge will be pleasant to your soul. Discretion will protect you, and understanding will guard you.
Proverbs 2:10–11

Love is sound in mind, self-controlled, moderate as to opinion or passion. Love is sober, safe.

Lord of Love, with You in control, my emotions do not rule; fear cannot cause panic. Be Lord over every part of my being and teach me discretion in my words and deeds.

. . . Train the younger women to love their husbands and children, to be self-controlled [*discreet* KJV] and pure, to be busy at home, to be kind, and to be subject to their husbands. . . .
Titus 2:4–5

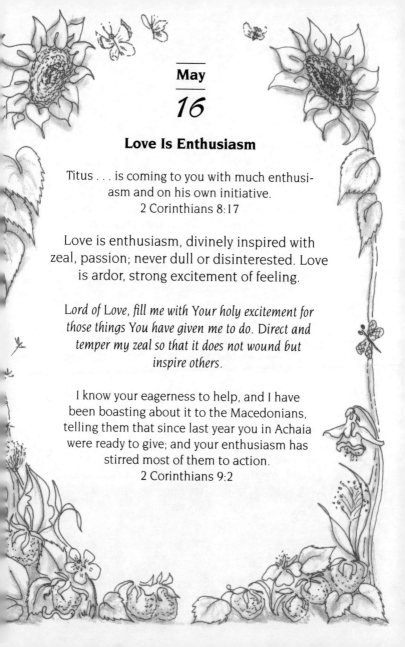

Love Is Enthusiasm

Titus . . . is coming to you with much enthusiasm and on his own initiative.
2 Corinthians 8:17

Love is enthusiasm, divinely inspired with zeal, passion; never dull or disinterested. Love is ardor, strong excitement of feeling.

Lord of Love, fill me with Your holy excitement for those things You have given me to do. Direct and temper my zeal so that it does not wound but inspire others.

I know your eagerness to help, and I have been boasting about it to the Macedonians, telling them that since last year you in Achaia were ready to give; and your enthusiasm has stirred most of them to action.
2 Corinthians 9:2

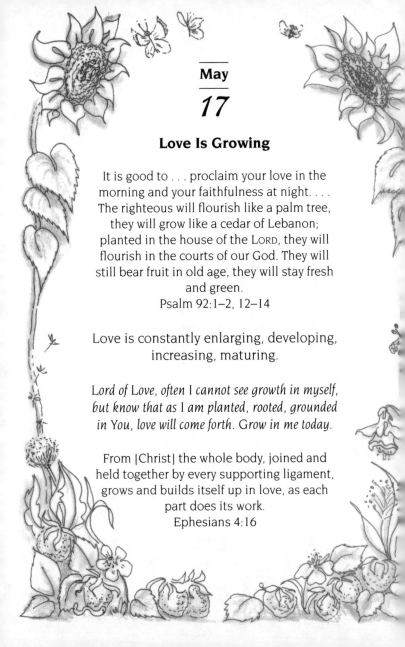

May

17

Love Is Growing

It is good to . . . proclaim your love in the morning and your faithfulness at night. . . . The righteous will flourish like a palm tree, they will grow like a cedar of Lebanon; planted in the house of the LORD, they will flourish in the courts of our God. They will still bear fruit in old age, they will stay fresh and green.
Psalm 92:1–2, 12–14

Love is constantly enlarging, developing, increasing, maturing.

Lord of Love, often I cannot see growth in myself, but know that as I am planted, rooted, grounded in You, love will come forth. Grow in me today.

From [Christ] the whole body, joined and held together by every supporting ligament, grows and builds itself up in love, as each part does its work.
Ephesians 4:16

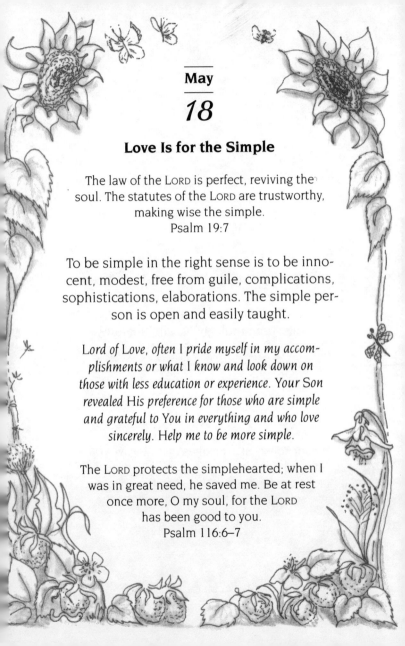

Love Is for the Simple

The law of the LORD is perfect, reviving the
soul. The statutes of the LORD are trustworthy,
making wise the simple.
Psalm 19:7

To be simple in the right sense is to be innocent, modest, free from guile, complications,
sophistications, elaborations. The simple person is open and easily taught.

*Lord of Love, often I pride myself in my accom-
plishments or what I know and look down on
those with less education or experience. Your Son
revealed His preference for those who are simple
and grateful to You in everything and who love
sincerely. Help me to be more simple.*

The LORD protects the simplehearted; when I
was in great need, he saved me. Be at rest
once more, O my soul, for the LORD
has been good to you.
Psalm 116:6–7

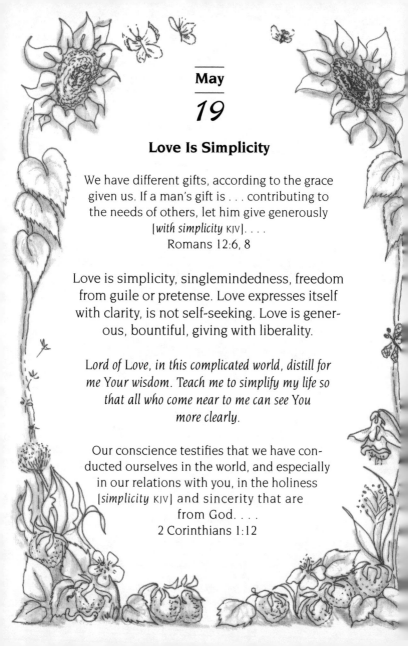

Love Is Simplicity

We have different gifts, according to the grace
given us. If a man's gift is . . . contributing to
the needs of others, let him give generously
[*with simplicity* KJV]. . . .
Romans 12:6, 8

Love is simplicity, singlemindedness, freedom
from guile or pretense. Love expresses itself
with clarity, is not self-seeking. Love is generous, bountiful, giving with liberality.

*Lord of Love, in this complicated world, distill for
me Your wisdom. Teach me to simplify my life so
that all who come near to me can see You
more clearly.*

Our conscience testifies that we have con-
ducted ourselves in the world, and especially
in our relations with you, in the holiness
[*simplicity* KJV] and sincerity that are
from God. . . .
2 Corinthians 1:12

May

20

Love Is Truthful

Speaking the truth in love, we will in all
things grow up into him who is the Head,
that is, Christ.
Ephesians 4:15

Love tells the truth with fidelity, constancy.
Love is sincere in action, character and
utterance.

Lord of Love, shine the light of Your truth into
every darkened part of my mind and memories.
Reveal to me Your perspective so that my words,
purified with the flames of Your love, will bring
kindly light to others.

Grace, mercy and peace from God the Father
and from Jesus Christ, the Father's Son, will
be with us in truth and love. It has given me
great joy to find some of your children
walking in the truth, just as the Father
commanded us.
2 John 3–4

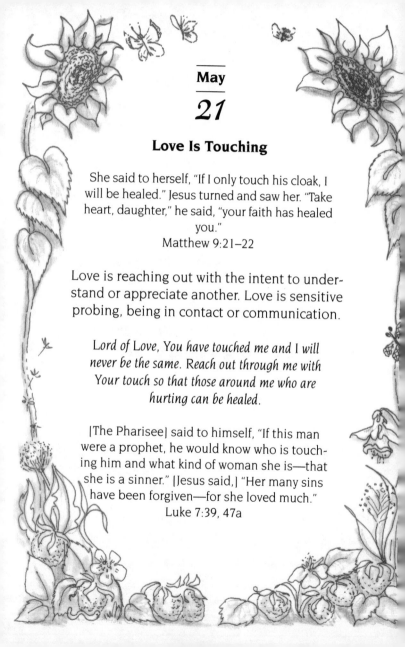

Love Is Touching

She said to herself, "If I only touch his cloak, I
will be healed." Jesus turned and saw her. "Take
heart, daughter," he said, "your faith has healed
you."
Matthew 9:21–22

Love is reaching out with the intent to understand or appreciate another. Love is sensitive
probing, being in contact or communication.

*Lord of Love, You have touched me and I will
never be the same. Reach out through me with
Your touch so that those around me who are
hurting can be healed.*

[The Pharisee] said to himself, "If this man
were a prophet, he would know who is touching him and what kind of woman she is—that
she is a sinner." [Jesus said,] "Her many sins
have been forgiven—for she loved much."
Luke 7:39, 47a

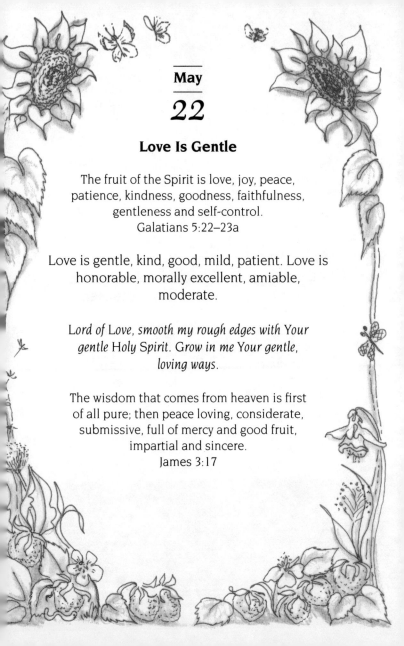

Love Is Gentle

The fruit of the Spirit is love, joy, peace,
patience, kindness, goodness, faithfulness,
gentleness and self-control.
Galatians 5:22–23a

Love is gentle, kind, good, mild, patient. Love is
honorable, morally excellent, amiable,
moderate.

*Lord of Love, smooth my rough edges with Your
gentle Holy Spirit. Grow in me Your gentle,
loving ways.*

The wisdom that comes from heaven is first
of all pure; then peace loving, considerate,
submissive, full of mercy and good fruit,
impartial and sincere.
James 3:17

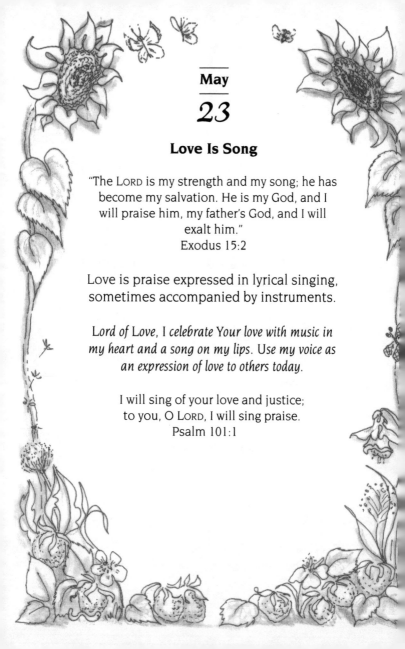

Love Is Song

"The LORD is my strength and my song; he has become my salvation. He is my God, and I will praise him, my father's God, and I will exalt him."
Exodus 15:2

Love is praise expressed in lyrical singing, sometimes accompanied by instruments.

Lord of Love, I celebrate Your love with music in my heart and a song on my lips. Use my voice as an expression of love to others today.

I will sing of your love and justice;
to you, O LORD, I will sing praise.
Psalm 101:1

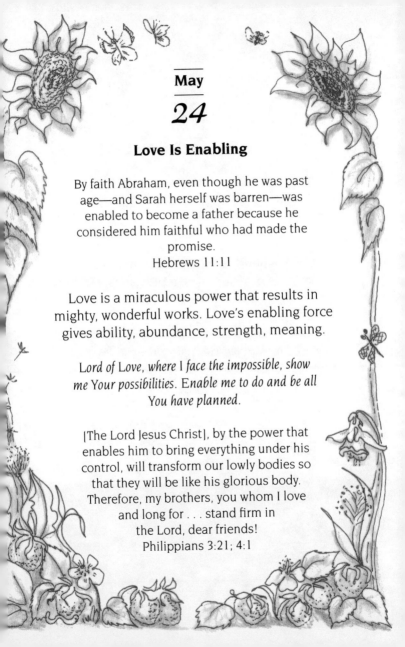

May

24

Love Is Enabling

By faith Abraham, even though he was past
age—and Sarah herself was barren—was
enabled to become a father because he
considered him faithful who had made the
promise.
Hebrews 11:11

Love is a miraculous power that results in
mighty, wonderful works. Love's enabling force
gives ability, abundance, strength, meaning.

*Lord of Love, where I face the impossible, show
me Your possibilities. Enable me to do and be all
You have planned.*

[The Lord Jesus Christ], by the power that
enables him to bring everything under his
control, will transform our lowly bodies so
that they will be like his glorious body.
Therefore, my brothers, you whom I love
and long for . . . stand firm in
the Lord, dear friends!
Philippians 3:21; 4:1

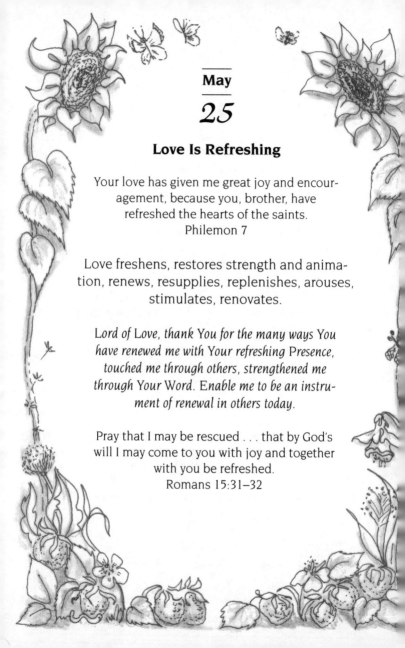

May
25

Love Is Refreshing

Your love has given me great joy and encouragement, because you, brother, have refreshed the hearts of the saints.
Philemon 7

Love freshens, restores strength and animation, renews, resupplies, replenishes, arouses, stimulates, renovates.

Lord of Love, thank You for the many ways You have renewed me with Your refreshing Presence, touched me through others, strengthened me through Your Word. Enable me to be an instrument of renewal in others today.

Pray that I may be rescued . . . that by God's will I may come to you with joy and together with you be refreshed.
Romans 15:31–32

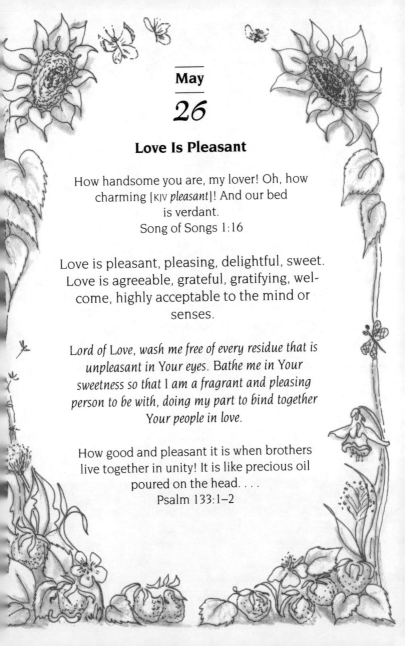

Love Is Pleasant

How handsome you are, my lover! Oh, how
charming [KJV *pleasant*]! And our bed
is verdant.
Song of Songs 1:16

Love is pleasant, pleasing, delightful, sweet.
Love is agreeable, grateful, gratifying, welcome, highly acceptable to the mind or
senses.

*Lord of Love, wash me free of every residue that is
unpleasant in Your eyes. Bathe me in Your
sweetness so that I am a fragrant and pleasing
person to be with, doing my part to bind together
Your people in love.*

How good and pleasant it is when brothers
live together in unity! It is like precious oil
poured on the head. . . .
Psalm 133:1–2

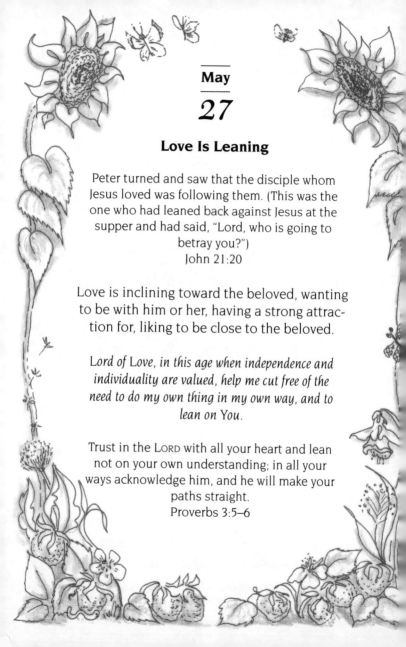

Love Is Leaning

Peter turned and saw that the disciple whom
Jesus loved was following them. (This was the
one who had leaned back against Jesus at the
supper and had said, "Lord, who is going to
betray you?")
John 21:20

Love is inclining toward the beloved, wanting
to be with him or her, having a strong attrac-
tion for, liking to be close to the beloved.

*Lord of Love, in this age when independence and
individuality are valued, help me cut free of the
need to do my own thing in my own way, and to
lean on You.*

Trust in the LORD with all your heart and lean
not on your own understanding; in all your
ways acknowledge him, and he will make your
paths straight.
Proverbs 3:5–6

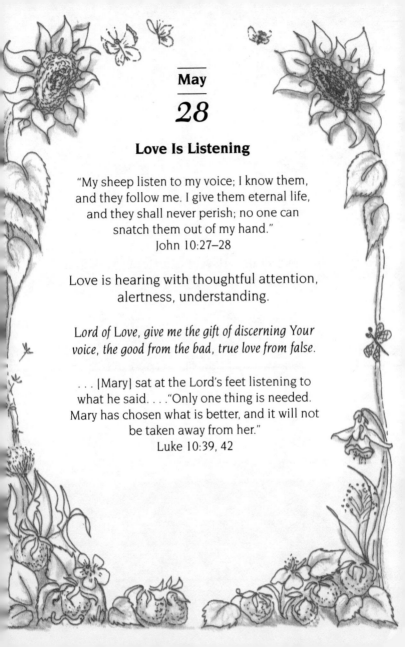

Love Is Listening

"My sheep listen to my voice; I know them,
and they follow me. I give them eternal life,
and they shall never perish; no one can
snatch them out of my hand."
John 10:27–28

Love is hearing with thoughtful attention,
alertness, understanding.

*Lord of Love, give me the gift of discerning Your
voice, the good from the bad, true love from false.*

. . . [Mary] sat at the Lord's feet listening to
what he said. . . ."Only one thing is needed.
Mary has chosen what is better, and it will not
be taken away from her."
Luke 10:39, 42

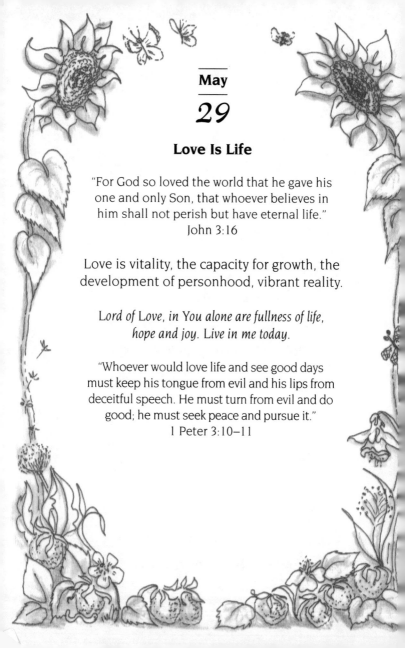

May

29

Love Is Life

"For God so loved the world that he gave his
one and only Son, that whoever believes in
him shall not perish but have eternal life."
John 3:16

Love is vitality, the capacity for growth, the
development of personhood, vibrant reality.

*Lord of Love, in You alone are fullness of life,
hope and joy. Live in me today.*

"Whoever would love life and see good days
must keep his tongue from evil and his lips from
deceitful speech. He must turn from evil and do
good; he must seek peace and pursue it."
1 Peter 3:10–11

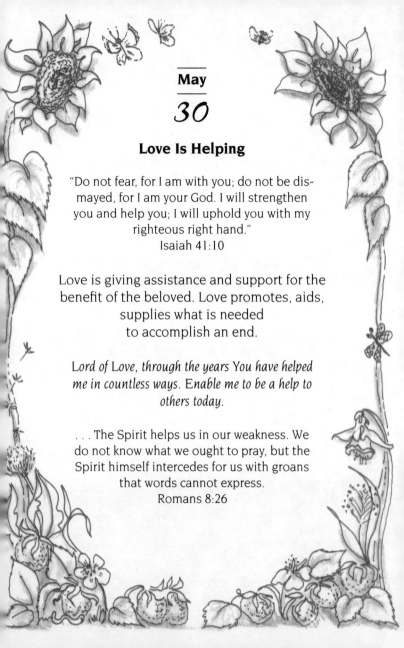

Love Is Helping

"Do not fear, for I am with you; do not be dismayed, for I am your God. I will strengthen you and help you; I will uphold you with my righteous right hand."
Isaiah 41:10

Love is giving assistance and support for the benefit of the beloved. Love promotes, aids, supplies what is needed to accomplish an end.

Lord of Love, through the years You have helped me in countless ways. Enable me to be a help to others today.

. . . The Spirit helps us in our weakness. We do not know what we ought to pray, but the Spirit himself intercedes for us with groans that words cannot express.
Romans 8:26

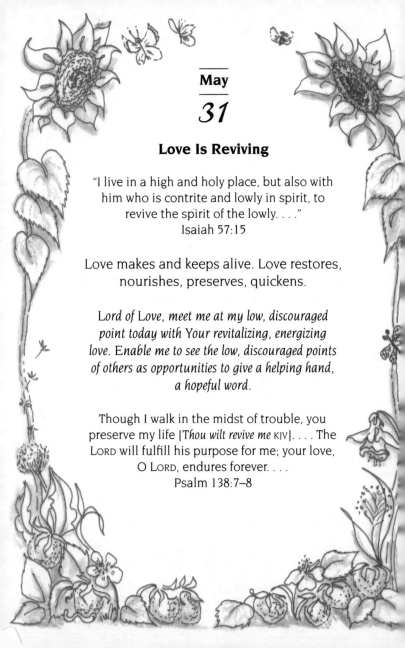

Love Is Reviving

"I live in a high and holy place, but also with
him who is contrite and lowly in spirit, to
revive the spirit of the lowly. . . ."
Isaiah 57:15

Love makes and keeps alive. Love restores,
nourishes, preserves, quickens.

*Lord of Love, meet me at my low, discouraged
point today with Your revitalizing, energizing
love. Enable me to see the low, discouraged points
of others as opportunities to give a helping hand,
a hopeful word.*

Though I walk in the midst of trouble, you
preserve my life [*Thou wilt revive me* KJV]. . . . The
LORD will fulfill his purpose for me; your love,
O LORD, endures forever. . . .
Psalm 138:7–8

June
Love Is a Banner

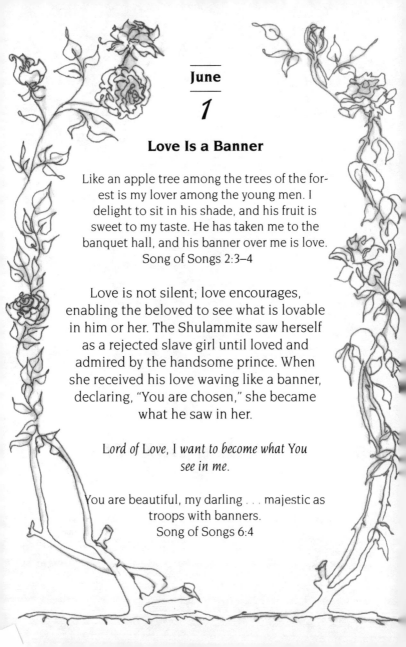

Love Is a Banner

Like an apple tree among the trees of the forest is my lover among the young men. I delight to sit in his shade, and his fruit is sweet to my taste. He has taken me to the banquet hall, and his banner over me is love.
Song of Songs 2:3–4

Love is not silent; love encourages, enabling the beloved to see what is lovable in him or her. The Shulammite saw herself as a rejected slave girl until loved and admired by the handsome prince. When she received his love waving like a banner, declaring, "You are chosen," she became what he saw in her.

Lord of Love, I want to become what You see in me.

You are beautiful, my darling . . . majestic as troops with banners.
Song of Songs 6:4

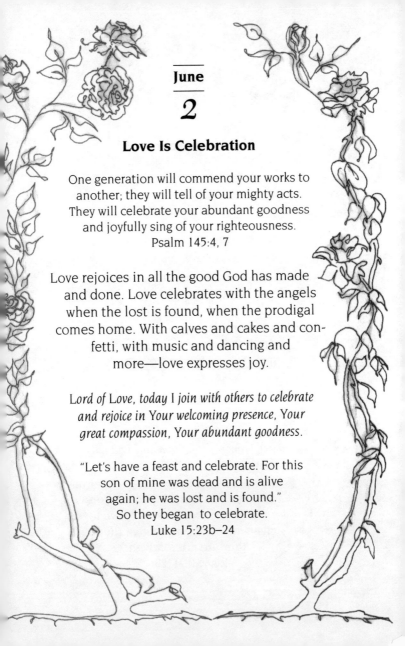

June

2

Love Is Celebration

One generation will commend your works to
another; they will tell of your mighty acts.
They will celebrate your abundant goodness
and joyfully sing of your righteousness.
Psalm 145:4, 7

Love rejoices in all the good God has made
and done. Love celebrates with the angels
when the lost is found, when the prodigal
comes home. With calves and cakes and con-
fetti, with music and dancing and
more—love expresses joy.

*Lord of Love, today I join with others to celebrate
and rejoice in Your welcoming presence, Your
great compassion, Your abundant goodness.*

"Let's have a feast and celebrate. For this
son of mine was dead and is alive
again; he was lost and is found."
So they began to celebrate.
Luke 15:23b–24

June

3

Love Is Agreement

". . . If two of you on earth agree about anything you ask for, it will be done for you by my Father in heaven. For where two or three come together in my name, there am I with them."
Matthew 18:19–20

Love is agreement, coming together in harmony, being of one mind and heart—or at least working toward that goal without giving up! It is easier to see the faults, to criticize destructively, to exclude those who disagree with me.

Lord of Love, help me to exercise my love muscles today by stretching beyond my feelings to include that person or group not like me (and who may not like me, either). I can keep practicing until I get it right!

". . . Peace be with you! As the Father has sent me, I am sending you. If you forgive anyone his sins, they are forgiven; if you do not forgive them, they are not forgiven."
John 20:21, 23

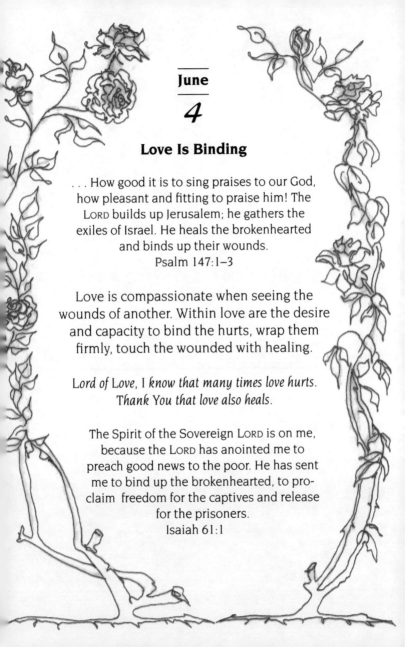

June
4

Love Is Binding

. . . How good it is to sing praises to our God,
how pleasant and fitting to praise him! The
LORD builds up Jerusalem; he gathers the
exiles of Israel. He heals the brokenhearted
and binds up their wounds.
Psalm 147:1–3

Love is compassionate when seeing the
wounds of another. Within love are the desire
and capacity to bind the hurts, wrap them
firmly, touch the wounded with healing.

*Lord of Love, I know that many times love hurts.
Thank You that love also heals.*

The Spirit of the Sovereign LORD is on me,
because the LORD has anointed me to
preach good news to the poor. He has sent
me to bind up the brokenhearted, to proclaim freedom for the captives and release
for the prisoners.
Isaiah 61:1

June
5

Love Is Cleaving

The man said, "This is now bone of my bones and flesh of my flesh. . . ." For this reason a man will leave his father and mother and be united to his wife, and they will become one flesh.
Genesis 2:23–24

Love is loyal, sticking close, adhering firmly, unwaveringly to the beloved.

Lord of Love, Your love is the bonding agent that enables two fragmented lives to join as one whole. It is never easy for two to become one—mathematically impossible!—but spiritually vital.

". . . Hold fast [*cleave* KJV] to the LORD your God, as you have until now. Be very careful to love the LORD your God."
Joshua 23:8, 11

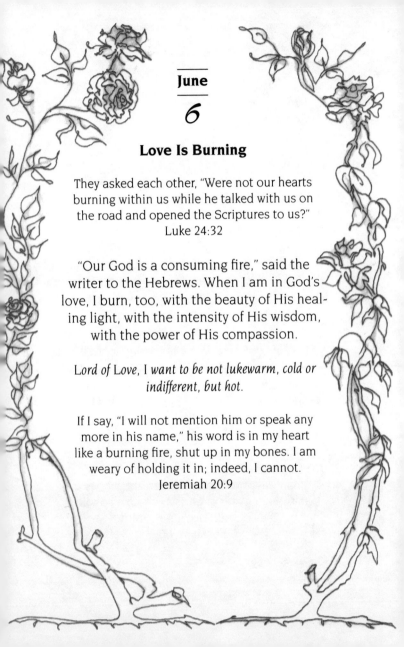

June

6

Love Is Burning

They asked each other, "Were not our hearts
burning within us while he talked with us on
the road and opened the Scriptures to us?"
Luke 24:32

"Our God is a consuming fire," said the
writer to the Hebrews. When I am in God's
love, I burn, too, with the beauty of His healing light, with the intensity of His wisdom,
with the power of His compassion.

*Lord of Love, I want to be not lukewarm, cold or
indifferent, but hot.*

If I say, "I will not mention him or speak any
more in his name," his word is in my heart
like a burning fire, shut up in my bones. I am
weary of holding it in; indeed, I cannot.
Jeremiah 20:9

June

7

Love Is Spirit

The fruit of the Spirit is love. . . . Since we live
by the Spirit, let us keep in step with the
Spirit.
Galatians 5:22, 25

Love is as basic as breath and breathing,
infused in my being as spirit and life;
light; fresh, clean air. This love spirit produces
fearless courage, cheerful vitality.

*Lord of Love, breathe in and through me today
with Your overcoming Spirit. Grow in me all
Your gifts. Shower me with all Your gifts that
enable me to function as an integral part of Jesus'
body on planet earth.*

. . . All over the world this gospel is producing
fruit and growing. . . . You learned it from
Epaphras, our dear fellow servant, who is a
faithful minister of Christ . . . who also told
us of your love in the Spirit.
Colossians 1:6–8

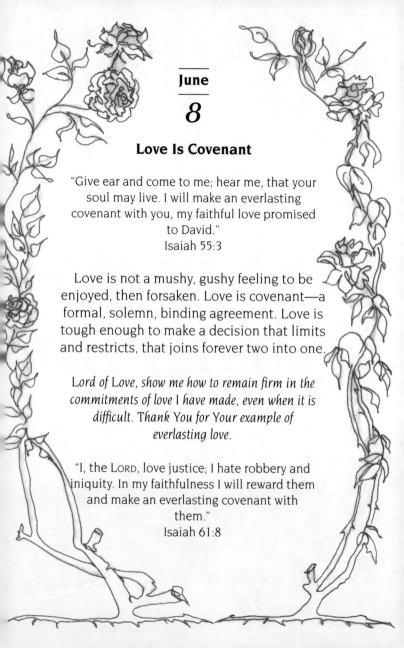

June
8

Love Is Covenant

"Give ear and come to me; hear me, that your soul may live. I will make an everlasting covenant with you, my faithful love promised to David."
Isaiah 55:3

Love is not a mushy, gushy feeling to be enjoyed, then forsaken. Love is covenant—a formal, solemn, binding agreement. Love is tough enough to make a decision that limits and restricts, that joins forever two into one.

Lord of Love, show me how to remain firm in the commitments of love I have made, even when it is difficult. Thank You for Your example of everlasting love.

"I, the LORD, love justice; I hate robbery and iniquity. In my faithfulness I will reward them and make an everlasting covenant with them."
Isaiah 61:8

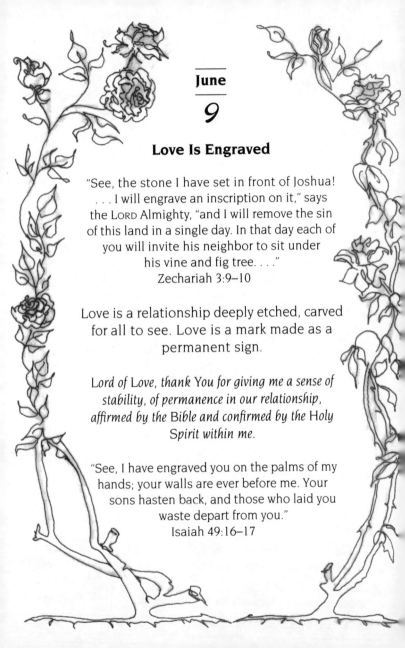

June

9

Love Is Engraved

"See, the stone I have set in front of Joshua!
. . . I will engrave an inscription on it," says
the LORD Almighty, "and I will remove the sin
of this land in a single day. In that day each of
you will invite his neighbor to sit under
his vine and fig tree. . . ."
Zechariah 3:9–10

Love is a relationship deeply etched, carved
for all to see. Love is a mark made as a
permanent sign.

*Lord of Love, thank You for giving me a sense of
stability, of permanence in our relationship,
affirmed by the Bible and confirmed by the Holy
Spirit within me.*

"See, I have engraved you on the palms of my
hands; your walls are ever before me. Your
sons hasten back, and those who laid you
waste depart from you."
Isaiah 49:16–17

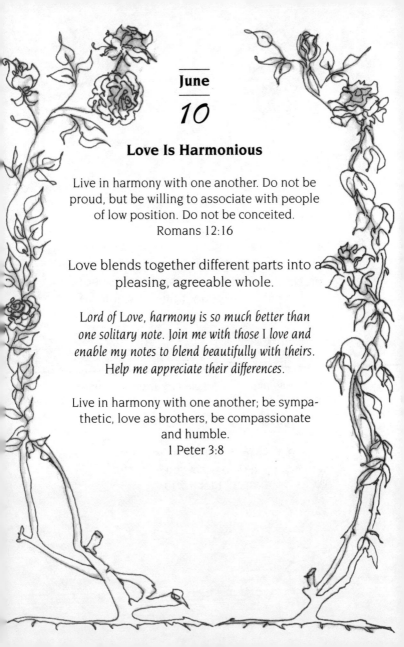

Love Is Harmonious

Live in harmony with one another. Do not be
proud, but be willing to associate with people
of low position. Do not be conceited.
Romans 12:16

Love blends together different parts into a
pleasing, agreeable whole.

*Lord of Love, harmony is so much better than
one solitary note. Join me with those I love and
enable my notes to blend beautifully with theirs.
Help me appreciate their differences.*

Live in harmony with one another; be sympathetic, love as brothers, be compassionate
and humble.
1 Peter 3:8

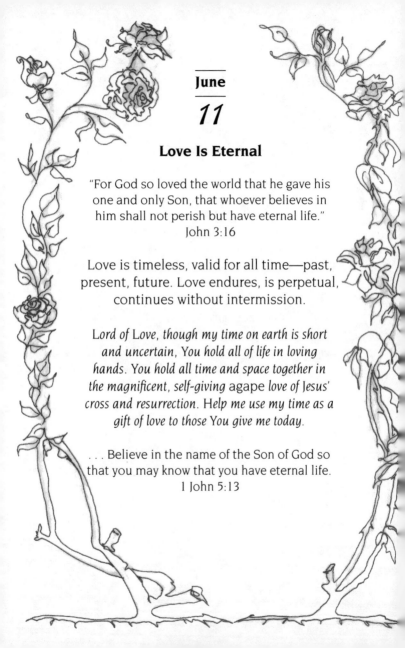

June

11

Love Is Eternal

"For God so loved the world that he gave his
one and only Son, that whoever believes in
him shall not perish but have eternal life."
John 3:16

Love is timeless, valid for all time—past,
present, future. Love endures, is perpetual,
continues without intermission.

*Lord of Love, though my time on earth is short
and uncertain, You hold all of life in loving
hands. You hold all time and space together in
the magnificent, self-giving agape love of Jesus'
cross and resurrection. Help me use my time as a
gift of love to those You give me today.*

. . . Believe in the name of the Son of God so
that you may know that you have eternal life.
1 John 5:13

June

12

Love Is Fellowship

We proclaim to you what we have seen and heard, so that you also may have fellowship with us. And our fellowship is with the Father and with his Son, Jesus Christ.
1 John 1:3

Love is *koinonia*, from the Greek word meaning fellowship, communion, shared partnership, communication, participation.

Lord of Love, help me have the courage to put aside things that keep me from having meaningful fellowship with the loved ones You have given me.

God, who has called you into fellowship with his Son Jesus Christ our Lord, is faithful. I appeal to you, brothers, in the name of our Lord Jesus Christ, that all of you agree with one another so that . . . you may be perfectly united in mind and thought.
1 Corinthians 1:9–10

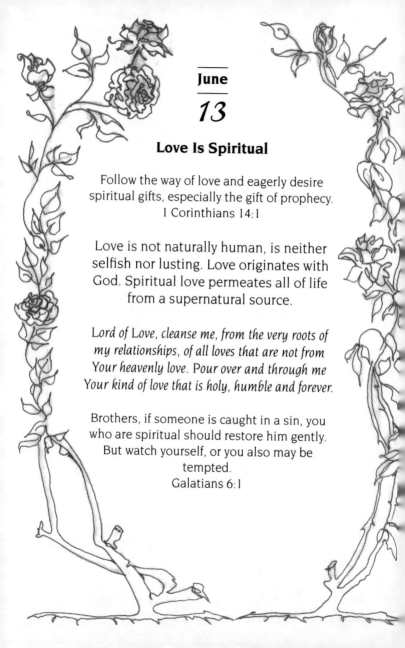

June

13

Love Is Spiritual

Follow the way of love and eagerly desire
spiritual gifts, especially the gift of prophecy.
1 Corinthians 14:1

Love is not naturally human, is neither
selfish nor lusting. Love originates with
God. Spiritual love permeates all of life
from a supernatural source.

*Lord of Love, cleanse me, from the very roots of
my relationships, of all loves that are not from
Your heavenly love. Pour over and through me
Your kind of love that is holy, humble and forever.*

Brothers, if someone is caught in a sin, you
who are spiritual should restore him gently.
But watch yourself, or you also may be
tempted.
Galatians 6:1

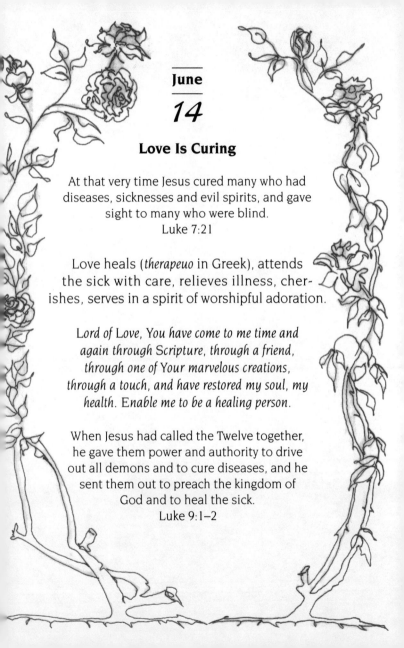

June

14

Love Is Curing

At that very time Jesus cured many who had
diseases, sicknesses and evil spirits, and gave
sight to many who were blind.
Luke 7:21

Love heals (*therapeuo* in Greek), attends
the sick with care, relieves illness, cherishes, serves in a spirit of worshipful adoration.

*Lord of Love, You have come to me time and
again through Scripture, through a friend,
through one of Your marvelous creations,
through a touch, and have restored my soul, my
health. Enable me to be a healing person.*

When Jesus had called the Twelve together,
he gave them power and authority to drive
out all demons and to cure diseases, and he
sent them out to preach the kingdom of
God and to heal the sick.
Luke 9:1–2

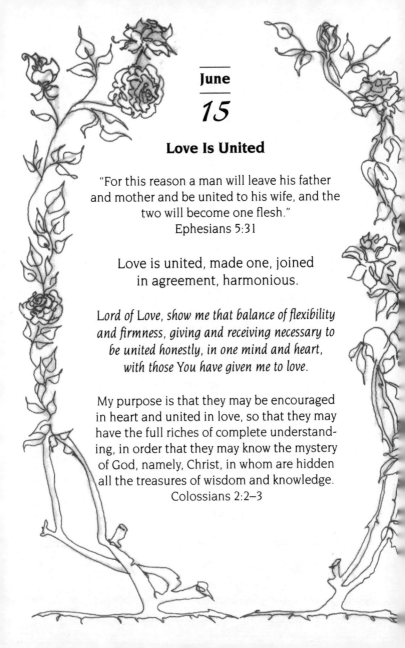

June

15

Love Is United

"For this reason a man will leave his father and mother and be united to his wife, and the two will become one flesh."
Ephesians 5:31

Love is united, made one, joined in agreement, harmonious.

Lord of Love, show me that balance of flexibility and firmness, giving and receiving necessary to be united honestly, in one mind and heart, with those You have given me to love.

My purpose is that they may be encouraged in heart and united in love, so that they may have the full riches of complete understanding, in order that they may know the mystery of God, namely, Christ, in whom are hidden all the treasures of wisdom and knowledge.
Colossians 2:2–3

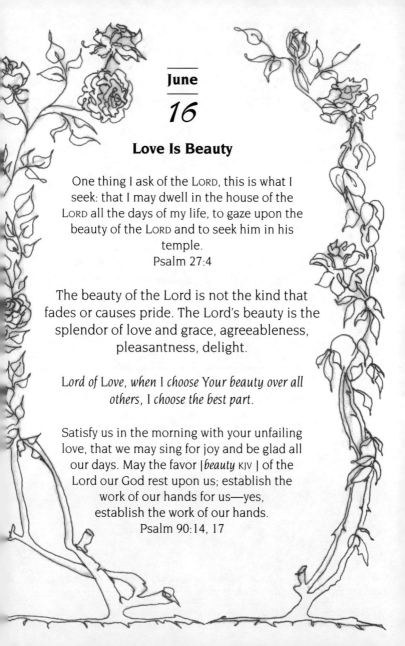

June

16

Love Is Beauty

One thing I ask of the LORD, this is what I seek: that I may dwell in the house of the LORD all the days of my life, to gaze upon the beauty of the LORD and to seek him in his temple.
Psalm 27:4

The beauty of the Lord is not the kind that fades or causes pride. The Lord's beauty is the splendor of love and grace, agreeableness, pleasantness, delight.

Lord of Love, when I choose Your beauty over all others, I choose the best part.

Satisfy us in the morning with your unfailing love, that we may sing for joy and be glad all our days. May the favor [*beauty* KJV] of the Lord our God rest upon us; establish the work of our hands for us—yes, establish the work of our hands.
Psalm 90:14, 17

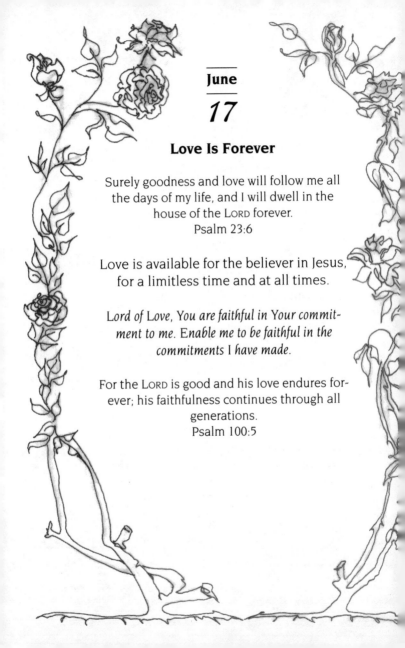

June

17

Love Is Forever

Surely goodness and love will follow me all
the days of my life, and I will dwell in the
house of the Lord forever.
Psalm 23:6

Love is available for the believer in Jesus,
for a limitless time and at all times.

*Lord of Love, You are faithful in Your commit-
ment to me. Enable me to be faithful in the
commitments I have made.*

For the Lord is good and his love endures forever; his faithfulness continues through all
generations.
Psalm 100:5

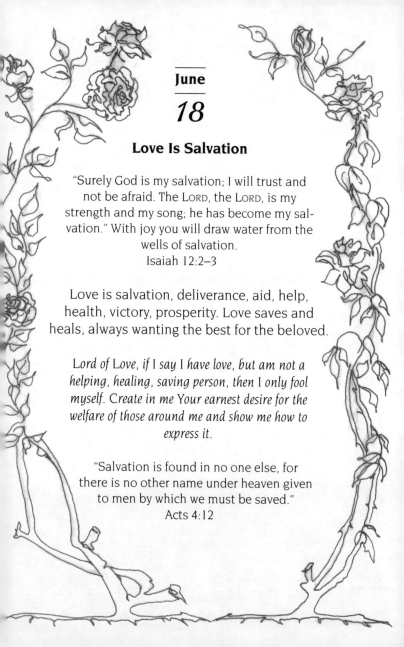

June

18

Love Is Salvation

"Surely God is my salvation; I will trust and
not be afraid. The LORD, the LORD, is my
strength and my song; he has become my salvation." With joy you will draw water from the
wells of salvation.
Isaiah 12:2–3

Love is salvation, deliverance, aid, help,
health, victory, prosperity. Love saves and
heals, always wanting the best for the beloved.

Lord of Love, if I say I have love, but am not a
helping, healing, saving person, then I only fool
myself. Create in me Your earnest desire for the
welfare of those around me and show me how to
express it.

"Salvation is found in no one else, for
there is no other name under heaven given
to men by which we must be saved."
Acts 4:12

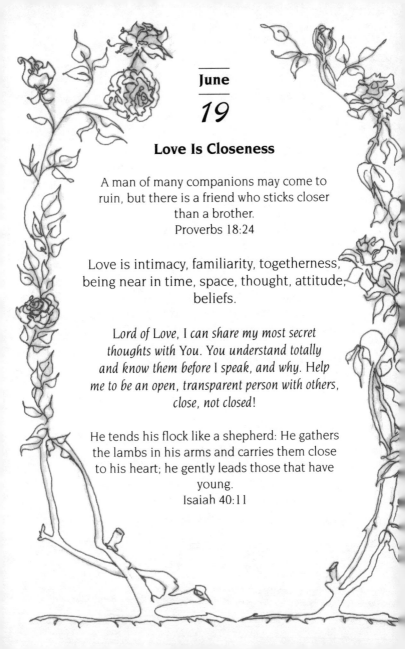

June

19

Love Is Closeness

A man of many companions may come to
ruin, but there is a friend who sticks closer
than a brother.
Proverbs 18:24

Love is intimacy, familiarity, togetherness,
being near in time, space, thought, attitude,
beliefs.

*Lord of Love, I can share my most secret
thoughts with You. You understand totally
and know them before I speak, and why. Help
me to be an open, transparent person with others,
close, not closed!*

He tends his flock like a shepherd: He gathers
the lambs in his arms and carries them close
to his heart; he gently leads those that have
young.
Isaiah 40:11

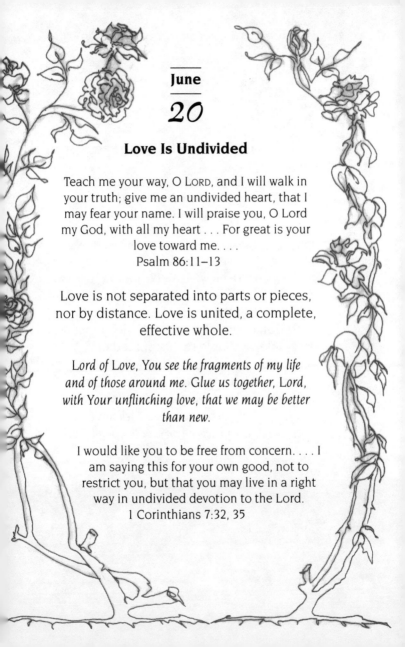

June

20

Love Is Undivided

Teach me your way, O LORD, and I will walk in
your truth; give me an undivided heart, that I
may fear your name. I will praise you, O Lord
my God, with all my heart . . . For great is your
love toward me. . . .
Psalm 86:11–13

Love is not separated into parts or pieces,
nor by distance. Love is united, a complete,
effective whole.

*Lord of Love, You see the fragments of my life
and of those around me. Glue us together, Lord,
with Your unflinching love, that we may be better
than new.*

I would like you to be free from concern. . . . I
am saying this for your own good, not to
restrict you, but that you may live in a right
way in undivided devotion to the Lord.
1 Corinthians 7:32, 35

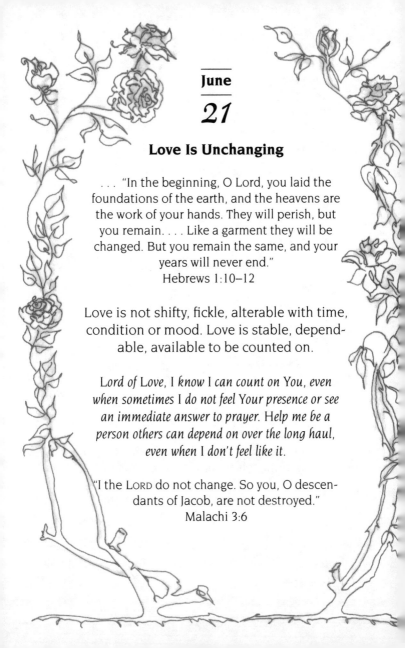

June

21

Love Is Unchanging

. . . "In the beginning, O Lord, you laid the foundations of the earth, and the heavens are the work of your hands. They will perish, but you remain. . . . Like a garment they will be changed. But you remain the same, and your years will never end."
Hebrews 1:10–12

Love is not shifty, fickle, alterable with time, condition or mood. Love is stable, dependable, available to be counted on.

Lord of Love, I know I can count on You, even when sometimes I do not feel Your presence or see an immediate answer to prayer. Help me be a person others can depend on over the long haul, even when I don't feel like it.

"I the Lord do not change. So you, O descendants of Jacob, are not destroyed."
Malachi 3:6

June

22

Love Is Wonderful

I praise you because I am fearfully and wonderfully made; your works are wonderful. . . .
Psalm 139:14

Love is remarkable, marvelous, an
exciting wonder. Love is astonishing,
unusually good, admirable.

Lord of Love, Your name is wonderful. Nature is
wonderful. You made each person on earth
wonderful, too, with the capacity to be filled with
the wonder of Your love. Fill me today, Lord, with
the wonder that You are.

"There are three things that are too amazing
[*wonderful* KJV] for me, four that I do not understand: the way of an eagle in the sky, the way
of a snake on a rock, the way of a ship on the
high seas, and the way of a man with a
maiden."
Proverbs 30:18–19

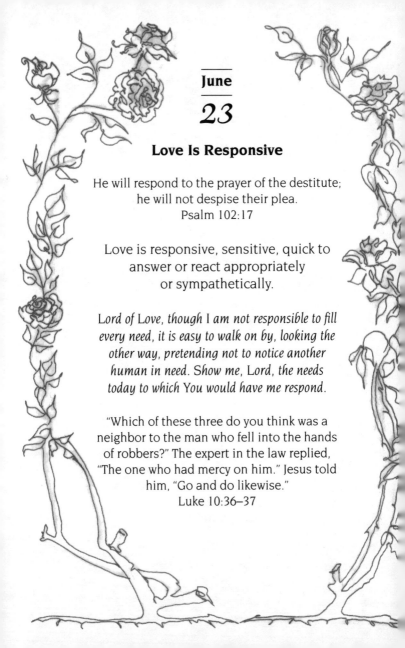

June

23

Love Is Responsive

He will respond to the prayer of the destitute;
he will not despise their plea.
Psalm 102:17

Love is responsive, sensitive, quick to
answer or react appropriately
or sympathetically.

*Lord of Love, though I am not responsible to fill
every need, it is easy to walk on by, looking the
other way, pretending not to notice another
human in need. Show me, Lord, the needs
today to which You would have me respond.*

"Which of these three do you think was a
neighbor to the man who fell into the hands
of robbers?" The expert in the law replied,
"The one who had mercy on him." Jesus told
him, "Go and do likewise."
Luke 10:36–37

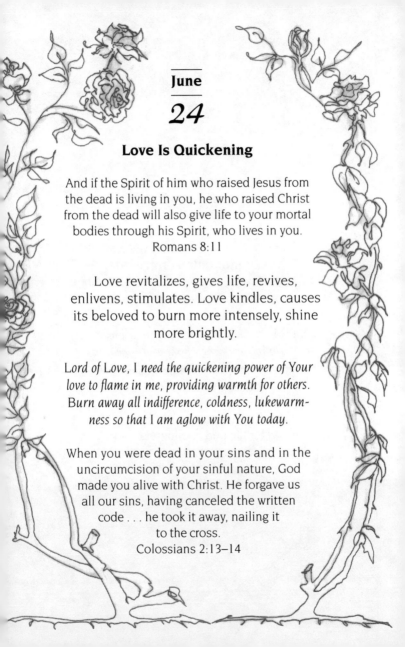

June
24

Love Is Quickening

And if the Spirit of him who raised Jesus from the dead is living in you, he who raised Christ from the dead will also give life to your mortal bodies through his Spirit, who lives in you.
Romans 8:11

Love revitalizes, gives life, revives, enlivens, stimulates. Love kindles, causes its beloved to burn more intensely, shine more brightly.

Lord of Love, I need the quickening power of Your love to flame in me, providing warmth for others. Burn away all indifference, coldness, lukewarmness so that I am aglow with You today.

When you were dead in your sins and in the uncircumcision of your sinful nature, God made you alive with Christ. He forgave us all our sins, having canceled the written code . . . he took it away, nailing it to the cross.
Colossians 2:13–14

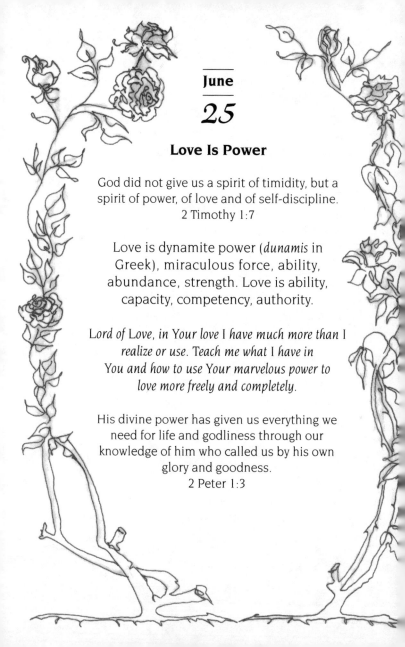

June

25

Love Is Power

God did not give us a spirit of timidity, but a spirit of power, of love and of self-discipline.
2 Timothy 1:7

Love is dynamite power (*dunamis* in Greek), miraculous force, ability, abundance, strength. Love is ability, capacity, competency, authority.

Lord of Love, in Your love I have much more than I realize or use. Teach me what I have in You and how to use Your marvelous power to love more freely and completely.

His divine power has given us everything we need for life and godliness through our knowledge of him who called us by his own glory and goodness.
2 Peter 1:3

June
26

Love Is Lovingkindness

He forgives all my sins and heals all my diseases; he redeems my life from the pit and
crowns me with love [*lovingkindness* KJV] and
compassion.
Psalm 103:3–4

Love is merciful kindness, good deeds,
beauty, favor. Love is tender, benevolent
affection.

Lord of Love, I affirm again all that Your love is.
It is worthy of all my days filled with praises of
thanksgiving. Today I trust that You are able to
carry every burden that weighs me down so that I
can dance before You.

. . . "I have loved you with an everlasting love; I
have drawn you with loving-kindness. I will
build you up again and you will be rebuilt, O
Virgin Israel. Again you will take up your
tambourines and go out to dance
with the joyful."
Jeremiah 31:3–4

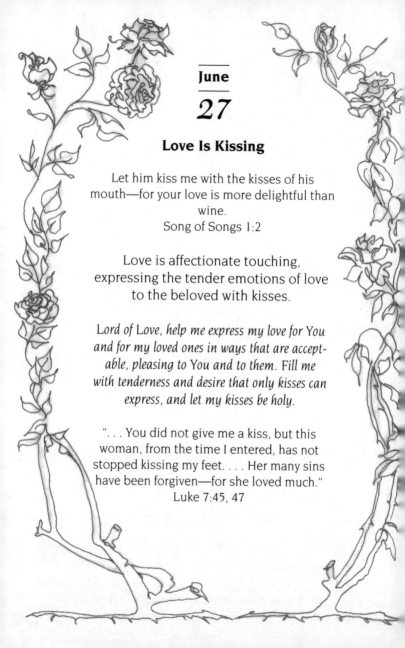

June

27

Love Is Kissing

Let him kiss me with the kisses of his mouth—for your love is more delightful than wine.
Song of Songs 1:2

Love is affectionate touching, expressing the tender emotions of love to the beloved with kisses.

Lord of Love, help me express my love for You and for my loved ones in ways that are acceptable, pleasing to You and to them. Fill me with tenderness and desire that only kisses can express, and let my kisses be holy.

". . . You did not give me a kiss, but this woman, from the time I entered, has not stopped kissing my feet. . . . Her many sins have been forgiven—for she loved much."
Luke 7:45, 47

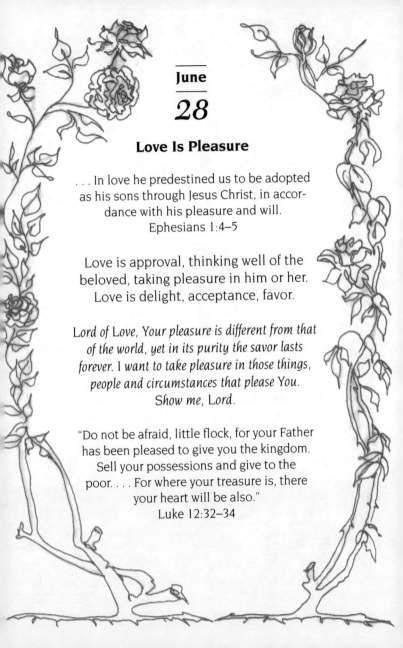

June
28

Love Is Pleasure

. . . In love he predestined us to be adopted
as his sons through Jesus Christ, in accordance with his pleasure and will.
Ephesians 1:4–5

Love is approval, thinking well of the
beloved, taking pleasure in him or her.
Love is delight, acceptance, favor.

*Lord of Love, Your pleasure is different from that
of the world, yet in its purity the savor lasts
forever. I want to take pleasure in those things,
people and circumstances that please You.
Show me, Lord.*

"Do not be afraid, little flock, for your Father
has been pleased to give you the kingdom.
Sell your possessions and give to the
poor. . . . For where your treasure is, there
your heart will be also."
Luke 12:32–34

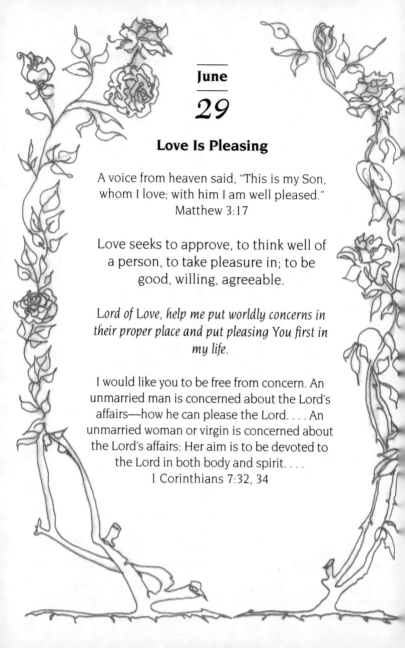

June

29

Love Is Pleasing

A voice from heaven said, "This is my Son,
whom I love; with him I am well pleased."
Matthew 3:17

Love seeks to approve, to think well of
a person, to take pleasure in; to be
good, willing, agreeable.

*Lord of Love, help me put worldly concerns in
their proper place and put pleasing You first in
my life.*

I would like you to be free from concern. An
unmarried man is concerned about the Lord's
affairs—how he can please the Lord. . . . An
unmarried woman or virgin is concerned about
the Lord's affairs: Her aim is to be devoted to
the Lord in both body and spirit. . . .
1 Corinthians 7:32, 34

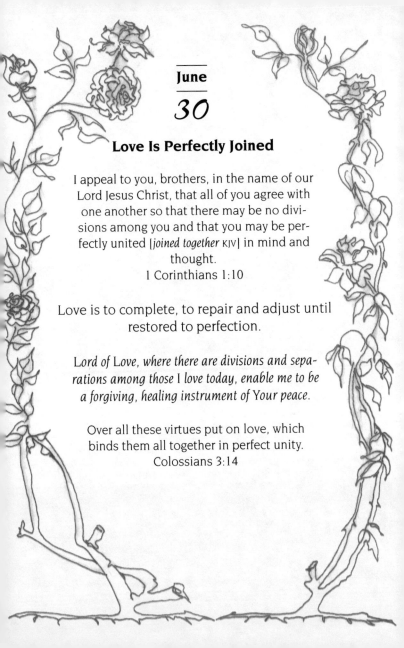

June

30

Love Is Perfectly Joined

I appeal to you, brothers, in the name of our
Lord Jesus Christ, that all of you agree with
one another so that there may be no divisions among you and that you may be perfectly united [*joined together* KJV] in mind and
thought.
1 Corinthians 1:10

Love is to complete, to repair and adjust until
restored to perfection.

*Lord of Love, where there are divisions and sepa-
rations among those I love today, enable me to be
a forgiving, healing instrument of Your peace.*

Over all these virtues put on love, which
binds them all together in perfect unity.
Colossians 3:14

July
Love Is Bountiful

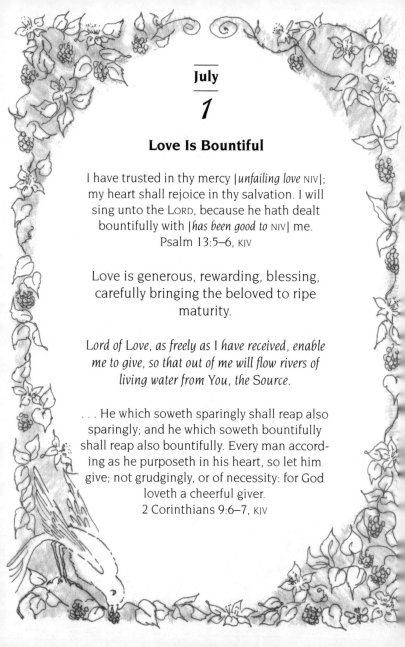

July

1

Love Is Bountiful

I have trusted in thy mercy [*unfailing love* NIV];
my heart shall rejoice in thy salvation. I will
sing unto the LORD, because he hath dealt
bountifully with [*has been good to* NIV] me.
Psalm 13:5–6, KJV

Love is generous, rewarding, blessing,
carefully bringing the beloved to ripe
maturity.

*Lord of Love, as freely as I have received, enable
me to give, so that out of me will flow rivers of
living water from You, the Source.*

. . . He which soweth sparingly shall reap also
sparingly; and he which soweth bountifully
shall reap also bountifully. Every man according as he purposeth in his heart, so let him
give; not grudgingly, or of necessity: for God
loveth a cheerful giver.
2 Corinthians 9:6–7, KJV

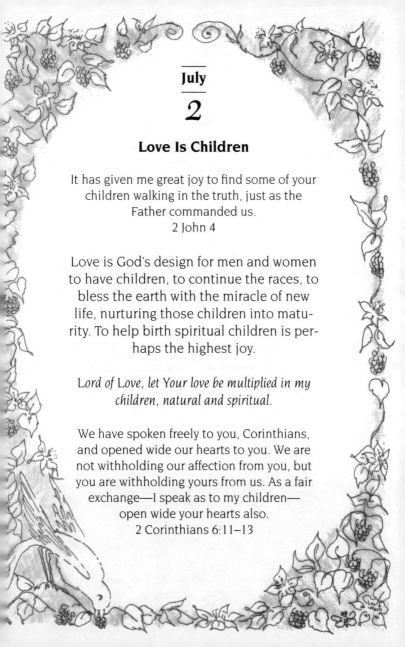

July

2

Love Is Children

It has given me great joy to find some of your
children walking in the truth, just as the
Father commanded us.
2 John 4

Love is God's design for men and women
to have children, to continue the races, to
bless the earth with the miracle of new
life, nurturing those children into maturity. To help birth spiritual children is per-
haps the highest joy.

*Lord of Love, let Your love be multiplied in my
children, natural and spiritual.*

We have spoken freely to you, Corinthians,
and opened wide our hearts to you. We are
not withholding our affection from you, but
you are withholding yours from us. As a fair
exchange—I speak as to my children—
open wide your hearts also.
2 Corinthians 6:11–13

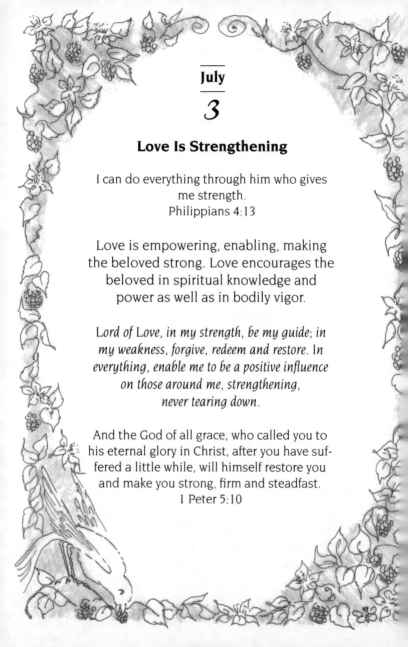

July
3

Love Is Strengthening

I can do everything through him who gives
me strength.
Philippians 4:13

Love is empowering, enabling, making
the beloved strong. Love encourages the
beloved in spiritual knowledge and
power as well as in bodily vigor.

*Lord of Love, in my strength, be my guide; in
my weakness, forgive, redeem and restore. In
everything, enable me to be a positive influence
on those around me, strengthening,
never tearing down.*

And the God of all grace, who called you to
his eternal glory in Christ, after you have suffered a little while, will himself restore you
and make you strong, firm and steadfast.
1 Peter 5:10

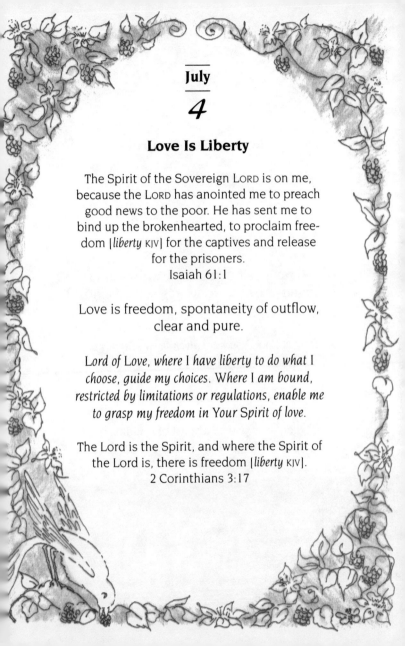

July
4

Love Is Liberty

The Spirit of the Sovereign LORD is on me,
because the LORD has anointed me to preach
good news to the poor. He has sent me to
bind up the brokenhearted, to proclaim freedom [*liberty* KJV] for the captives and release
for the prisoners.
Isaiah 61:1

Love is freedom, spontaneity of outflow,
clear and pure.

*Lord of Love, where I have liberty to do what I
choose, guide my choices. Where I am bound,
restricted by limitations or regulations, enable me
to grasp my freedom in Your Spirit of love.*

The Lord is the Spirit, and where the Spirit of
the Lord is, there is freedom [*liberty* KJV].
2 Corinthians 3:17

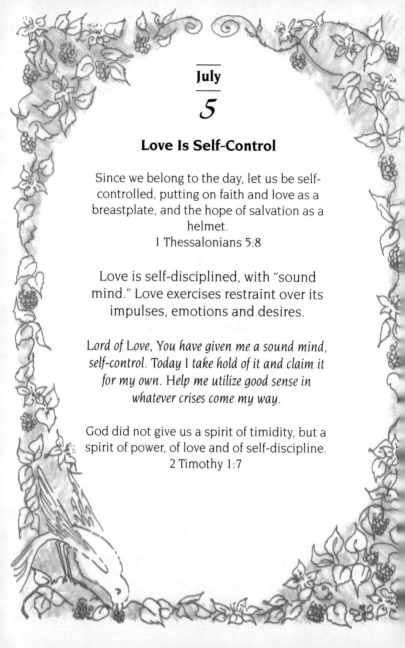

July
5

Love Is Self-Control

Since we belong to the day, let us be self-controlled, putting on faith and love as a breastplate, and the hope of salvation as a helmet.
1 Thessalonians 5:8

Love is self-disciplined, with "sound mind." Love exercises restraint over its impulses, emotions and desires.

Lord of Love, You have given me a sound mind, self-control. Today I take hold of it and claim it for my own. Help me utilize good sense in whatever crises come my way.

God did not give us a spirit of timidity, but a spirit of power, of love and of self-discipline.
2 Timothy 1:7

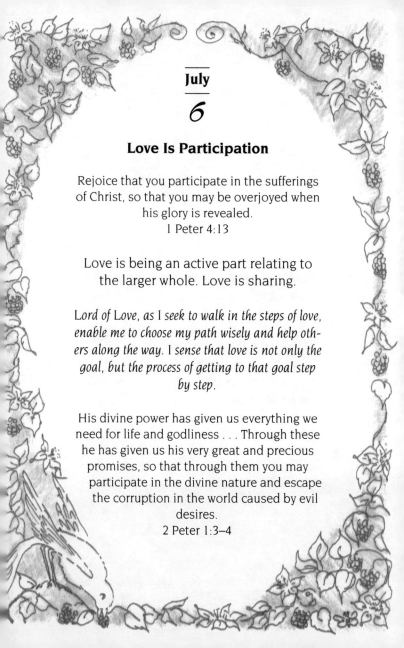

July

6

Love Is Participation

Rejoice that you participate in the sufferings of Christ, so that you may be overjoyed when his glory is revealed.
1 Peter 4:13

Love is being an active part relating to the larger whole. Love is sharing.

Lord of Love, as I seek to walk in the steps of love, enable me to choose my path wisely and help others along the way. I sense that love is not only the goal, but the process of getting to that goal step by step.

His divine power has given us everything we need for life and godliness . . . Through these he has given us his very great and precious promises, so that through them you may participate in the divine nature and escape the corruption in the world caused by evil desires.
2 Peter 1:3–4

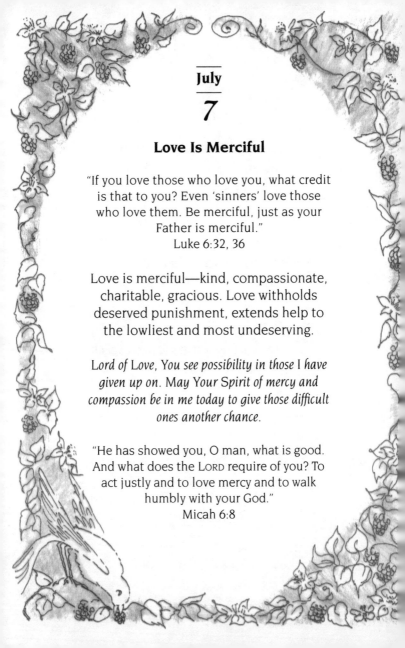

July
7

Love Is Merciful

"If you love those who love you, what credit
is that to you? Even 'sinners' love those
who love them. Be merciful, just as your
Father is merciful."
Luke 6:32, 36

Love is merciful—kind, compassionate,
charitable, gracious. Love withholds
deserved punishment, extends help to
the lowliest and most undeserving.

*Lord of Love, You see possibility in those I have
given up on. May Your Spirit of mercy and
compassion be in me today to give those difficult
ones another chance.*

"He has showed you, O man, what is good.
And what does the LORD require of you? To
act justly and to love mercy and to walk
humbly with your God."
Micah 6:8

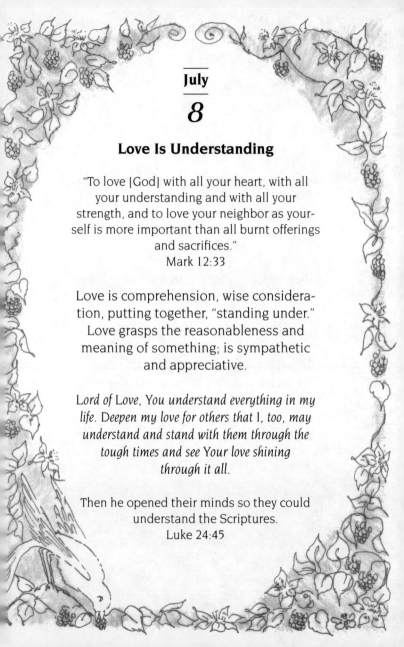

July

8

Love Is Understanding

"To love [God] with all your heart, with all
your understanding and with all your
strength, and to love your neighbor as yourself is more important than all burnt offerings
and sacrifices."
Mark 12:33

Love is comprehension, wise consideration, putting together, "standing under."
Love grasps the reasonableness and
meaning of something; is sympathetic
and appreciative.

*Lord of Love, You understand everything in my
life. Deepen my love for others that I, too, may
understand and stand with them through the
tough times and see Your love shining
through it all.*

Then he opened their minds so they could
understand the Scriptures.
Luke 24:45

July
9

Love Is Applying

Pay attention and listen to the sayings of the
wise; apply your heart to what I teach, for it is
pleasing when you keep them in your heart
and have all of them ready on your lips.
Proverbs 22:17–18

Whether love is active, going and coming,
or stays at home, it applies wisdom to
every situation. Love is always learning—
flexible, fluid, yet firm in the truth.

*Lord of Love, guard in my heart the good,
planted like seeds that take root and grow in my
life. Use and apply the bad as fertilizer!*

Apply your heart to instruction and your ears
to words of knowledge.
Proverbs 23:12

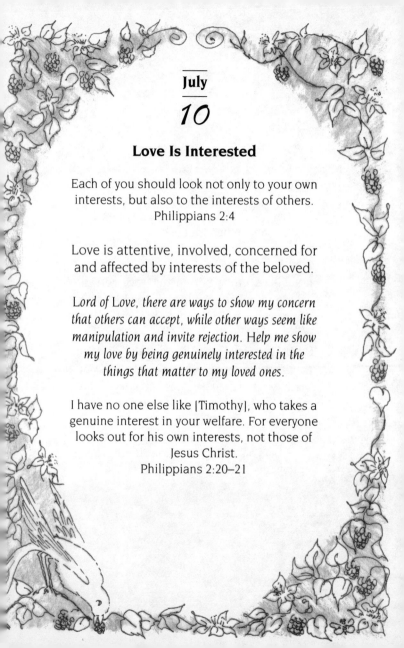

Love Is Interested

Each of you should look not only to your own
interests, but also to the interests of others.
Philippians 2:4

Love is attentive, involved, concerned for
and affected by interests of the beloved.

*Lord of Love, there are ways to show my concern
that others can accept, while other ways seem like
manipulation and invite rejection. Help me show
my love by being genuinely interested in the
things that matter to my loved ones.*

I have no one else like [Timothy], who takes a
genuine interest in your welfare. For everyone
looks out for his own interests, not those of
Jesus Christ.
Philippians 2:20–21

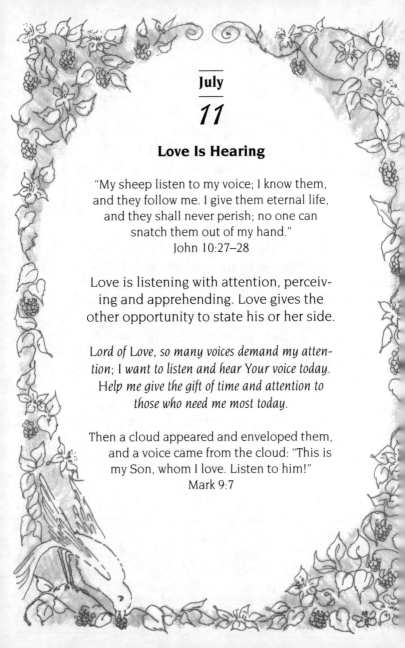

July

11

Love Is Hearing

"My sheep listen to my voice; I know them,
and they follow me. I give them eternal life,
and they shall never perish; no one can
snatch them out of my hand."
John 10:27–28

Love is listening with attention, perceiving and apprehending. Love gives the
other opportunity to state his or her side.

*Lord of Love, so many voices demand my atten-
tion; I want to listen and hear Your voice today.
Help me give the gift of time and attention to
those who need me most today.*

Then a cloud appeared and enveloped them,
and a voice came from the cloud: "This is
my Son, whom I love. Listen to him!"
Mark 9:7

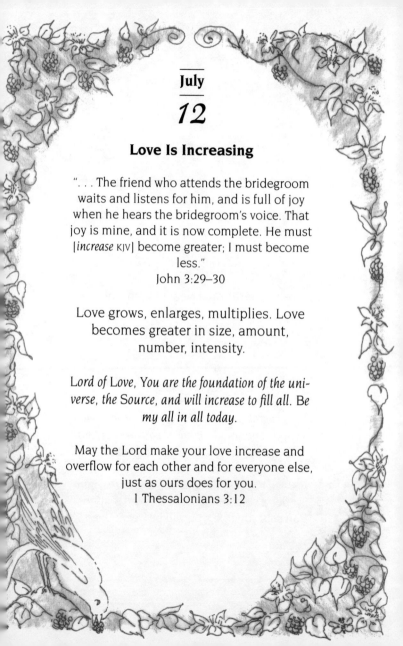

July
12

Love Is Increasing

". . . The friend who attends the bridegroom
waits and listens for him, and is full of joy
when he hears the bridegroom's voice. That
joy is mine, and it is now complete. He must
[*increase* KJV] become greater; I must become
less."
John 3:29–30

Love grows, enlarges, multiplies. Love
becomes greater in size, amount,
number, intensity.

Lord of Love, You are the foundation of the uni-
verse, the Source, and will increase to fill all. Be
my all in all today.

May the Lord make your love increase and
overflow for each other and for everyone else,
just as ours does for you.
1 Thessalonians 3:12

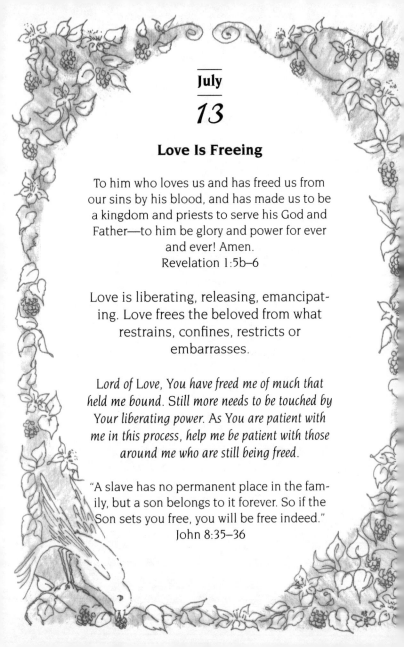

July

13

Love Is Freeing

To him who loves us and has freed us from our sins by his blood, and has made us to be a kingdom and priests to serve his God and Father—to him be glory and power for ever and ever! Amen.
Revelation 1:5b–6

Love is liberating, releasing, emancipating. Love frees the beloved from what restrains, confines, restricts or embarrasses.

Lord of Love, You have freed me of much that held me bound. Still more needs to be touched by Your liberating power. As You are patient with me in this process, help me be patient with those around me who are still being freed.

"A slave has no permanent place in the family, but a son belongs to it forever. So if the Son sets you free, you will be free indeed."
John 8:35–36

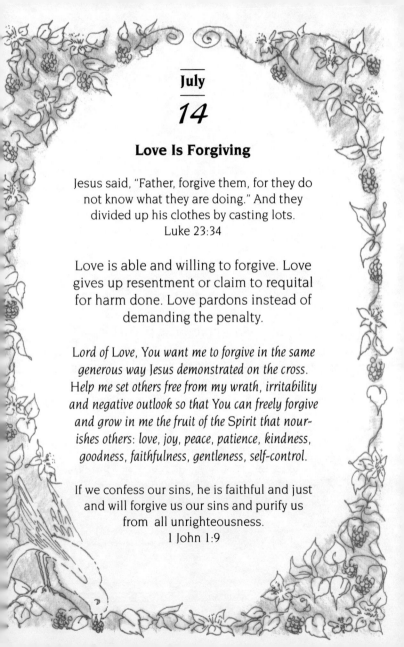

July
14

Love Is Forgiving

Jesus said, "Father, forgive them, for they do
not know what they are doing." And they
divided up his clothes by casting lots.
Luke 23:34

Love is able and willing to forgive. Love
gives up resentment or claim to requital
for harm done. Love pardons instead of
demanding the penalty.

*Lord of Love, You want me to forgive in the same
generous way Jesus demonstrated on the cross.
Help me set others free from my wrath, irritability
and negative outlook so that You can freely forgive
and grow in me the fruit of the Spirit that nourishes others: love, joy, peace, patience, kindness,
goodness, faithfulness, gentleness, self-control.*

If we confess our sins, he is faithful and just
and will forgive us our sins and purify us
from all unrighteousness.
1 John 1:9

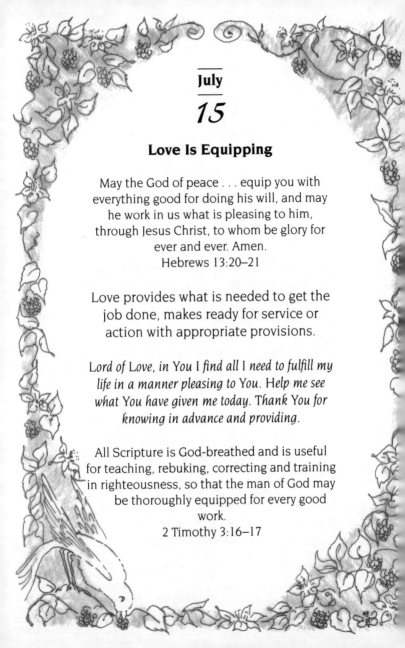

July

15

Love Is Equipping

May the God of peace . . . equip you with
everything good for doing his will, and may
he work in us what is pleasing to him,
through Jesus Christ, to whom be glory for
ever and ever. Amen.
Hebrews 13:20–21

Love provides what is needed to get the
job done, makes ready for service or
action with appropriate provisions.

*Lord of Love, in You I find all I need to fulfill my
life in a manner pleasing to You. Help me see
what You have given me today. Thank You for
knowing in advance and providing.*

All Scripture is God-breathed and is useful
for teaching, rebuking, correcting and training
in righteousness, so that the man of God may
be thoroughly equipped for every good
work.
2 Timothy 3:16–17

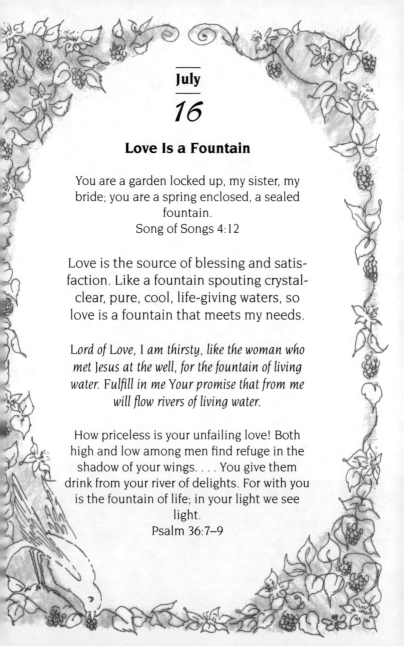

July

16

Love Is a Fountain

You are a garden locked up, my sister, my bride; you are a spring enclosed, a sealed fountain.
Song of Songs 4:12

Love is the source of blessing and satisfaction. Like a fountain spouting crystal-clear, pure, cool, life-giving waters, so love is a fountain that meets my needs.

Lord of Love, I am thirsty, like the woman who met Jesus at the well, for the fountain of living water. Fulfill in me Your promise that from me will flow rivers of living water.

How priceless is your unfailing love! Both high and low among men find refuge in the shadow of your wings. . . . You give them drink from your river of delights. For with you is the fountain of life; in your light we see light.
Psalm 36:7–9

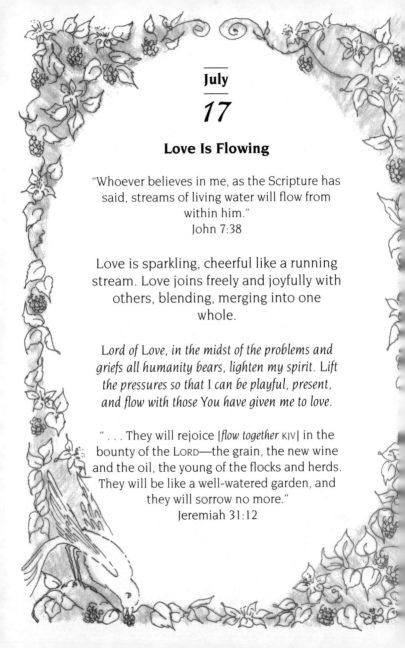

July

17

Love Is Flowing

"Whoever believes in me, as the Scripture has
said, streams of living water will flow from
within him."
John 7:38

Love is sparkling, cheerful like a running
stream. Love joins freely and joyfully with
others, blending, merging into one
whole.

*Lord of Love, in the midst of the problems and
griefs all humanity bears, lighten my spirit. Lift
the pressures so that I can be playful, present,
and flow with those You have given me to love.*

" . . . They will rejoice [*flow together* KJV] in the
bounty of the LORD—the grain, the new wine
and the oil, the young of the flocks and herds.
They will be like a well-watered garden, and
they will sorrow no more."
Jeremiah 31:12

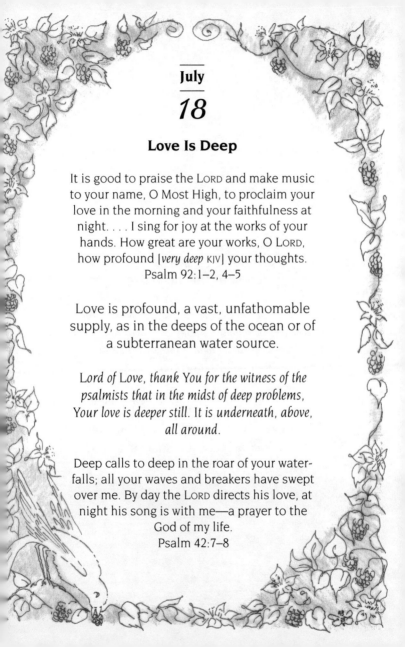

July

18

Love Is Deep

It is good to praise the LORD and make music to your name, O Most High, to proclaim your love in the morning and your faithfulness at night. . . . I sing for joy at the works of your hands. How great are your works, O LORD, how profound [*very deep* KJV] your thoughts.
Psalm 92:1–2, 4–5

Love is profound, a vast, unfathomable supply, as in the deeps of the ocean or of a subterranean water source.

Lord of Love, thank You for the witness of the psalmists that in the midst of deep problems, Your love is deeper still. It is underneath, above, all around.

Deep calls to deep in the roar of your waterfalls; all your waves and breakers have swept over me. By day the LORD directs his love, at night his song is with me—a prayer to the God of my life.
Psalm 42:7–8

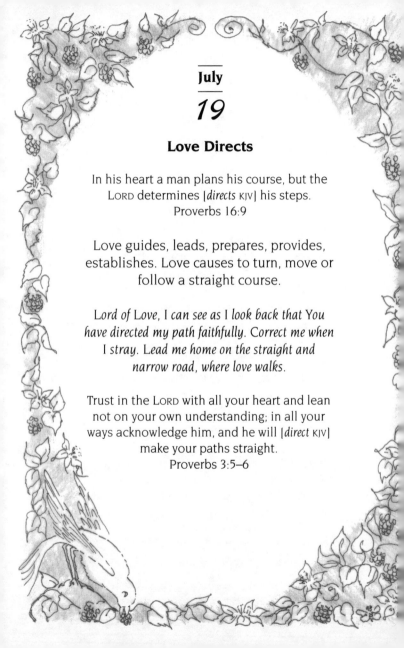

July
19

Love Directs

In his heart a man plans his course, but the
Lord determines [*directs* KJV] his steps.
Proverbs 16:9

Love guides, leads, prepares, provides,
establishes. Love causes to turn, move or
follow a straight course.

*Lord of Love, I can see as I look back that You
have directed my path faithfully. Correct me when
I stray. Lead me home on the straight and
narrow road, where love walks.*

Trust in the Lord with all your heart and lean
not on your own understanding; in all your
ways acknowledge him, and he will [*direct* KJV]
make your paths straight.
Proverbs 3:5–6

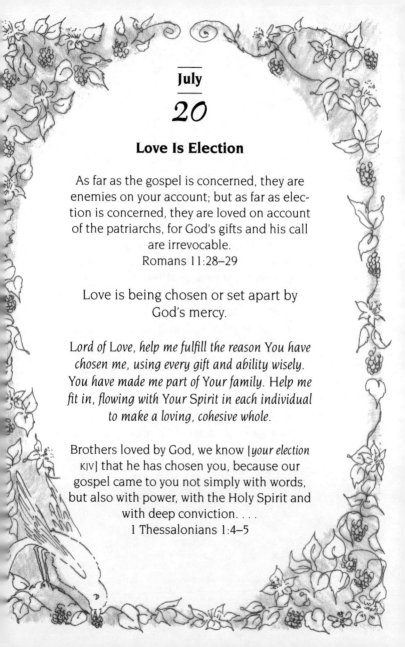

July
20

Love Is Election

As far as the gospel is concerned, they are
enemies on your account; but as far as election is concerned, they are loved on account
of the patriarchs, for God's gifts and his call
are irrevocable.
Romans 11:28–29

Love is being chosen or set apart by
God's mercy.

*Lord of Love, help me fulfill the reason You have
chosen me, using every gift and ability wisely.
You have made me part of Your family. Help me
fit in, flowing with Your Spirit in each individual
to make a loving, cohesive whole.*

Brothers loved by God, we know [*your election*
KJV] that he has chosen you, because our
gospel came to you not simply with words,
but also with power, with the Holy Spirit and
with deep conviction. . . .
1 Thessalonians 1:4–5

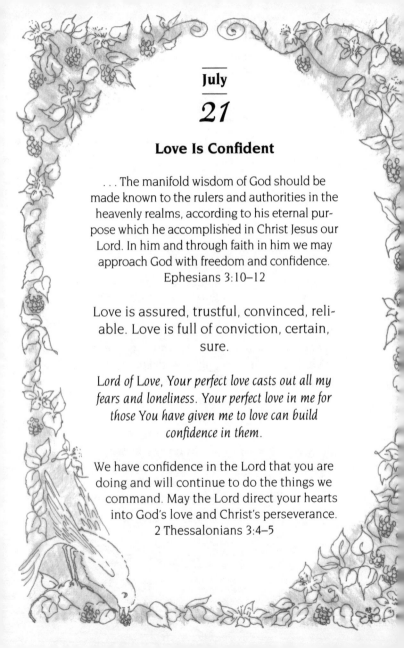

July
21

Love Is Confident

. . . The manifold wisdom of God should be
made known to the rulers and authorities in the
heavenly realms, according to his eternal purpose which he accomplished in Christ Jesus our
Lord. In him and through faith in him we may
approach God with freedom and confidence.
Ephesians 3:10–12

Love is assured, trustful, convinced, reli-
able. Love is full of conviction, certain,
sure.

Lord of Love, Your perfect love casts out all my
fears and loneliness. Your perfect love in me for
those You have given me to love can build
confidence in them.

We have confidence in the Lord that you are
doing and will continue to do the things we
command. May the Lord direct your hearts
into God's love and Christ's perseverance.
2 Thessalonians 3:4–5

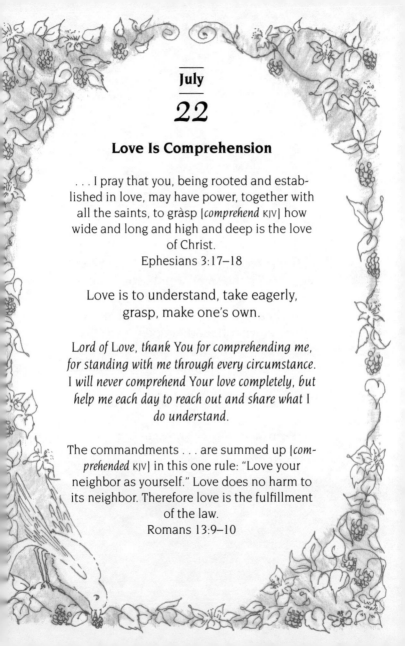

Love Is Comprehension

. . . I pray that you, being rooted and established in love, may have power, together with all the saints, to gràsp [*comprehend* KJV] how wide and long and high and deep is the love of Christ.
Ephesians 3:17–18

Love is to understand, take eagerly, grasp, make one's own.

Lord of Love, thank You for comprehending me, for standing with me through every circumstance. I will never comprehend Your love completely, but help me each day to reach out and share what I do understand.

The commandments . . . are summed up [*comprehended* KJV] in this one rule: "Love your neighbor as yourself." Love does no harm to its neighbor. Therefore love is the fulfillment of the law.
Romans 13:9–10

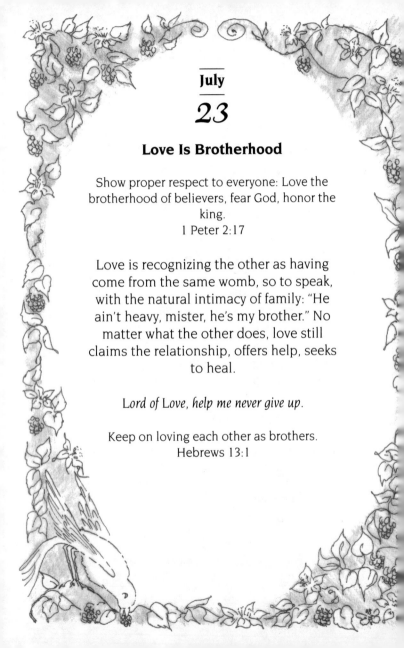

Love Is Brotherhood

Show proper respect to everyone: Love the
brotherhood of believers, fear God, honor the
king.
1 Peter 2:17

Love is recognizing the other as having
come from the same womb, so to speak,
with the natural intimacy of family: "He
ain't heavy, mister, he's my brother." No
matter what the other does, love still
claims the relationship, offers help, seeks
to heal.

Lord of Love, help me never give up.

Keep on loving each other as brothers.
Hebrews 13:1

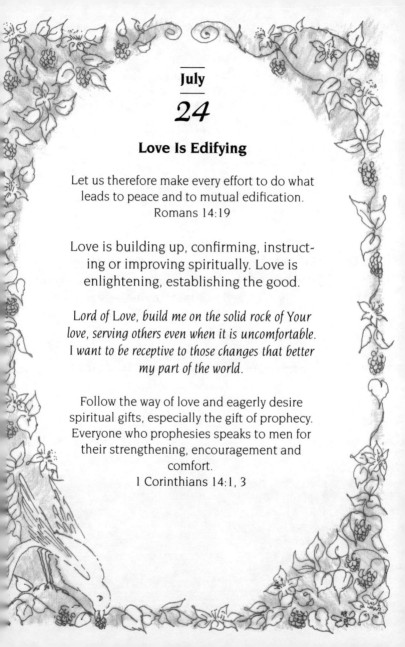

July

24

Love Is Edifying

Let us therefore make every effort to do what leads to peace and to mutual edification.
Romans 14:19

Love is building up, confirming, instructing or improving spiritually. Love is enlightening, establishing the good.

Lord of Love, build me on the solid rock of Your love, serving others even when it is uncomfortable. I want to be receptive to those changes that better my part of the world.

Follow the way of love and eagerly desire spiritual gifts, especially the gift of prophecy. Everyone who prophesies speaks to men for their strengthening, encouragement and comfort.
1 Corinthians 14:1, 3

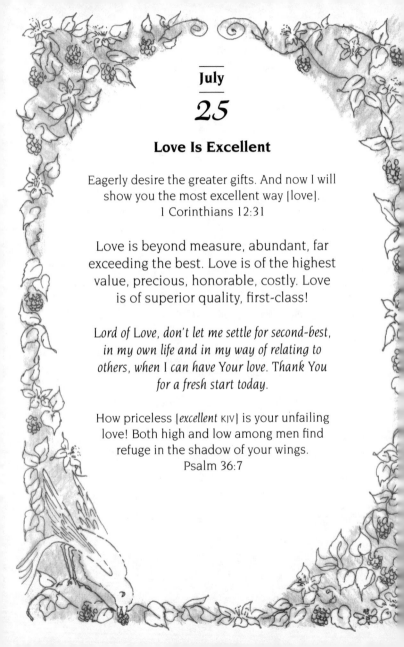

July
25

Love Is Excellent

Eagerly desire the greater gifts. And now I will
show you the most excellent way [love].
1 Corinthians 12:31

Love is beyond measure, abundant, far
exceeding the best. Love is of the highest
value, precious, honorable, costly. Love
is of superior quality, first-class!

*Lord of Love, don't let me settle for second-best,
in my own life and in my way of relating to
others, when I can have Your love. Thank You
for a fresh start today.*

How priceless [*excellent* KJV] is your unfailing
love! Both high and low among men find
refuge in the shadow of your wings.
Psalm 36:7

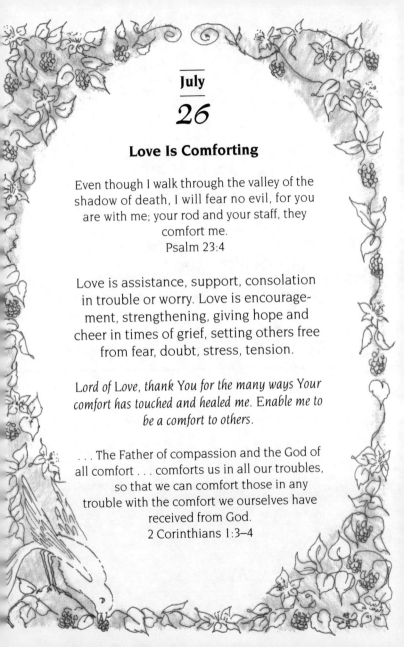

July

26

Love Is Comforting

Even though I walk through the valley of the
shadow of death, I will fear no evil, for you
are with me; your rod and your staff, they
comfort me.
Psalm 23:4

Love is assistance, support, consolation
in trouble or worry. Love is encouragement, strengthening, giving hope and
cheer in times of grief, setting others free
from fear, doubt, stress, tension.

*Lord of Love, thank You for the many ways Your
comfort has touched and healed me. Enable me to
be a comfort to others.*

. . . The Father of compassion and the God of
all comfort . . . comforts us in all our troubles,
so that we can comfort those in any
trouble with the comfort we ourselves have
received from God.
2 Corinthians 1:3–4

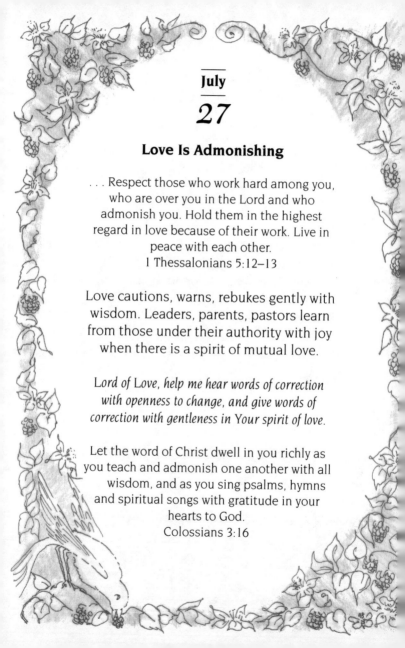

Love Is Admonishing

. . . Respect those who work hard among you,
who are over you in the Lord and who
admonish you. Hold them in the highest
regard in love because of their work. Live in
peace with each other.
1 Thessalonians 5:12–13

Love cautions, warns, rebukes gently with
wisdom. Leaders, parents, pastors learn
from those under their authority with joy
when there is a spirit of mutual love.

*Lord of Love, help me hear words of correction
with openness to change, and give words of
correction with gentleness in Your spirit of love.*

Let the word of Christ dwell in you richly as
you teach and admonish one another with all
wisdom, and as you sing psalms, hymns
and spiritual songs with gratitude in your
hearts to God.
Colossians 3:16

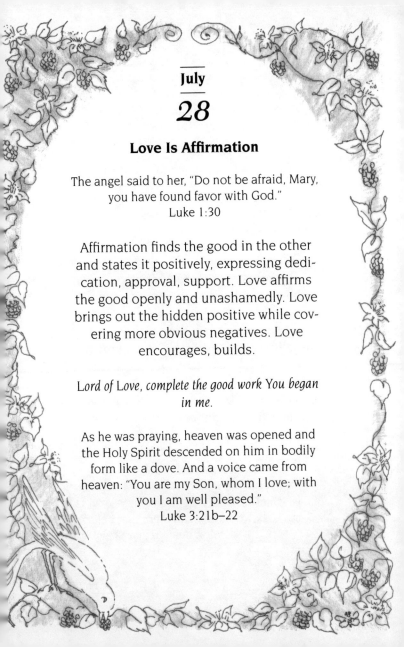

Love Is Affirmation

The angel said to her, "Do not be afraid, Mary,
you have found favor with God."
Luke 1:30

Affirmation finds the good in the other
and states it positively, expressing dedi-
cation, approval, support. Love affirms
the good openly and unashamedly. Love
brings out the hidden positive while covering more obvious negatives. Love
encourages, builds.

*Lord of Love, complete the good work You began
in me.*

As he was praying, heaven was opened and
the Holy Spirit descended on him in bodily
form like a dove. And a voice came from
heaven: "You are my Son, whom I love; with
you I am well pleased."
Luke 3:21b–22

July

29

Love Is Admirable

. . . Whatever is noble . . . right . . . pure . . .
lovely . . . admirable . . . excellent or praiseworthy—think about such things. . . . And the
God of peace will be with you.
Philippians 4:8, 9b

Love causes me to be filled with wonder,
admiration. Love enables me to see the
good, overlook hundreds of faults, forgive
seventy times seven. Love lifts me out of
myself, focuses my vision beyond my tiny
circle.

*Lord of Love, I love You with exalting, praising
admiration. Let my love of my neighbor be
forgiving, encouraging, admiring. Let my love of
myself be thankful, humble admiration of what
You have done in me.*

. . He shall come to be glorified in his saints,
and to be admired in all them that believe.
2 Thessalonians 1:10, KJV

July

30

Love Is Great

Great is your love, reaching to the heavens;
your faithfulness reaches to the skies.
Psalm 57:10

"God is great, God is good" is the first
prayer I remember. God is superior in
character and quality to every other
being. He is noble and remarkable in
every way—in magnitude, degree and
effectiveness. God expresses every
attribute of His greatness as love.

*Lord of Love, when I am overwhelmed by
seemingly insurmountable circumstances and feel
my own inadequacy, lift my eyes to see Your
greatness, Your ability to overcome.*

How great is the love the Father has lavished
on us, that we should be called children of
God!
1 John 3:1a

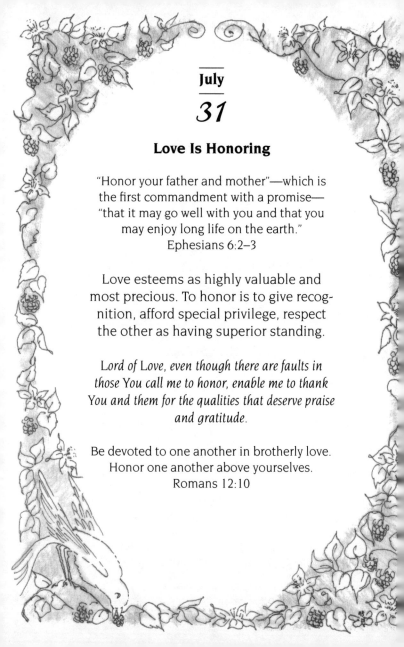

Love Is Honoring

"Honor your father and mother"—which is
the first commandment with a promise—
"that it may go well with you and that you
may enjoy long life on the earth."
Ephesians 6:2–3

Love esteems as highly valuable and
most precious. To honor is to give recognition, afford special privilege, respect
the other as having superior standing.

*Lord of Love, even though there are faults in
those You call me to honor, enable me to thank
You and them for the qualities that deserve praise
and gratitude.*

Be devoted to one another in brotherly love.
Honor one another above yourselves.
Romans 12:10

August
Love Is Strength

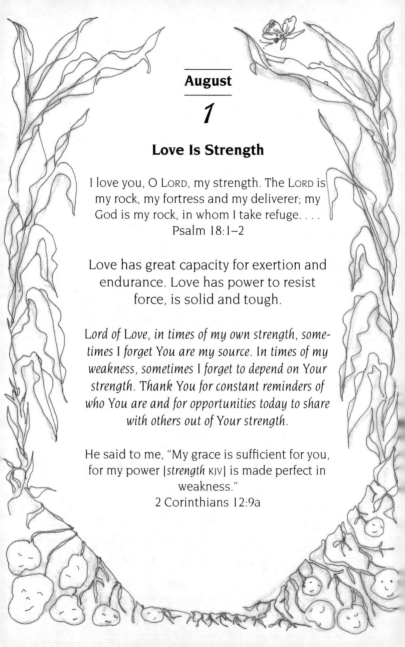

August

1

Love Is Strength

I love you, O LORD, my strength. The LORD is my rock, my fortress and my deliverer; my God is my rock, in whom I take refuge. . . .
Psalm 18:1–2

Love has great capacity for exertion and endurance. Love has power to resist force, is solid and tough.

Lord of Love, in times of my own strength, sometimes I forget You are my source. In times of my weakness, sometimes I forget to depend on Your strength. Thank You for constant reminders of who You are and for opportunities today to share with others out of Your strength.

He said to me, "My grace is sufficient for you, for my power [*strength* KJV] is made perfect in weakness."
2 Corinthians 12:9a

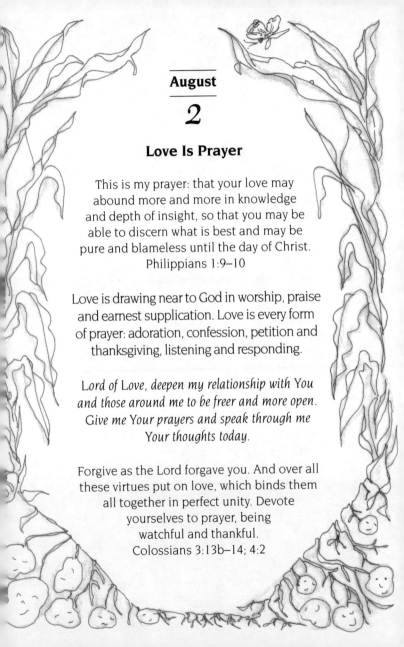

Love Is Prayer

This is my prayer: that your love may
abound more and more in knowledge
and depth of insight, so that you may be
able to discern what is best and may be
pure and blameless until the day of Christ.
Philippians 1:9–10

Love is drawing near to God in worship, praise
and earnest supplication. Love is every form
of prayer: adoration, confession, petition and
thanksgiving, listening and responding.

*Lord of Love, deepen my relationship with You
and those around me to be freer and more open.
Give me Your prayers and speak through me
Your thoughts today.*

Forgive as the Lord forgave you. And over all
these virtues put on love, which binds them
all together in perfect unity. Devote
yourselves to prayer, being
watchful and thankful.
Colossians 3:13b–14; 4:2

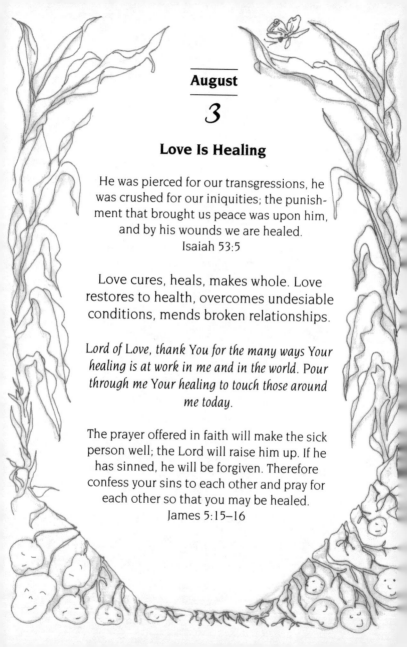

August

3

Love Is Healing

He was pierced for our transgressions, he was crushed for our iniquities; the punishment that brought us peace was upon him, and by his wounds we are healed.

Isaiah 53:5

Love cures, heals, makes whole. Love restores to health, overcomes undesiable conditions, mends broken relationships.

Lord of Love, thank You for the many ways Your healing is at work in me and in the world. Pour through me Your healing to touch those around me today.

The prayer offered in faith will make the sick person well; the Lord will raise him up. If he has sinned, he will be forgiven. Therefore confess your sins to each other and pray for each other so that you may be healed.

James 5:15–16

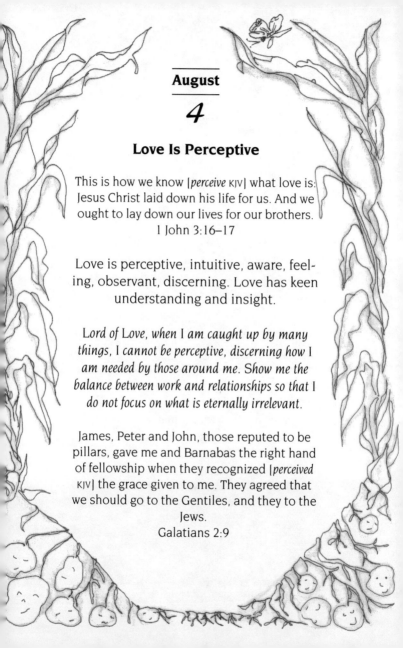

Love Is Perceptive

This is how we know [*perceive* KJV] what love is:
Jesus Christ laid down his life for us. And we
ought to lay down our lives for our brothers.
1 John 3:16–17

Love is perceptive, intuitive, aware, feeling, observant, discerning. Love has keen
understanding and insight.

*Lord of Love, when I am caught up by many
things, I cannot be perceptive, discerning how I
am needed by those around me. Show me the
balance between work and relationships so that I
do not focus on what is eternally irrelevant.*

James, Peter and John, those reputed to be
pillars, gave me and Barnabas the right hand
of fellowship when they recognized [*perceived*
KJV] the grace given to me. They agreed that
we should go to the Gentiles, and they to the
Jews.
Galatians 2:9

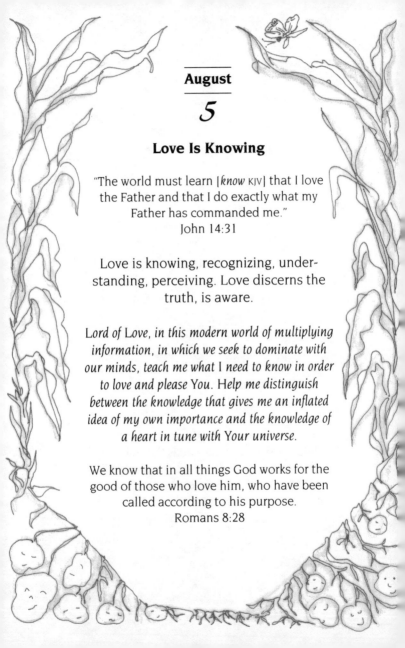

August

5

Love Is Knowing

"The world must learn [*know* KJV] that I love
the Father and that I do exactly what my
Father has commanded me."
John 14:31

Love is knowing, recognizing, understanding, perceiving. Love discerns the
truth, is aware.

Lord of Love, in this modern world of multiplying
information, in which we seek to dominate with
our minds, teach me what I need to know in order
to love and please You. Help me distinguish
between the knowledge that gives me an inflated
idea of my own importance and the knowledge of
a heart in tune with Your universe.

We know that in all things God works for the
good of those who love him, who have been
called according to his purpose.
Romans 8:28

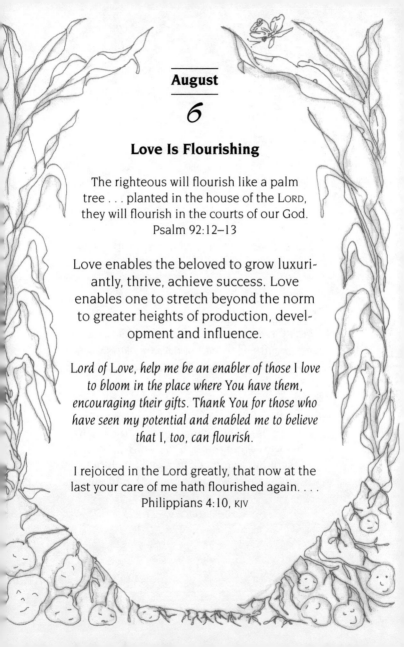

August

6

Love Is Flourishing

The righteous will flourish like a palm
tree . . . planted in the house of the LORD,
they will flourish in the courts of our God.
Psalm 92:12–13

Love enables the beloved to grow luxuri-
antly, thrive, achieve success. Love
enables one to stretch beyond the norm
to greater heights of production, development and influence.

*Lord of Love, help me be an enabler of those I love
to bloom in the place where You have them,
encouraging their gifts. Thank You for those who
have seen my potential and enabled me to believe
that I, too, can flourish.*

I rejoiced in the Lord greatly, that now at the
last your care of me hath flourished again. . . .
Philippians 4:10, KJV

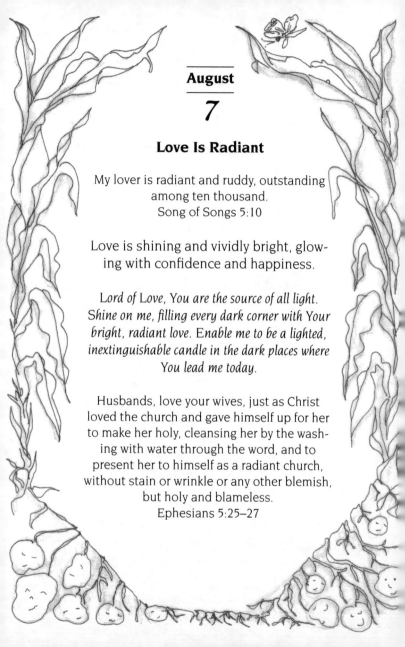

Love Is Radiant

My lover is radiant and ruddy, outstanding among ten thousand.
Song of Songs 5:10

Love is shining and vividly bright, glowing with confidence and happiness.

Lord of Love, You are the source of all light. Shine on me, filling every dark corner with Your bright, radiant love. Enable me to be a lighted, inextinguishable candle in the dark places where You lead me today.

Husbands, love your wives, just as Christ loved the church and gave himself up for her to make her holy, cleansing her by the washing with water through the word, and to present her to himself as a radiant church, without stain or wrinkle or any other blemish, but holy and blameless.
Ephesians 5:25–27

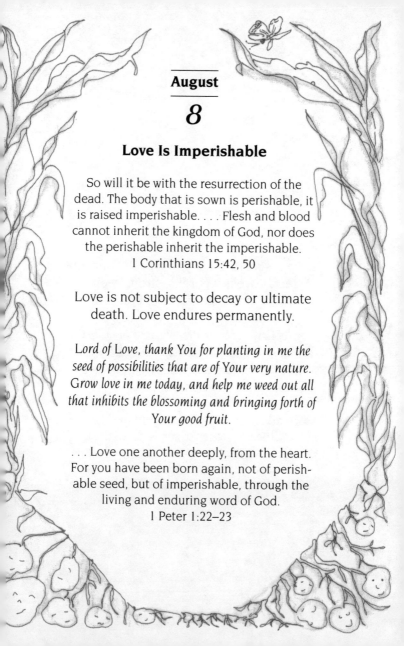

Love Is Imperishable

So will it be with the resurrection of the
dead. The body that is sown is perishable, it
is raised imperishable. . . . Flesh and blood
cannot inherit the kingdom of God, nor does
the perishable inherit the imperishable.
1 Corinthians 15:42, 50

Love is not subject to decay or ultimate
death. Love endures permanently.

*Lord of Love, thank You for planting in me the
seed of possibilities that are of Your very nature.
Grow love in me today, and help me weed out all
that inhibits the blossoming and bringing forth of
Your good fruit.*

. . . Love one another deeply, from the heart.
For you have been born again, not of perishable seed, but of imperishable, through the
living and enduring word of God.
1 Peter 1:22–23

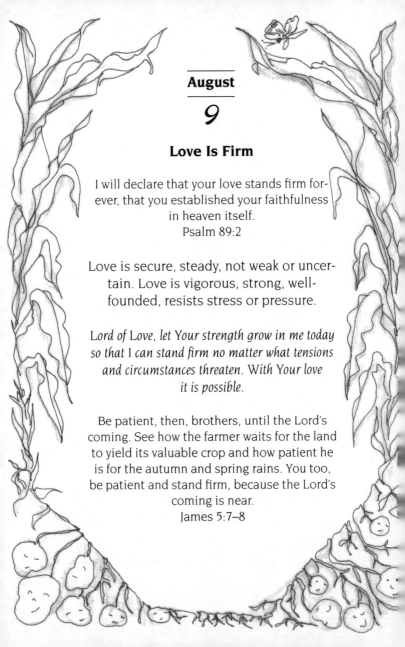

August

9

Love Is Firm

I will declare that your love stands firm forever, that you established your faithfulness
in heaven itself.
Psalm 89:2

Love is secure, steady, not weak or uncertain. Love is vigorous, strong, wellfounded, resists stress or pressure.

*Lord of Love, let Your strength grow in me today
so that I can stand firm no matter what tensions
and circumstances threaten. With Your love
it is possible.*

Be patient, then, brothers, until the Lord's
coming. See how the farmer waits for the land
to yield its valuable crop and how patient he
is for the autumn and spring rains. You too,
be patient and stand firm, because the Lord's
coming is near.
James 5:7–8

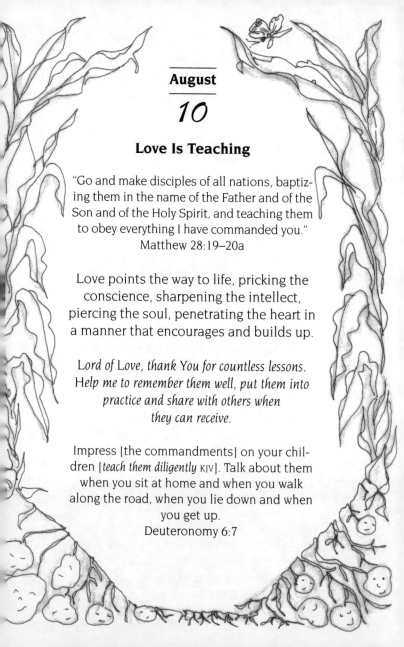

Love Is Teaching

"Go and make disciples of all nations, baptizing them in the name of the Father and of the Son and of the Holy Spirit, and teaching them to obey everything I have commanded you."
Matthew 28:19–20a

Love points the way to life, pricking the conscience, sharpening the intellect, piercing the soul, penetrating the heart in a manner that encourages and builds up.

Lord of Love, thank You for countless lessons. Help me to remember them well, put them into practice and share with others when they can receive.

Impress [the commandments] on your children [*teach them diligently* KJV]. Talk about them when you sit at home and when you walk along the road, when you lie down and when you get up.
Deuteronomy 6:7

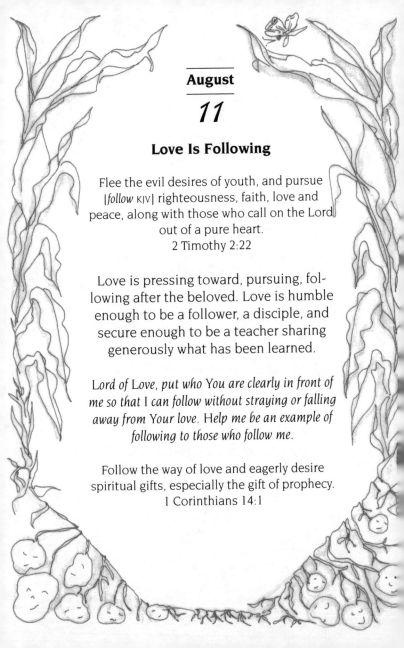

August

11

Love Is Following

Flee the evil desires of youth, and pursue
[*follow* KJV] righteousness, faith, love and
peace, along with those who call on the Lord
out of a pure heart.
2 Timothy 2:22

Love is pressing toward, pursuing, following after the beloved. Love is humble
enough to be a follower, a disciple, and
secure enough to be a teacher sharing
generously what has been learned.

*Lord of Love, put who You are clearly in front of
me so that I can follow without straying or falling
away from Your love. Help me be an example of
following to those who follow me.*

Follow the way of love and eagerly desire
spiritual gifts, especially the gift of prophecy.
1 Corinthians 14:1

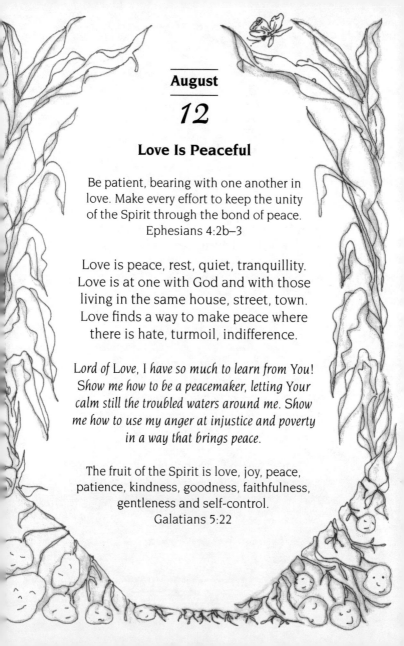

August

12

Love Is Peaceful

Be patient, bearing with one another in
love. Make every effort to keep the unity
of the Spirit through the bond of peace.
Ephesians 4:2b–3

Love is peace, rest, quiet, tranquillity.
Love is at one with God and with those
living in the same house, street, town.
Love finds a way to make peace where
there is hate, turmoil, indifference.

*Lord of Love, I have so much to learn from You!
Show me how to be a peacemaker, letting Your
calm still the troubled waters around me. Show
me how to use my anger at injustice and poverty
in a way that brings peace.*

The fruit of the Spirit is love, joy, peace,
patience, kindness, goodness, faithfulness,
gentleness and self-control.
Galatians 5:22

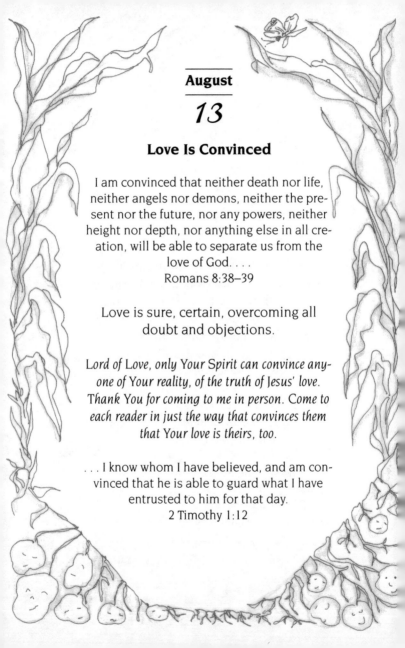

August

13

Love Is Convinced

I am convinced that neither death nor life,
neither angels nor demons, neither the present nor the future, nor any powers, neither
height nor depth, nor anything else in all creation, will be able to separate us from the
love of God. . . .
Romans 8:38–39

Love is sure, certain, overcoming all
doubt and objections.

Lord of Love, only Your Spirit can convince any-
one of Your reality, of the truth of Jesus' love.
Thank You for coming to me in person. Come to
each reader in just the way that convinces them
that Your love is theirs, too.

. . . I know whom I have believed, and am convinced that he is able to guard what I have
entrusted to him for that day.
2 Timothy 1:12

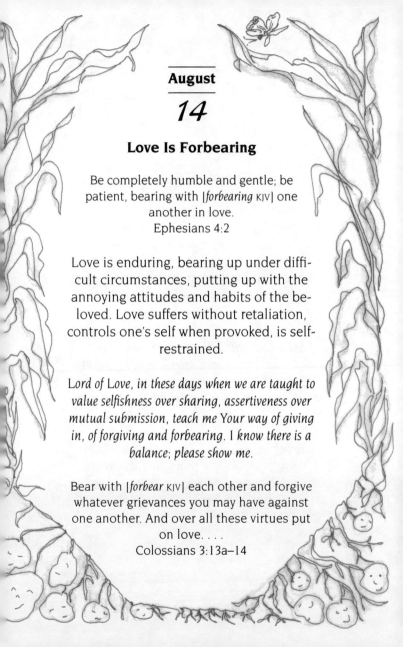

August

14

Love Is Forbearing

Be completely humble and gentle; be
patient, bearing with [*forbearing* KJV] one
another in love.
Ephesians 4:2

Love is enduring, bearing up under difficult circumstances, putting up with the
annoying attitudes and habits of the beloved. Love suffers without retaliation,
controls one's self when provoked, is self-
restrained.

Lord of Love, in these days when we are taught to
value selfishness over sharing, assertiveness over
mutual submission, teach me Your way of giving
in, of forgiving and forbearing. I know there is a
balance; please show me.

Bear with [*forbear* KJV] each other and forgive
whatever grievances you may have against
one another. And over all these virtues put
on love. . . .
Colossians 3:13a–14

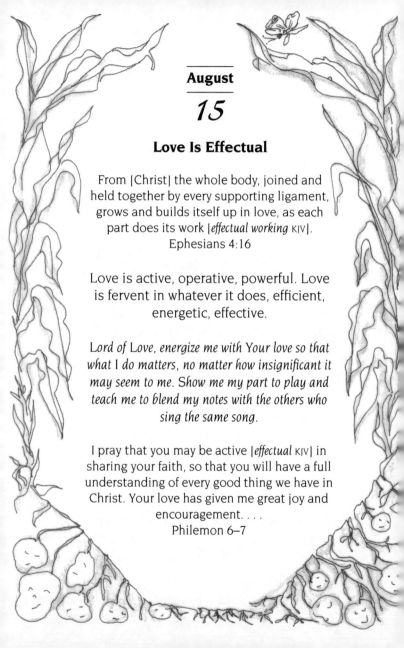

August

15

Love Is Effectual

From [Christ] the whole body, joined and
held together by every supporting ligament,
grows and builds itself up in love, as each
part does its work [*effectual working* KJV].
Ephesians 4:16

Love is active, operative, powerful. Love
is fervent in whatever it does, efficient,
energetic, effective.

*Lord of Love, energize me with Your love so that
what I do matters, no matter how insignificant it
may seem to me. Show me my part to play and
teach me to blend my notes with the others who
sing the same song.*

I pray that you may be active [*effectual* KJV] in
sharing your faith, so that you will have a full
understanding of every good thing we have in
Christ. Your love has given me great joy and
encouragement. . . .
Philemon 6–7

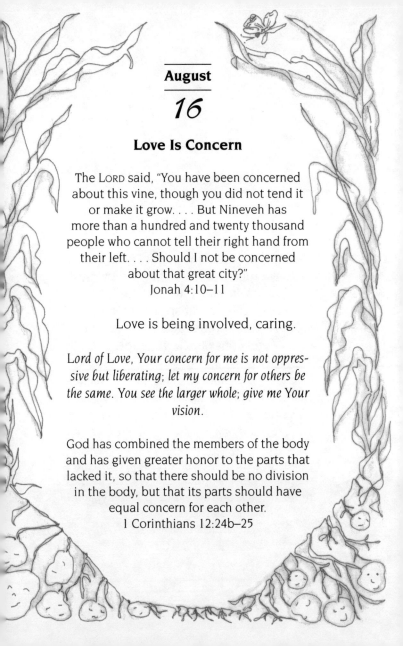

Love Is Concern

The LORD said, "You have been concerned
about this vine, though you did not tend it
or make it grow. . . . But Nineveh has
more than a hundred and twenty thousand
people who cannot tell their right hand from
their left. . . . Should I not be concerned
about that great city?"
Jonah 4:10–11

Love is being involved, caring.

Lord of Love, Your concern for me is not oppres-
sive but liberating; let my concern for others be
the same. You see the larger whole; give me Your
vision.

God has combined the members of the body
and has given greater honor to the parts that
lacked it, so that there should be no division
in the body, but that its parts should have
equal concern for each other.
1 Corinthians 12:24b–25

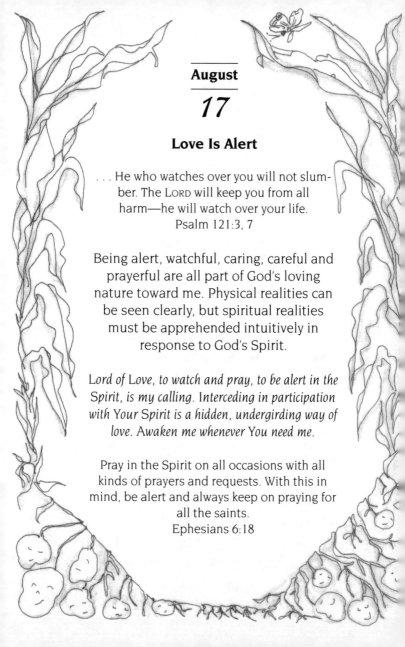

August

17

Love Is Alert

. . . He who watches over you will not slumber. The Lord will keep you from all harm—he will watch over your life.
Psalm 121:3, 7

Being alert, watchful, caring, careful and prayerful are all part of God's loving nature toward me. Physical realities can be seen clearly, but spiritual realities must be apprehended intuitively in response to God's Spirit.

Lord of Love, to watch and pray, to be alert in the Spirit, is my calling. Interceding in participation with Your Spirit is a hidden, undergirding way of love. Awaken me whenever You need me.

Pray in the Spirit on all occasions with all kinds of prayers and requests. With this in mind, be alert and always keep on praying for all the saints.
Ephesians 6:18

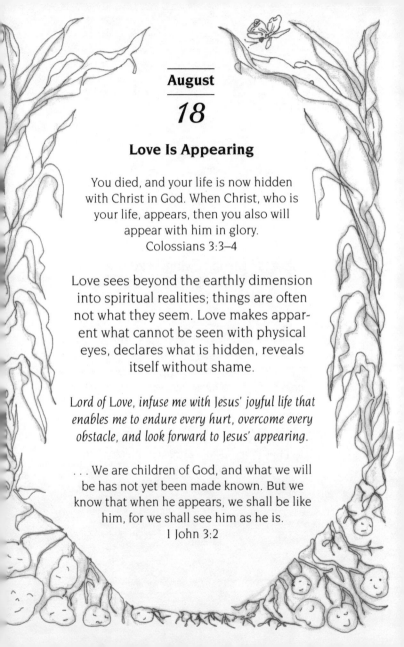

August

18

Love Is Appearing

You died, and your life is now hidden
with Christ in God. When Christ, who is
your life, appears, then you also will
appear with him in glory.
Colossians 3:3–4

Love sees beyond the earthly dimension
into spiritual realities; things are often
not what they seem. Love makes appar-
ent what cannot be seen with physical
eyes, declares what is hidden, reveals
itself without shame.

*Lord of Love, infuse me with Jesus' joyful life that
enables me to endure every hurt, overcome every
obstacle, and look forward to Jesus' appearing.*

. . . We are children of God, and what we will
be has not yet been made known. But we
know that when he appears, we shall be like
him, for we shall see him as he is.
1 John 3:2

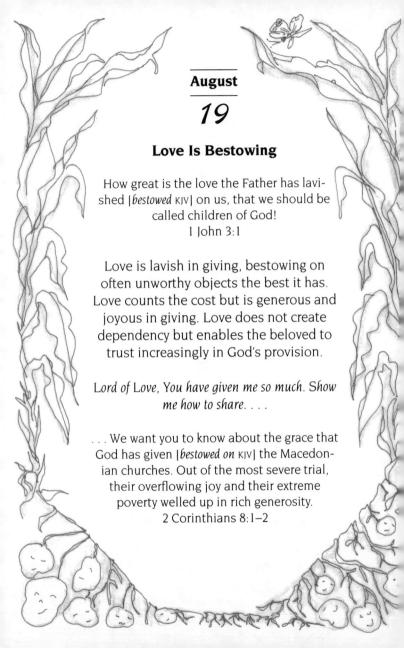

August

19

Love Is Bestowing

How great is the love the Father has lavished [*bestowed* KJV] on us, that we should be called children of God!
1 John 3:1

Love is lavish in giving, bestowing on often unworthy objects the best it has. Love counts the cost but is generous and joyous in giving. Love does not create dependency but enables the beloved to trust increasingly in God's provision.

Lord of Love, You have given me so much. Show me how to share. . . .

. . . We want you to know about the grace that God has given [*bestowed on* KJV] the Macedonian churches. Out of the most severe trial, their overflowing joy and their extreme poverty welled up in rich generosity.
2 Corinthians 8:1–2

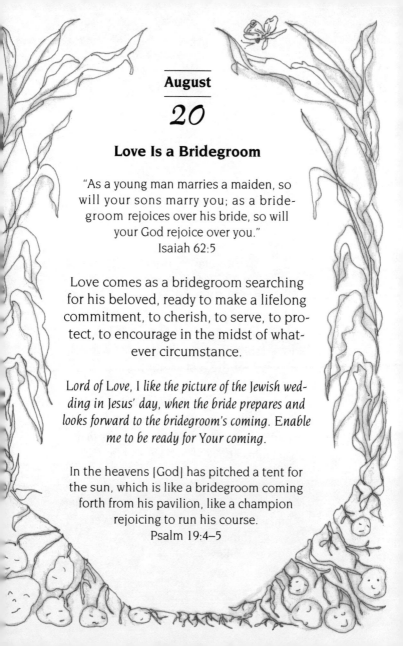

August

20

Love Is a Bridegroom

"As a young man marries a maiden, so
will your sons marry you; as a bridegroom rejoices over his bride, so will
your God rejoice over you."
Isaiah 62:5

Love comes as a bridegroom searching
for his beloved, ready to make a lifelong
commitment, to cherish, to serve, to protect, to encourage in the midst of whatever circumstance.

*Lord of Love, I like the picture of the Jewish wed-
ding in Jesus' day, when the bride prepares and
looks forward to the bridegroom's coming. Enable
me to be ready for Your coming.*

In the heavens [God] has pitched a tent for
the sun, which is like a bridegroom coming
forth from his pavilion, like a champion
rejoicing to run his course.
Psalm 19:4–5

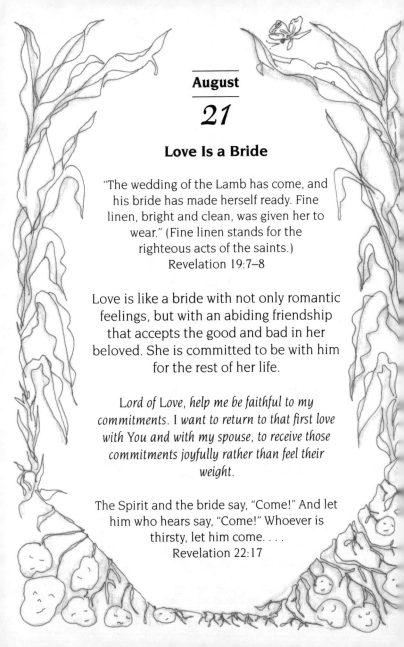

August

21

Love Is a Bride

"The wedding of the Lamb has come, and his bride has made herself ready. Fine linen, bright and clean, was given her to wear." (Fine linen stands for the righteous acts of the saints.)
Revelation 19:7–8

Love is like a bride with not only romantic feelings, but with an abiding friendship that accepts the good and bad in her beloved. She is committed to be with him for the rest of her life.

Lord of Love, help me be faithful to my commitments. I want to return to that first love with You and with my spouse, to receive those commitments joyfully rather than feel their weight.

The Spirit and the bride say, "Come!" And let him who hears say, "Come!" Whoever is thirsty, let him come. . . .
Revelation 22:17

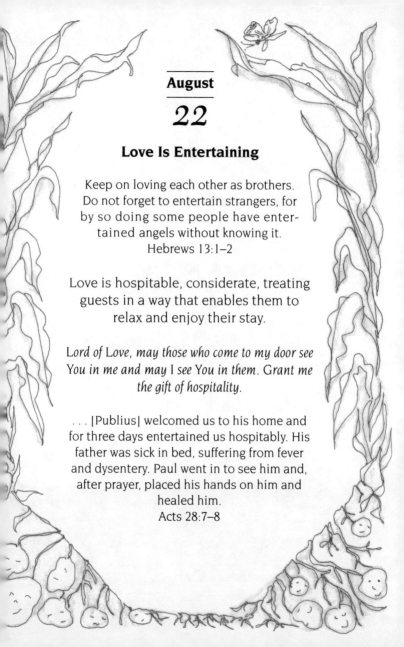

Love Is Entertaining

Keep on loving each other as brothers.
Do not forget to entertain strangers, for
by so doing some people have entertained angels without knowing it.
Hebrews 13:1–2

Love is hospitable, considerate, treating
guests in a way that enables them to
relax and enjoy their stay.

*Lord of Love, may those who come to my door see
You in me and may I see You in them. Grant me
the gift of hospitality.*

. . . [Publius] welcomed us to his home and
for three days entertained us hospitably. His
father was sick in bed, suffering from fever
and dysentery. Paul went in to see him and,
after prayer, placed his hands on him and
healed him.
Acts 28:7–8

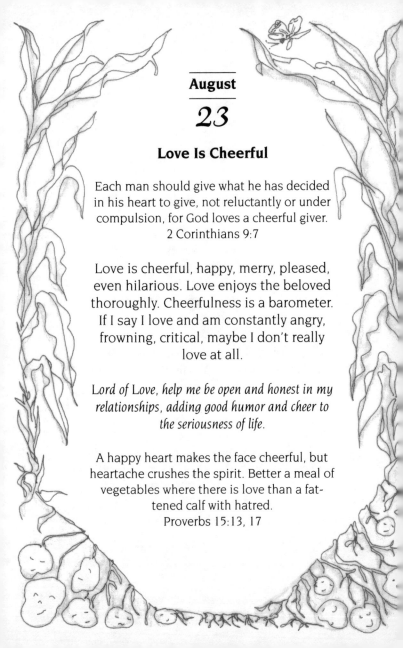

August

23

Love Is Cheerful

Each man should give what he has decided in his heart to give, not reluctantly or under compulsion, for God loves a cheerful giver.
2 Corinthians 9:7

Love is cheerful, happy, merry, pleased, even hilarious. Love enjoys the beloved thoroughly. Cheerfulness is a barometer. If I say I love and am constantly angry, frowning, critical, maybe I don't really love at all.

Lord of Love, help me be open and honest in my relationships, adding good humor and cheer to the seriousness of life.

A happy heart makes the face cheerful, but heartache crushes the spirit. Better a meal of vegetables where there is love than a fattened calf with hatred.
Proverbs 15:13, 17

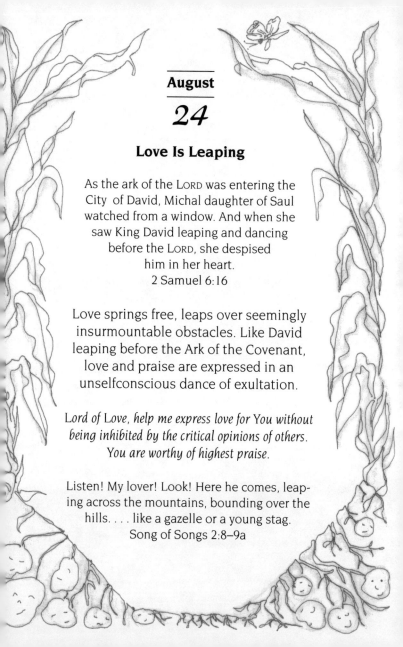

August

24

Love Is Leaping

As the ark of the LORD was entering the
City of David, Michal daughter of Saul
watched from a window. And when she
saw King David leaping and dancing
before the LORD, she despised
him in her heart.
2 Samuel 6:16

Love springs free, leaps over seemingly
insurmountable obstacles. Like David
leaping before the Ark of the Covenant,
love and praise are expressed in an
unselfconscious dance of exultation.

*Lord of Love, help me express love for You without
being inhibited by the critical opinions of others.
You are worthy of highest praise.*

Listen! My lover! Look! Here he comes, leaping across the mountains, bounding over the
hills. . . . like a gazelle or a young stag.
Song of Songs 2:8–9a

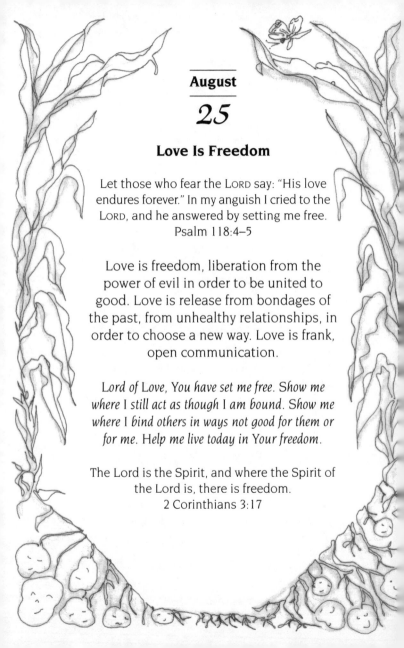

Love Is Freedom

Let those who fear the LORD say: "His love
endures forever." In my anguish I cried to the
LORD, and he answered by setting me free.
Psalm 118:4–5

Love is freedom, liberation from the
power of evil in order to be united to
good. Love is release from bondages of
the past, from unhealthy relationships, in
order to choose a new way. Love is frank,
open communication.

*Lord of Love, You have set me free. Show me
where I still act as though I am bound. Show me
where I bind others in ways not good for them or
for me. Help me live today in Your freedom.*

The Lord is the Spirit, and where the Spirit of
the Lord is, there is freedom.
2 Corinthians 3:17

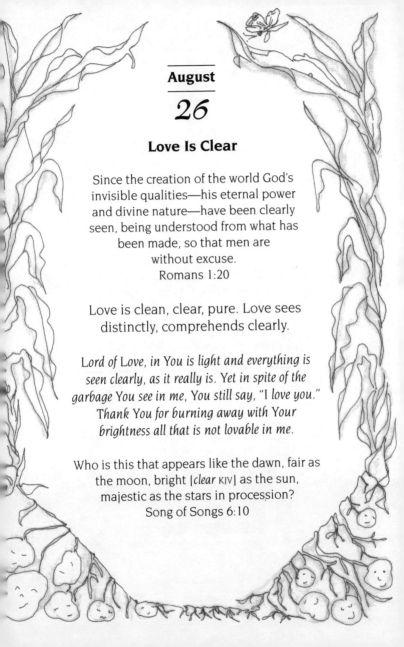

August

26

Love Is Clear

Since the creation of the world God's invisible qualities—his eternal power and divine nature—have been clearly seen, being understood from what has been made, so that men are without excuse.
Romans 1:20

Love is clean, clear, pure. Love sees distinctly, comprehends clearly.

Lord of Love, in You is light and everything is seen clearly, as it really is. Yet in spite of the garbage You see in me, You still say, "I love you." Thank You for burning away with Your brightness all that is not lovable in me.

Who is this that appears like the dawn, fair as the moon, bright [*clear* KJV] as the sun, majestic as the stars in procession?
Song of Songs 6:10

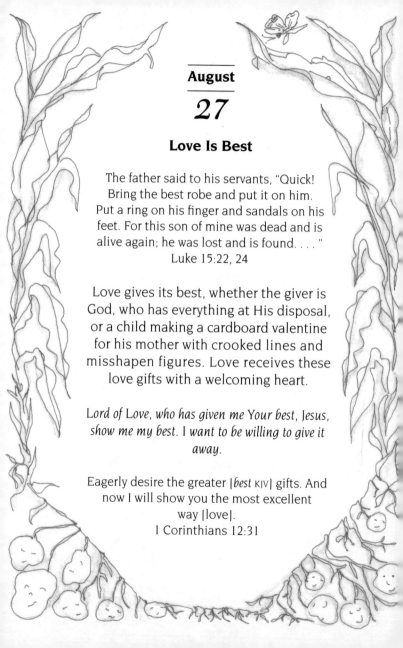

August

27

Love Is Best

The father said to his servants, "Quick!
Bring the best robe and put it on him.
Put a ring on his finger and sandals on his
feet. For this son of mine was dead and is
alive again; he was lost and is found. . . ."
Luke 15:22, 24

Love gives its best, whether the giver is
God, who has everything at His disposal,
or a child making a cardboard valentine
for his mother with crooked lines and
misshapen figures. Love receives these
love gifts with a welcoming heart.

*Lord of Love, who has given me Your best, Jesus,
show me my best. I want to be willing to give it
away.*

Eagerly desire the greater [*best* KJV] gifts. And
now I will show you the most excellent
way [love].
1 Corinthians 12:31

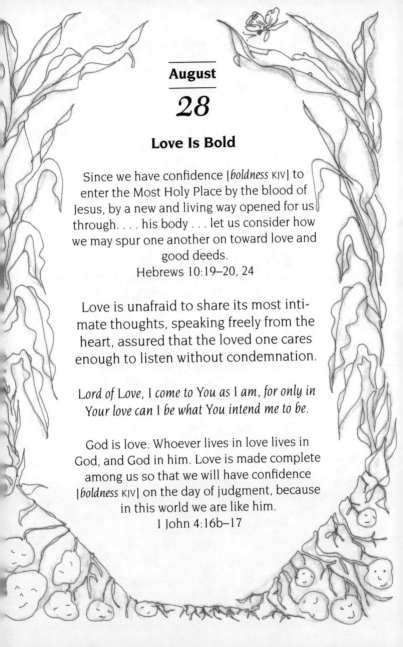

Love Is Bold

Since we have confidence [*boldness* KJV] to enter the Most Holy Place by the blood of Jesus, by a new and living way opened for us through. . . . his body . . . let us consider how we may spur one another on toward love and good deeds.
Hebrews 10:19–20, 24

Love is unafraid to share its most intimate thoughts, speaking freely from the heart, assured that the loved one cares enough to listen without condemnation.

Lord of Love, I come to You as I am, for only in Your love can I be what You intend me to be.

God is love. Whoever lives in love lives in God, and God in him. Love is made complete among us so that we will have confidence [*boldness* KJV] on the day of judgment, because in this world we are like him.
1 John 4:16b–17

August

29

Love Is Appointing

May [the king] be enthroned in God's presence forever; appoint your love and faithfulness to protect him.
Psalm 61:7

In love God has chosen me for a purpose. As I lay aside every other choice, I commit myself to receive the appointment, to fulfill in my body, soul and spirit His godly purpose.

Lord of Love, as Jesus appointed the disciples to go forth, placing in them all they needed of Your Spirit to do the very things Jesus did, so this surging, powerful love is for me today. I, too, am appointed! Thank You!

. . . [Put] on faith and love as a breastplate. . . For God did not appoint us to suffer wrath but to receive salvation through our Lord Jesus Christ.
1 Thessalonians 5:8–9

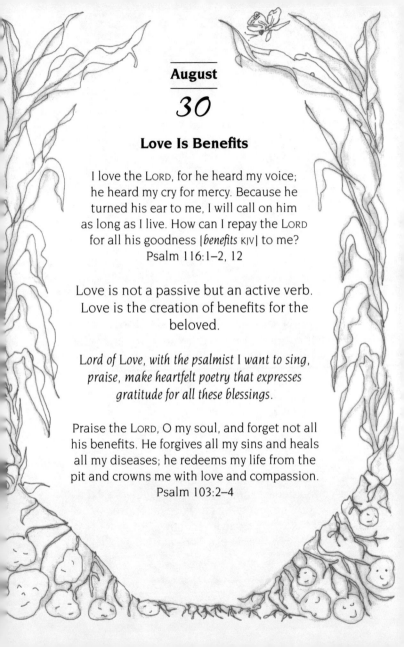

Love Is Benefits

I love the LORD, for he heard my voice;
he heard my cry for mercy. Because he
turned his ear to me, I will call on him
as long as I live. How can I repay the LORD
for all his goodness [*benefits* KJV] to me?
Psalm 116:1–2, 12

Love is not a passive but an active verb.
Love is the creation of benefits for the
beloved.

*Lord of Love, with the psalmist I want to sing,
praise, make heartfelt poetry that expresses
gratitude for all these blessings.*

Praise the LORD, O my soul, and forget not all
his benefits. He forgives all my sins and heals
all my diseases; he redeems my life from the
pit and crowns me with love and compassion.
Psalm 103:2–4

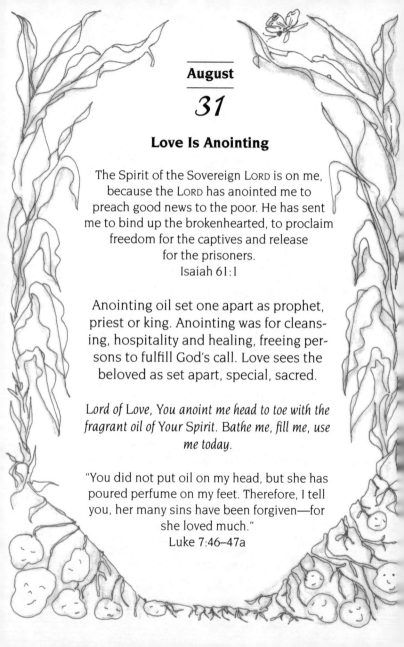

Love Is Anointing

The Spirit of the Sovereign LORD is on me,
because the LORD has anointed me to
preach good news to the poor. He has sent
me to bind up the brokenhearted, to proclaim
freedom for the captives and release
for the prisoners.
Isaiah 61:1

Anointing oil set one apart as prophet,
priest or king. Anointing was for cleansing, hospitality and healing, freeing persons to fulfill God's call. Love sees the
beloved as set apart, special, sacred.

*Lord of Love, You anoint me head to toe with the
fragrant oil of Your Spirit. Bathe me, fill me, use
me today.*

"You did not put oil on my head, but she has
poured perfume on my feet. Therefore, I tell
you, her many sins have been forgiven—for
she loved much."
Luke 7:46–47a

September
Love Is Labor

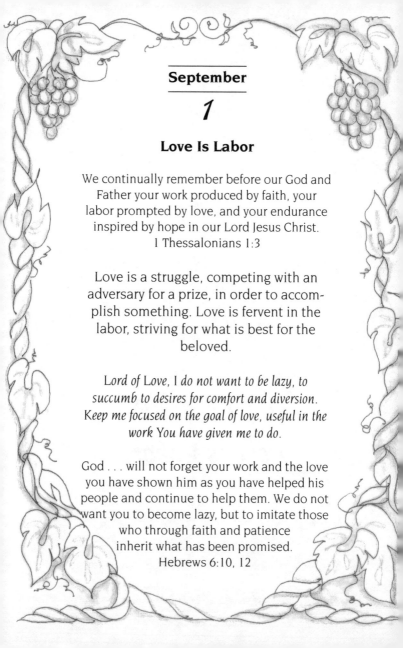

September

1

Love Is Labor

We continually remember before our God and
Father your work produced by faith, your
labor prompted by love, and your endurance
inspired by hope in our Lord Jesus Christ.
1 Thessalonians 1:3

Love is a struggle, competing with an
adversary for a prize, in order to accomplish something. Love is fervent in the
labor, striving for what is best for the
beloved.

*Lord of Love, I do not want to be lazy, to
succumb to desires for comfort and diversion.
Keep me focused on the goal of love, useful in the
work You have given me to do.*

God . . . will not forget your work and the love
you have shown him as you have helped his
people and continue to help them. We do not
want you to become lazy, but to imitate those
who through faith and patience
inherit what has been promised.
Hebrews 6:10, 12

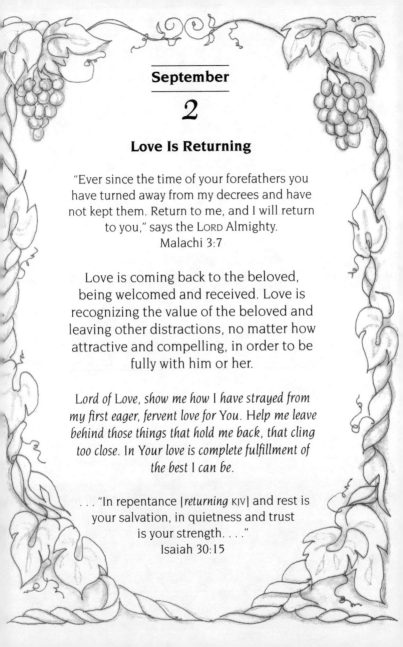

September

2

Love Is Returning

"Ever since the time of your forefathers you
have turned away from my decrees and have
not kept them. Return to me, and I will return
to you," says the LORD Almighty.
Malachi 3:7

Love is coming back to the beloved,
being welcomed and received. Love is
recognizing the value of the beloved and
leaving other distractions, no matter how
attractive and compelling, in order to be
fully with him or her.

*Lord of Love, show me how I have strayed from
my first eager, fervent love for You. Help me leave
behind those things that hold me back, that cling
too close. In Your love is complete fulfillment of
the best I can be.*

. . . "In repentance [*returning* KJV] and rest is
your salvation, in quietness and trust
is your strength. . . ."
Isaiah 30:15

September

3

Love Is Neighborly

"To love [God] with all your heart, with all
your understanding and with all your
strength, and to love your neighbor as yourself is more important than all burnt offerings
and sacrifices."
Mark 12:33

Love is being friendly, helpful. Jesus'
illustration of the Good Samaritan showed
a "neighbor" in action. Despite racial or
religious prejudice or anything that divides
human beings, a good neighbor shares,
helps, cares for the one at hand.

*Lord of Love, cleanse my heart of anything that
would prevent me from helping my neighbors.
Help me forgive them for their qualities that
irritate, so that I can see the good.*

Love does no harm to its neighbor. Therefore
love is the fulfillment of the law.
Romans 13:10

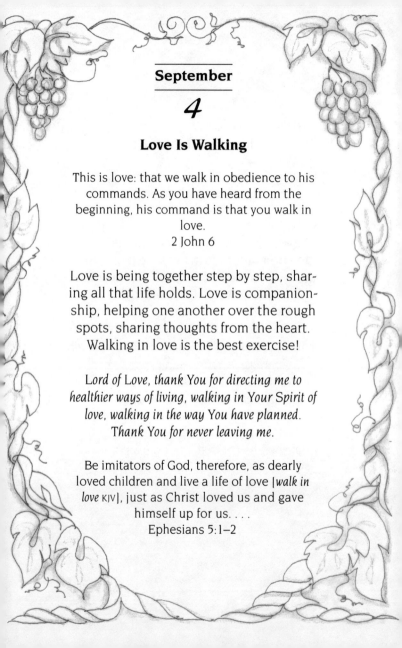

September

4

Love Is Walking

This is love: that we walk in obedience to his commands. As you have heard from the beginning, his command is that you walk in love.
2 John 6

Love is being together step by step, sharing all that life holds. Love is companionship, helping one another over the rough spots, sharing thoughts from the heart. Walking in love is the best exercise!

Lord of Love, thank You for directing me to healthier ways of living, walking in Your Spirit of love, walking in the way You have planned. Thank You for never leaving me.

Be imitators of God, therefore, as dearly loved children and live a life of love [*walk in love* KJV], just as Christ loved us and gave himself up for us. . . .
Ephesians 5:1–2

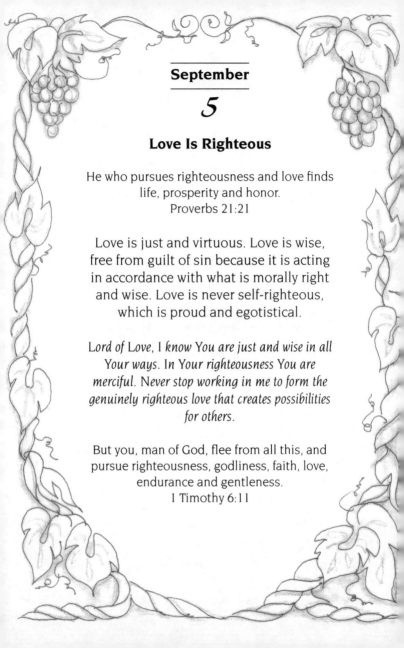

September

5

Love Is Righteous

He who pursues righteousness and love finds
life, prosperity and honor.
Proverbs 21:21

Love is just and virtuous. Love is wise,
free from guilt of sin because it is acting
in accordance with what is morally right
and wise. Love is never self-righteous,
which is proud and egotistical.

*Lord of Love, I know You are just and wise in all
Your ways. In Your righteousness You are
merciful. Never stop working in me to form the
genuinely righteous love that creates possibilities
for others.*

But you, man of God, flee from all this, and
pursue righteousness, godliness, faith, love,
endurance and gentleness.
1 Timothy 6:11

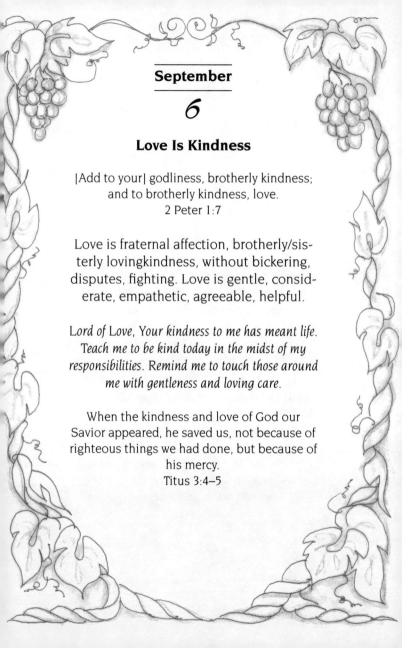

September

6

Love Is Kindness

[Add to your] godliness, brotherly kindness;
and to brotherly kindness, love.
2 Peter 1:7

Love is fraternal affection, brotherly/sis-
terly lovingkindness, without bickering,
disputes, fighting. Love is gentle, considerate, empathetic, agreeable, helpful.

Lord of Love, Your kindness to me has meant life.
Teach me to be kind today in the midst of my
responsibilities. Remind me to touch those around
me with gentleness and loving care.

When the kindness and love of God our
Savior appeared, he saved us, not because of
righteous things we had done, but because of
his mercy.
Titus 3:4–5

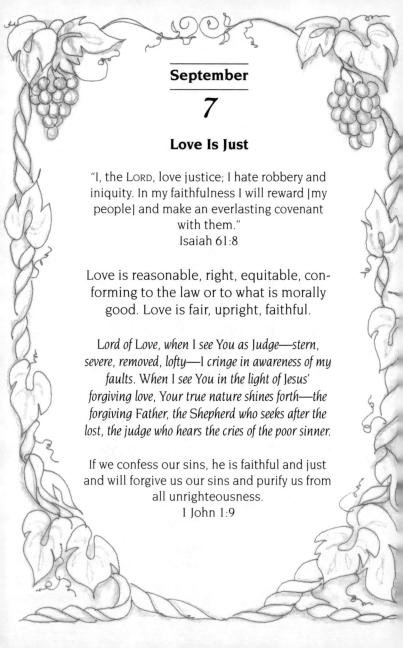

September

7

Love Is Just

"I, the Lord, love justice; I hate robbery and iniquity. In my faithfulness I will reward [my people] and make an everlasting covenant with them."
Isaiah 61:8

Love is reasonable, right, equitable, conforming to the law or to what is morally good. Love is fair, upright, faithful.

Lord of Love, when I see You as Judge—stern, severe, removed, lofty—I cringe in awareness of my faults. When I see You in the light of Jesus' forgiving love, Your true nature shines forth—the forgiving Father, the Shepherd who seeks after the lost, the judge who hears the cries of the poor sinner.

If we confess our sins, he is faithful and just and will forgive us our sins and purify us from all unrighteousness.
1 John 1:9

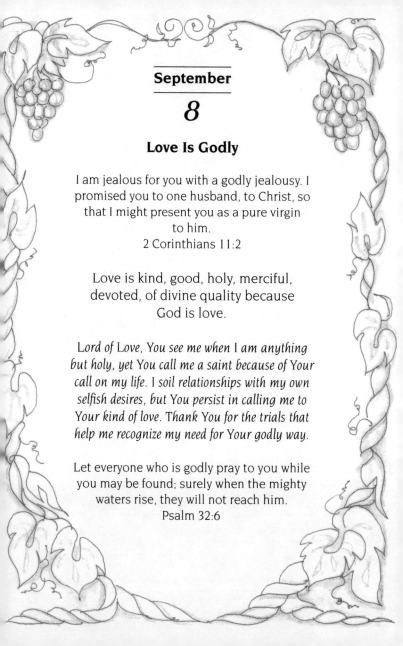

September

8

Love Is Godly

I am jealous for you with a godly jealousy. I
promised you to one husband, to Christ, so
that I might present you as a pure virgin
to him.
2 Corinthians 11:2

Love is kind, good, holy, merciful,
devoted, of divine quality because
God is love.

*Lord of Love, You see me when I am anything
but holy, yet You call me a saint because of Your
call on my life. I soil relationships with my own
selfish desires, but You persist in calling me to
Your kind of love. Thank You for the trials that
help me recognize my need for Your godly way.*

Let everyone who is godly pray to you while
you may be found; surely when the mighty
waters rise, they will not reach him.
Psalm 32:6

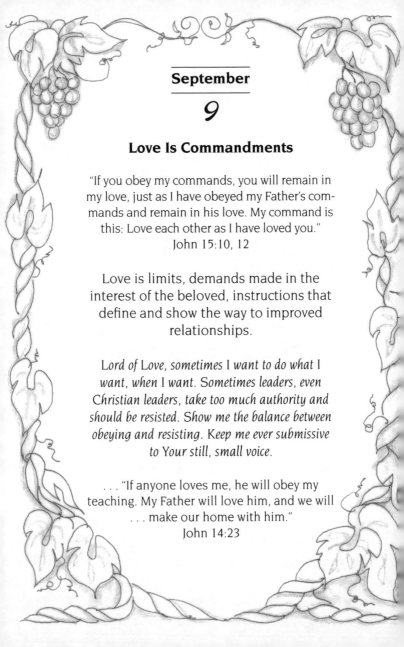

September

9

Love Is Commandments

"If you obey my commands, you will remain in my love, just as I have obeyed my Father's commands and remain in his love. My command is this: Love each other as I have loved you."
John 15:10, 12

Love is limits, demands made in the interest of the beloved, instructions that define and show the way to improved relationships.

Lord of Love, sometimes I want to do what I want, when I want. Sometimes leaders, even Christian leaders, take too much authority and should be resisted. Show me the balance between obeying and resisting. Keep me ever submissive to Your still, small voice.

. . . "If anyone loves me, he will obey my teaching. My Father will love him, and we will . . . make our home with him."
John 14:23

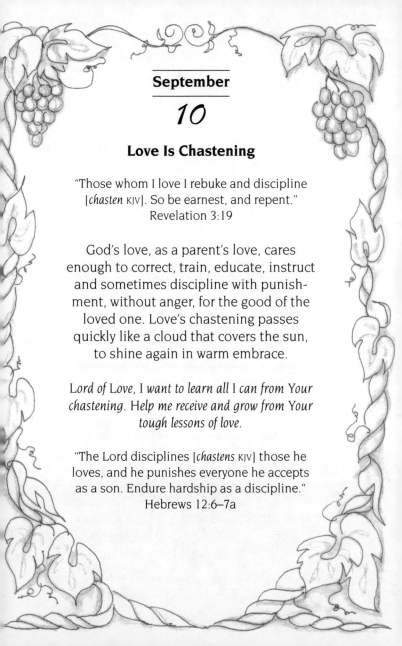

September

10

Love Is Chastening

"Those whom I love I rebuke and discipline
[*chasten* KJV]. So be earnest, and repent."
Revelation 3:19

God's love, as a parent's love, cares
enough to correct, train, educate, instruct
and sometimes discipline with punishment, without anger, for the good of the
loved one. Love's chastening passes
quickly like a cloud that covers the sun,
to shine again in warm embrace.

Lord of Love, I want to learn all I can from Your
chastening. Help me receive and grow from Your
tough lessons of love.

"The Lord disciplines [*chastens* KJV] those he
loves, and he punishes everyone he accepts
as a son. Endure hardship as a discipline."
Hebrews 12:6–7a

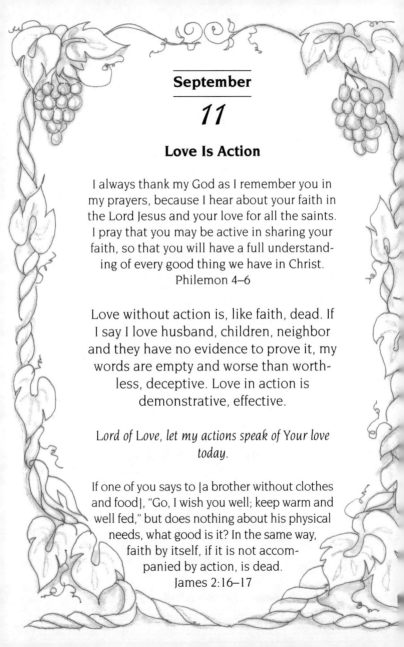

September

11

Love Is Action

I always thank my God as I remember you in my prayers, because I hear about your faith in the Lord Jesus and your love for all the saints. I pray that you may be active in sharing your faith, so that you will have a full understanding of every good thing we have in Christ.
Philemon 4–6

Love without action is, like faith, dead. If I say I love husband, children, neighbor and they have no evidence to prove it, my words are empty and worse than worthless, deceptive. Love in action is demonstrative, effective.

Lord of Love, let my actions speak of Your love today.

If one of you says to [a brother without clothes and food], "Go, I wish you well; keep warm and well fed," but does nothing about his physical needs, what good is it? In the same way, faith by itself, if it is not accompanied by action, is dead.
James 2:16–17

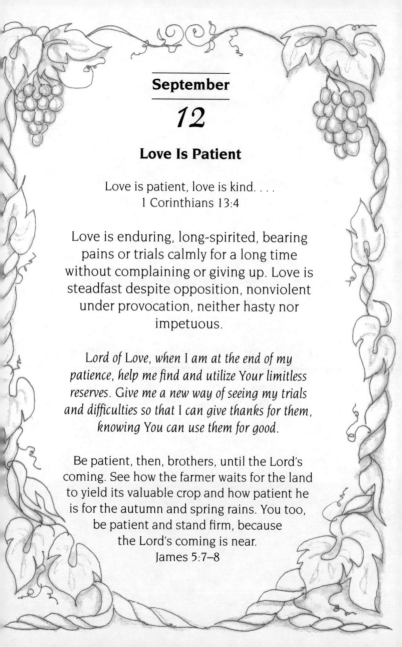

12

Love Is Patient

Love is patient, love is kind. . . .
1 Corinthians 13:4

Love is enduring, long-spirited, bearing
pains or trials calmly for a long time
without complaining or giving up. Love is
steadfast despite opposition, nonviolent
under provocation, neither hasty nor
impetuous.

*Lord of Love, when I am at the end of my
patience, help me find and utilize Your limitless
reserves. Give me a new way of seeing my trials
and difficulties so that I can give thanks for them,
knowing You can use them for good.*

Be patient, then, brothers, until the Lord's
coming. See how the farmer waits for the land
to yield its valuable crop and how patient he
is for the autumn and spring rains. You too,
be patient and stand firm, because
the Lord's coming is near.
James 5:7–8

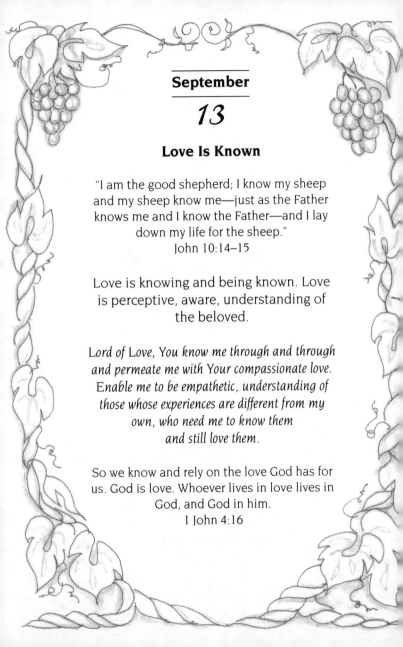

September

13

Love Is Known

"I am the good shepherd; I know my sheep
and my sheep know me—just as the Father
knows me and I know the Father—and I lay
down my life for the sheep."
John 10:14–15

Love is knowing and being known. Love
is perceptive, aware, understanding of
the beloved.

*Lord of Love, You know me through and through
and permeate me with Your compassionate love.
Enable me to be empathetic, understanding of
those whose experiences are different from my
own, who need me to know them
and still love them.*

So we know and rely on the love God has for
us. God is love. Whoever lives in love lives in
God, and God in him.
1 John 4:16

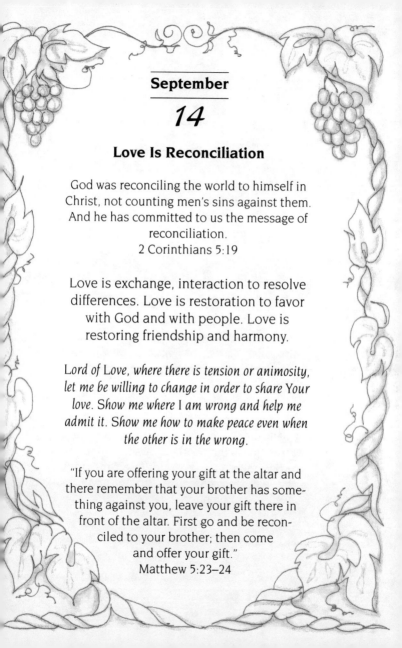

September

14

Love Is Reconciliation

God was reconciling the world to himself in
Christ, not counting men's sins against them.
And he has committed to us the message of
reconciliation.
2 Corinthians 5:19

Love is exchange, interaction to resolve
differences. Love is restoration to favor
with God and with people. Love is
restoring friendship and harmony.

*Lord of Love, where there is tension or animosity,
let me be willing to change in order to share Your
love. Show me where I am wrong and help me
admit it. Show me how to make peace even when
the other is in the wrong.*

"If you are offering your gift at the altar and
there remember that your brother has something against you, leave your gift there in
front of the altar. First go and be recon-
ciled to your brother; then come
and offer your gift."
Matthew 5:23–24

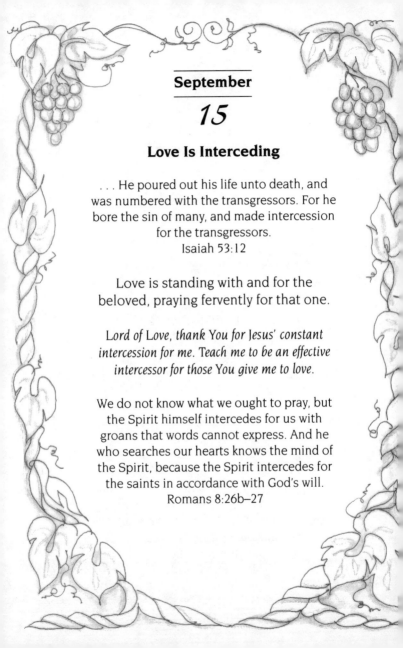

September

15

Love Is Interceding

. . . He poured out his life unto death, and
was numbered with the transgressors. For he
bore the sin of many, and made intercession
for the transgressors.
Isaiah 53:12

Love is standing with and for the
beloved, praying fervently for that one.

*Lord of Love, thank You for Jesus' constant
intercession for me. Teach me to be an effective
intercessor for those You give me to love.*

We do not know what we ought to pray, but
the Spirit himself intercedes for us with
groans that words cannot express. And he
who searches our hearts knows the mind of
the Spirit, because the Spirit intercedes for
the saints in accordance with God's will.
Romans 8:26b–27

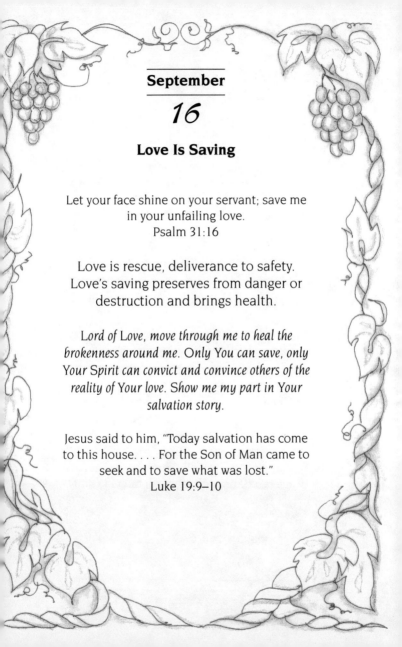

September

16

Love Is Saving

Let your face shine on your servant; save me
in your unfailing love.
Psalm 31:16

Love is rescue, deliverance to safety.
Love's saving preserves from danger or
destruction and brings health.

*Lord of Love, move through me to heal the
brokenness around me. Only You can save, only
Your Spirit can convict and convince others of the
reality of Your love. Show me my part in Your
salvation story.*

Jesus said to him, "Today salvation has come
to this house. . . . For the Son of Man came to
seek and to save what was lost."
Luke 19:9–10

Love Is Rescue

"Because he loves me," says the LORD, "I will
rescue him; I will protect him, for he acknowledges my name."
Psalm 91:14

Love sets free, delivers from danger, evil,
confinement, bondage. Love ransoms,
redeems, reclaims the beloved.

*Lord of Love, You have rescued me from many
perilous possibilities. Thank You for Your consistent, watchful care. Train me in rescuing those
around me without being domineering or control-
ling, being careful to give You all the glory.*

Grace and peace to you from God our Father
and the Lord Jesus Christ, who gave himself
for our sins to rescue us from the present evil
age, according to the will of our God and
Father.
Galatians 1:3–4

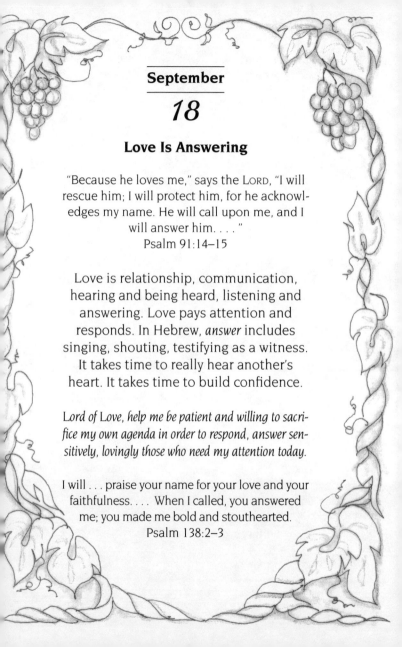

September

18

Love Is Answering

"Because he loves me," says the LORD, "I will
rescue him; I will protect him, for he acknowledges my name. He will call upon me, and I
will answer him. . . . "
Psalm 91:14–15

Love is relationship, communication,
hearing and being heard, listening and
answering. Love pays attention and
responds. In Hebrew, *answer* includes
singing, shouting, testifying as a witness.
It takes time to really hear another's
heart. It takes time to build confidence.

*Lord of Love, help me be patient and willing to sacri-
fice my own agenda in order to respond, answer sen-
sitively, lovingly those who need my attention today.*

I will . . . praise your name for your love and your
faithfulness. . . . When I called, you answered
me; you made me bold and stouthearted.
Psalm 138:2–3

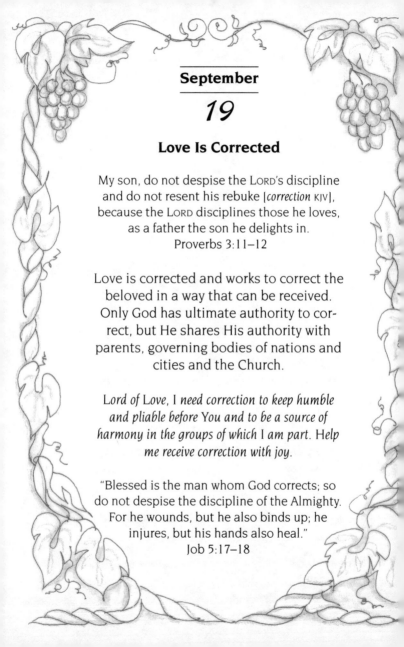

September

19

Love Is Corrected

My son, do not despise the LORD's discipline
and do not resent his rebuke [*correction* KJV],
because the LORD disciplines those he loves,
as a father the son he delights in.
Proverbs 3:11–12

Love is corrected and works to correct the
beloved in a way that can be received.
Only God has ultimate authority to correct, but He shares His authority with
parents, governing bodies of nations and
cities and the Church.

*Lord of Love, I need correction to keep humble
and pliable before You and to be a source of
harmony in the groups of which I am part. Help
me receive correction with joy.*

"Blessed is the man whom God corrects; so
do not despise the discipline of the Almighty.
For he wounds, but he also binds up; he
injures, but his hands also heal."
Job 5:17–18

September

20

Love Is Assurance

Since we have confidence to enter the Most Holy Place by the blood of Jesus, by a new and living way opened for us through the curtain, that is, his body . . . let us draw near to God with a sincere heart in full assurance [entire confidence] of faith. . . .
Hebrews 10:19–20, 22

"Do not be afraid" was the message of the angels when God's presence touched ordinary mortals like me. Love assures, overcomes fear. Love builds confidence, trust and intimacy.

Lord of Love, as I move freely in Your love, show me how to express Your love in the unique ways others can receive.

My little children, let us not love in word, neither in tongue; but in deed and in truth. And hereby we know that we are of the truth, and shall assure our hearts before him.
1 John 3:18–19, KJV

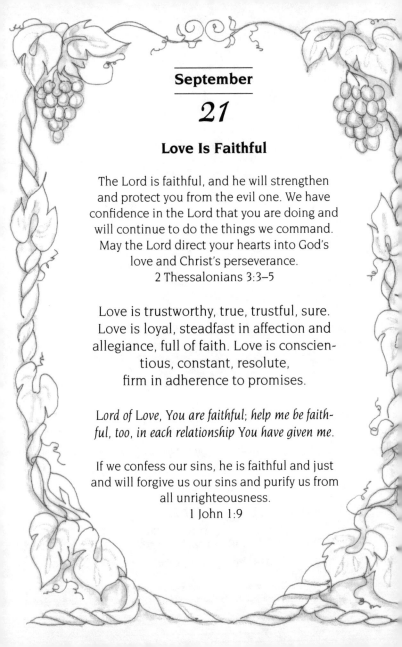

September

21

Love Is Faithful

The Lord is faithful, and he will strengthen and protect you from the evil one. We have confidence in the Lord that you are doing and will continue to do the things we command. May the Lord direct your hearts into God's love and Christ's perseverance.
2 Thessalonians 3:3–5

Love is trustworthy, true, trustful, sure. Love is loyal, steadfast in affection and allegiance, full of faith. Love is conscientious, constant, resolute, firm in adherence to promises.

Lord of Love, You are faithful; help me be faithful, too, in each relationship You have given me.

If we confess our sins, he is faithful and just and will forgive us our sins and purify us from all unrighteousness.
1 John 1:9

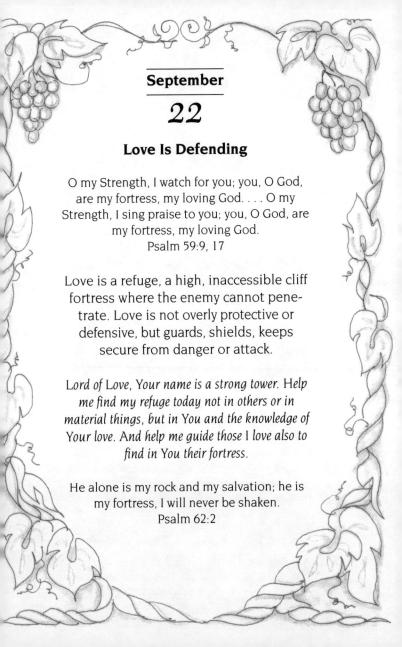

September

22

Love Is Defending

O my Strength, I watch for you; you, O God,
are my fortress, my loving God. . . . O my
Strength, I sing praise to you; you, O God, are
my fortress, my loving God.
Psalm 59:9, 17

Love is a refuge, a high, inaccessible cliff
fortress where the enemy cannot pene-
trate. Love is not overly protective or
defensive, but guards, shields, keeps
secure from danger or attack.

*Lord of Love, Your name is a strong tower. Help
me find my refuge today not in others or in
material things, but in You and the knowledge of
Your love. And help me guide those I love also to
find in You their fortress.*

He alone is my rock and my salvation; he is
my fortress, I will never be shaken.
Psalm 62:2

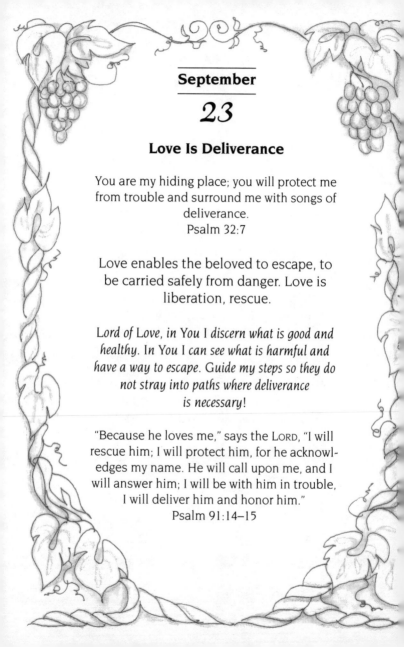

September

23

Love Is Deliverance

You are my hiding place; you will protect me
from trouble and surround me with songs of
deliverance.
Psalm 32:7

Love enables the beloved to escape, to
be carried safely from danger. Love is
liberation, rescue.

*Lord of Love, in You I discern what is good and
healthy. In You I can see what is harmful and
have a way to escape. Guide my steps so they do
not stray into paths where deliverance
is necessary!*

"Because he loves me," says the LORD, "I will
rescue him; I will protect him, for he acknowledges my name. He will call upon me, and I
will answer him; I will be with him in trouble,
I will deliver him and honor him."
Psalm 91:14–15

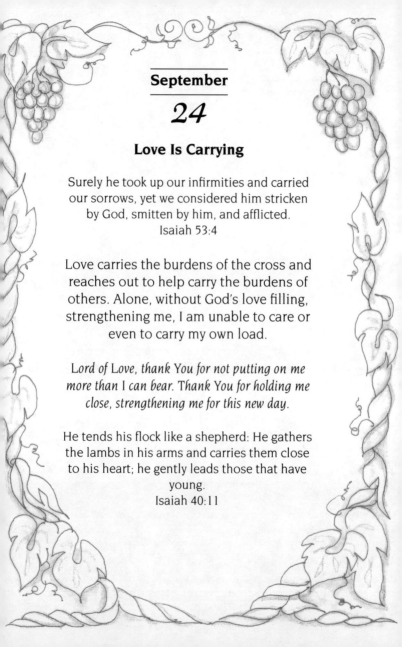

September

24

Love Is Carrying

Surely he took up our infirmities and carried
our sorrows, yet we considered him stricken
by God, smitten by him, and afflicted.
Isaiah 53:4

Love carries the burdens of the cross and
reaches out to help carry the burdens of
others. Alone, without God's love filling,
strengthening me, I am unable to care or
even to carry my own load.

*Lord of Love, thank You for not putting on me
more than I can bear. Thank You for holding me
close, strengthening me for this new day.*

He tends his flock like a shepherd: He gathers
the lambs in his arms and carries them close
to his heart; he gently leads those that have
young.
Isaiah 40:11

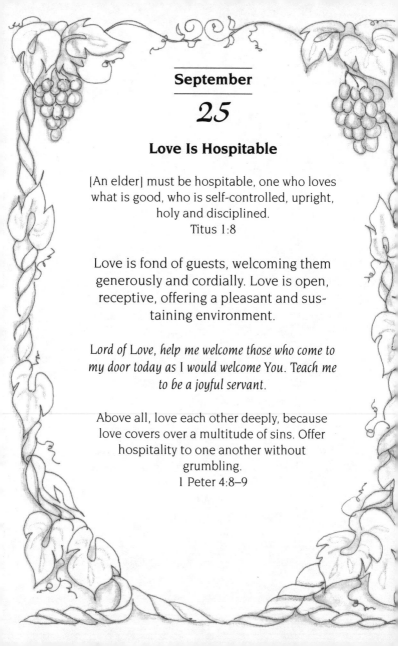

September

25

Love Is Hospitable

[An elder] must be hospitable, one who loves
what is good, who is self-controlled, upright,
holy and disciplined.
Titus 1:8

Love is fond of guests, welcoming them
generously and cordially. Love is open,
receptive, offering a pleasant and sustaining environment.

*Lord of Love, help me welcome those who come to
my door today as I would welcome You. Teach me
to be a joyful servant.*

Above all, love each other deeply, because
love covers over a multitude of sins. Offer
hospitality to one another without
grumbling.
1 Peter 4:8–9

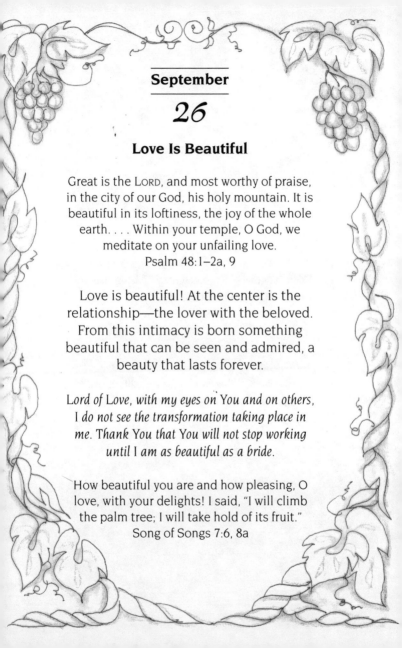

September

26

Love Is Beautiful

Great is the LORD, and most worthy of praise,
in the city of our God, his holy mountain. It is
beautiful in its loftiness, the joy of the whole
earth. . . . Within your temple, O God, we
meditate on your unfailing love.
Psalm 48:1–2a, 9

Love is beautiful! At the center is the
relationship—the lover with the beloved.
From this intimacy is born something
beautiful that can be seen and admired, a
beauty that lasts forever.

*Lord of Love, with my eyes on You and on others,
I do not see the transformation taking place in
me. Thank You that You will not stop working
until I am as beautiful as a bride.*

How beautiful you are and how pleasing, O
love, with your delights! I said, "I will climb
the palm tree; I will take hold of its fruit."
Song of Songs 7:6, 8a

September

27

Love Is Adorned

I saw the Holy City, the new Jerusalem, coming down out of heaven from God, prepared as a bride beautifully dressed [*adorned* KJV] for her husband.
Revelation 21:2

Love accepts, love covers. Love gives me beauty that cannot be destroyed. When I put on praise, humility, joy, peace, love, I glow with the radiance of a bride ready.

Lord of Love, how can I get ready for Jesus' coming, whether He comes on a white horse with thousands of saints and angels or as a lone beggar who wants a cup of water? My best adornment comes from "the unfading beauty of a gentle and quiet spirit" (1 Peter 3:4).

Again I will build thee . . . O virgin of Israel: thou shalt again be adorned with thy tabrets [*tambourines* NIV], and shalt go forth in the dances of them that make merry.
Jeremiah 31:4, KJV

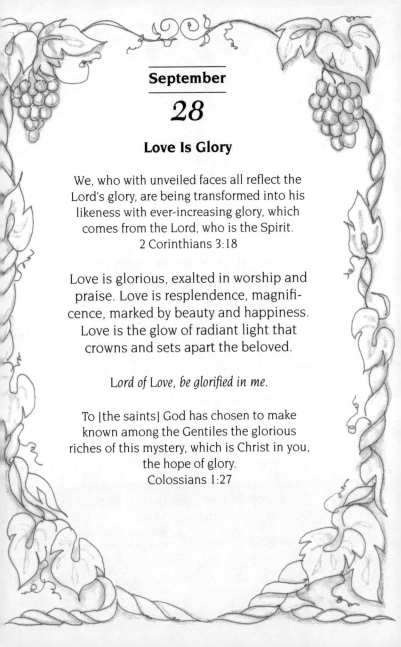

September

28

Love Is Glory

We, who with unveiled faces all reflect the
Lord's glory, are being transformed into his
likeness with ever-increasing glory, which
comes from the Lord, who is the Spirit.
2 Corinthians 3:18

Love is glorious, exalted in worship and
praise. Love is resplendence, magnifi-
cence, marked by beauty and happiness.
Love is the glow of radiant light that
crowns and sets apart the beloved.

Lord of Love, be glorified in me.

To [the saints] God has chosen to make
known among the Gentiles the glorious
riches of this mystery, which is Christ in you,
the hope of glory.
Colossians 1:27

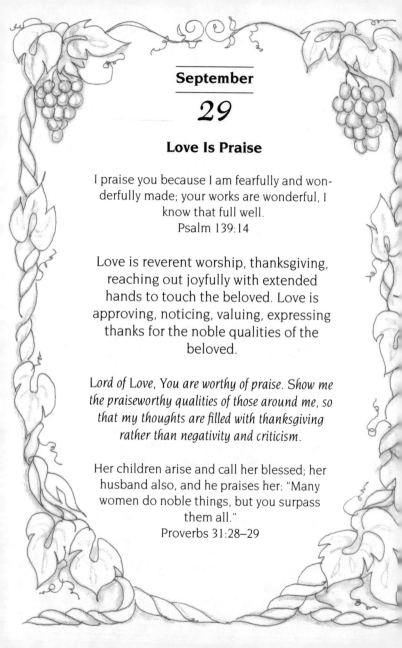

September

29

Love Is Praise

I praise you because I am fearfully and wonderfully made; your works are wonderful, I know that full well.
Psalm 139:14

Love is reverent worship, thanksgiving, reaching out joyfully with extended hands to touch the beloved. Love is approving, noticing, valuing, expressing thanks for the noble qualities of the beloved.

Lord of Love, You are worthy of praise. Show me the praiseworthy qualities of those around me, so that my thoughts are filled with thanksgiving rather than negativity and criticism.

Her children arise and call her blessed; her husband also, and he praises her: "Many women do noble things, but you surpass them all."
Proverbs 31:28–29

Love Is Awesome

Say to God, "How awesome are your deeds!
So great is your power that your enemies
cringe before you." God has surely listened
and heard my voice in prayer. Praise be to
God, who has not rejected my prayer or with-
held his love from me!
Psalm 66:3, 19–20

God is love. God is also holy, a consuming fire, not to be played with. The ele-
ments obey, the nations will tremble
before this God, but He calls me to sit on
His lap as a child, sharing my heart,
giving Him all my griefs.

*Lord of Love, thank You for inviting me to
intimacy in the midst of Your awesome power.*

. . . You did awesome things that we did not
expect. . . . No eye has seen any God besides
you, who acts on behalf of those
who wait for him.
Isaiah 64:3–4

October
Love Is Turning

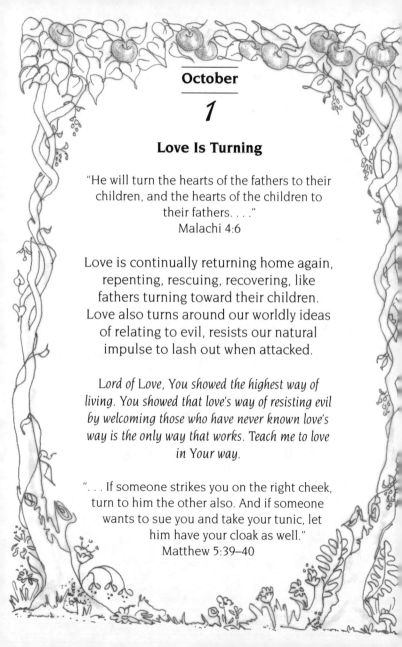

October

1

Love Is Turning

"He will turn the hearts of the fathers to their
children, and the hearts of the children to
their fathers. . . ."
Malachi 4:6

Love is continually returning home again,
repenting, rescuing, recovering, like
fathers turning toward their children.
Love also turns around our worldly ideas
of relating to evil, resists our natural
impulse to lash out when attacked.

*Lord of Love, You showed the highest way of
living. You showed that love's way of resisting evil
by welcoming those who have never known love's
way is the only way that works. Teach me to love
in Your way.*

". . . If someone strikes you on the right cheek,
turn to him the other also. And if someone
wants to sue you and take your tunic, let
him have your cloak as well."
Matthew 5:39–40

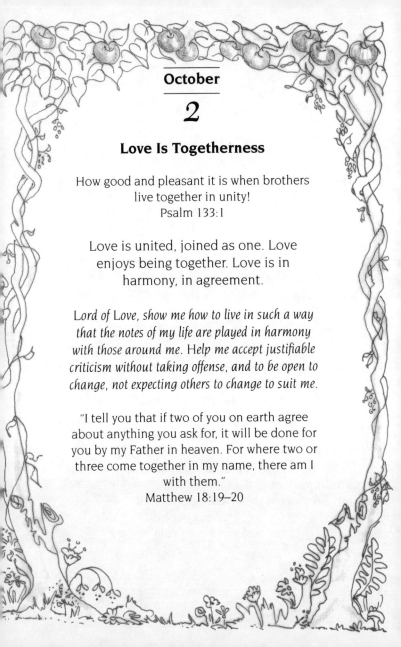

October

2

Love Is Togetherness

How good and pleasant it is when brothers
live together in unity!
Psalm 133:1

Love is united, joined as one. Love
enjoys being together. Love is in
harmony, in agreement.

*Lord of Love, show me how to live in such a way
that the notes of my life are played in harmony
with those around me. Help me accept justifiable
criticism without taking offense, and to be open to
change, not expecting others to change to suit me.*

"I tell you that if two of you on earth agree
about anything you ask for, it will be done for
you by my Father in heaven. For where two or
three come together in my name, there am I
with them."
Matthew 18:19–20

Love Is Respect

Each one of you also must love his wife as he loves himself, and the wife must respect her husband.
Ephesians 5:33

Love is high or special regard for the beloved. Love gives particular attention to and consideration for the beloved. Love is concerned for and esteems the beloved highly.

Lord of Love, sweep away my selfish ego so that with genuine enthusiasm I can reach out to love and respect my spouse. Open my eyes to see the many qualities I can admire in the partner You have given me. Make our love fresh and new.

Husbands, in the same way be considerate as you live with your wives, and treat them with respect as the weaker partner and as heirs with you of the gracious gift of life, so that nothing will hinder your prayers.
1 Peter 3:7

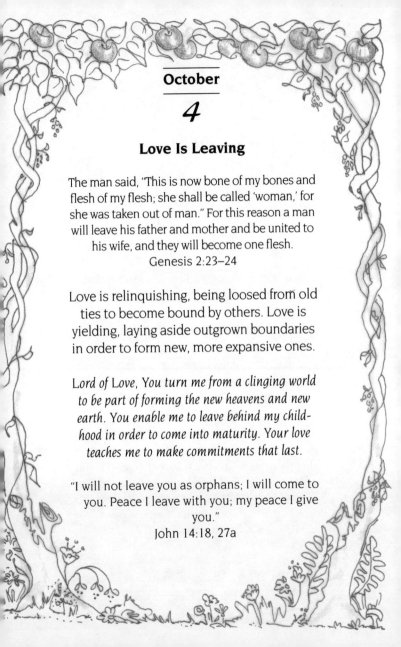

October

4

Love Is Leaving

The man said, "This is now bone of my bones and flesh of my flesh; she shall be called 'woman,' for she was taken out of man." For this reason a man will leave his father and mother and be united to his wife, and they will become one flesh.
Genesis 2:23–24

Love is relinquishing, being loosed from old ties to become bound by others. Love is yielding, laying aside outgrown boundaries in order to form new, more expansive ones.

Lord of Love, You turn me from a clinging world to be part of forming the new heavens and new earth. You enable me to leave behind my childhood in order to come into maturity. Your love teaches me to make commitments that last.

"I will not leave you as orphans; I will come to you. Peace I leave with you; my peace I give you."
John 14:18, 27a

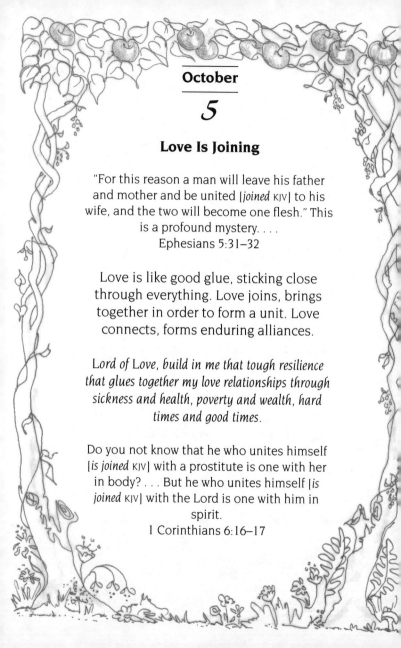

Love Is Joining

"For this reason a man will leave his father
and mother and be united [*joined* KJV] to his
wife, and the two will become one flesh." This
is a profound mystery. . . .
Ephesians 5:31–32

Love is like good glue, sticking close
through everything. Love joins, brings
together in order to form a unit. Love
connects, forms enduring alliances.

*Lord of Love, build in me that tough resilience
that glues together my love relationships through
sickness and health, poverty and wealth, hard
times and good times.*

Do you not know that he who unites himself
[*is joined* KJV] with a prostitute is one with her
in body? . . . But he who unites himself [*is
joined* KJV] with the Lord is one with him in
spirit.
1 Corinthians 6:16–17

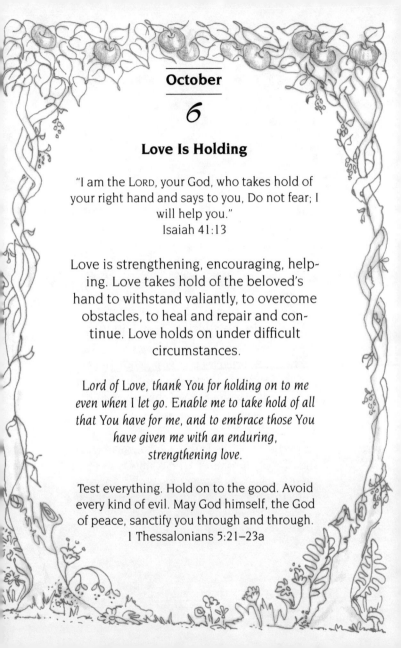

Love Is Holding

"I am the LORD, your God, who takes hold of
your right hand and says to you, Do not fear; I
will help you."
Isaiah 41:13

Love is strengthening, encouraging, helping. Love takes hold of the beloved's
hand to withstand valiantly, to overcome
obstacles, to heal and repair and continue. Love holds on under difficult
circumstances.

*Lord of Love, thank You for holding on to me
even when I let go. Enable me to take hold of all
that You have for me, and to embrace those You
have given me with an enduring,
strengthening love.*

Test everything. Hold on to the good. Avoid
every kind of evil. May God himself, the God
of peace, sanctify you through and through.
1 Thessalonians 5:21–23a

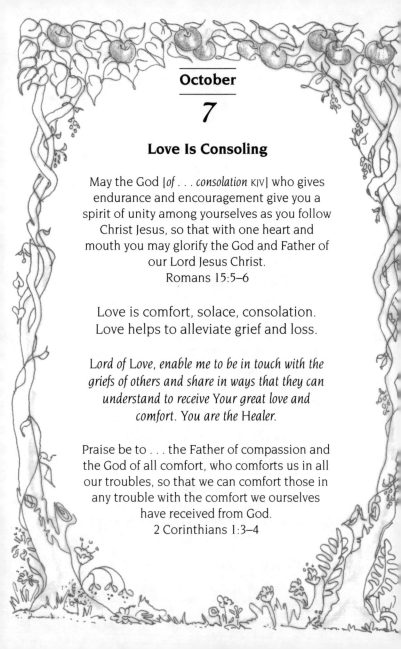

October

7

Love Is Consoling

May the God [*of . . . consolation* KJV] who gives
endurance and encouragement give you a
spirit of unity among yourselves as you follow
Christ Jesus, so that with one heart and
mouth you may glorify the God and Father of
our Lord Jesus Christ.
Romans 15:5–6

Love is comfort, solace, consolation.
Love helps to alleviate grief and loss.

Lord of Love, enable me to be in touch with the
griefs of others and share in ways that they can
understand to receive Your great love and
comfort. You are the Healer.

Praise be to . . . the Father of compassion and
the God of all comfort, who comforts us in all
our troubles, so that we can comfort those in
any trouble with the comfort we ourselves
have received from God.
2 Corinthians 1:3–4

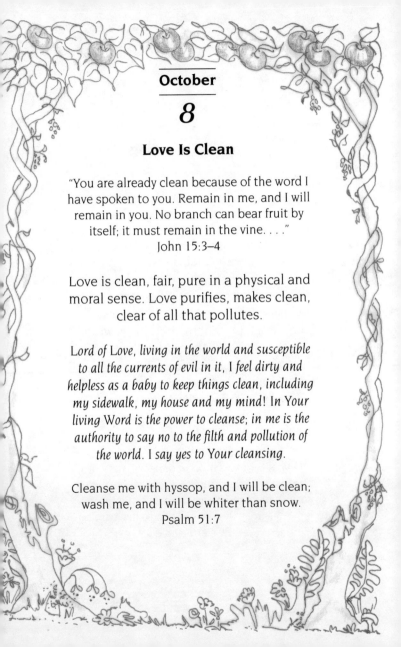

October

8

Love Is Clean

"You are already clean because of the word I have spoken to you. Remain in me, and I will remain in you. No branch can bear fruit by itself; it must remain in the vine. . . ."
John 15:3–4

Love is clean, fair, pure in a physical and moral sense. Love purifies, makes clean, clear of all that pollutes.

Lord of Love, living in the world and susceptible to all the currents of evil in it, I feel dirty and helpless as a baby to keep things clean, including my sidewalk, my house and my mind! In Your living Word is the power to cleanse; in me is the authority to say no to the filth and pollution of the world. I say yes to Your cleansing.

Cleanse me with hyssop, and I will be clean; wash me, and I will be whiter than snow.
Psalm 51:7

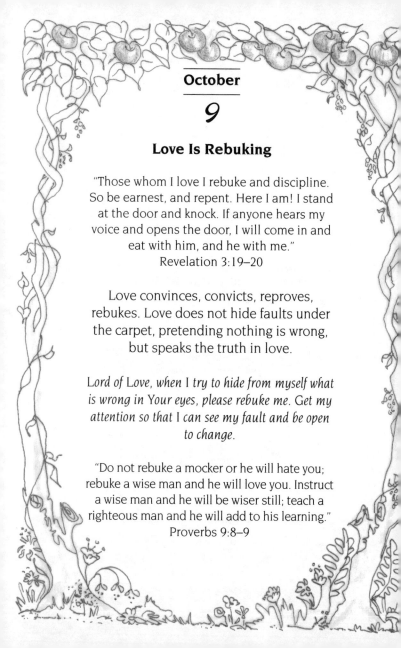

October

9

Love Is Rebuking

"Those whom I love I rebuke and discipline. So be earnest, and repent. Here I am! I stand at the door and knock. If anyone hears my voice and opens the door, I will come in and eat with him, and he with me."
Revelation 3:19–20

Love convinces, convicts, reproves, rebukes. Love does not hide faults under the carpet, pretending nothing is wrong, but speaks the truth in love.

Lord of Love, when I try to hide from myself what is wrong in Your eyes, please rebuke me. Get my attention so that I can see my fault and be open to change.

"Do not rebuke a mocker or he will hate you; rebuke a wise man and he will love you. Instruct a wise man and he will be wiser still; teach a righteous man and he will add to his learning."
Proverbs 9:8–9

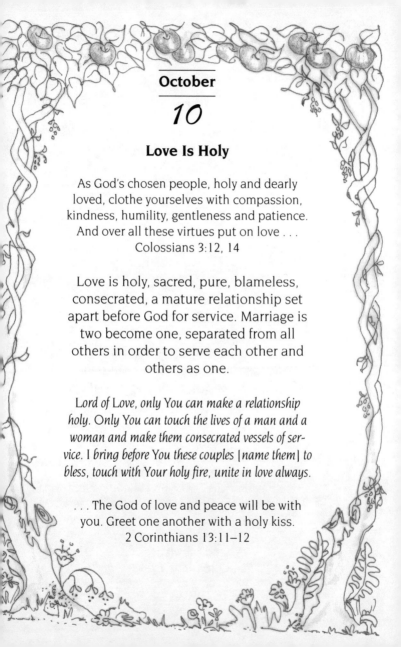

Love Is Holy

As God's chosen people, holy and dearly
loved, clothe yourselves with compassion,
kindness, humility, gentleness and patience.
And over all these virtues put on love . . .
Colossians 3:12, 14

Love is holy, sacred, pure, blameless,
consecrated, a mature relationship set
apart before God for service. Marriage is
two become one, separated from all
others in order to serve each other and
others as one.

*Lord of Love, only You can make a relationship
holy. Only You can touch the lives of a man and a
woman and make them consecrated vessels of service. I bring before You these couples [name them] to
bless, touch with Your holy fire, unite in love always.*

. . . The God of love and peace will be with
you. Greet one another with a holy kiss.
2 Corinthians 13:11–12

Love Is Wisdom

A man who loves wisdom brings joy to his
father.
Proverbs 29:3a

Love is wise in mind, word or act. Love
has discernment into relationships and
inner qualities. Love is understanding
and uses good sense in making
judgments.

*Lord of Love, where I lack understanding, teach
me Your wisdom. Where I am thoughtless, guide
me into discerning actions. Thank You that Your
wisdom created me for a purpose and will enable
that purpose to be completed.*

My purpose is that they may be encouraged
in heart and united in love, so that they may
have the full riches of complete understanding, in order that they may know the mystery
of God, namely, Christ, in whom are hidden
all the treasures of wisdom
and knowledge.
Colossians 2:2–3

12

Love Is Fragrant

Thanks be to God, who . . . through us
spreads everywhere the fragrance of the
knowledge of him. For we are to God the
aroma of Christ among those who are being
saved and those who are perishing.
2 Corinthians 2:14–15

Love has a sweet perfume, a pleasing
odor, like incense rising before the altar
or the natural, fresh fragrance of flowers
after rain.

*Lord of Love, in my relationships today, help me
be like a fragrant flower, to be and bring the sweet
fragrance of Jesus instead of the stench of my own
opinions.*

Be imitators of God, therefore, as dearly
loved children and live a life of love, just as
Christ loved us and gave himself up for us as
a fragrant offering and sacrifice to God.
Ephesians 5:1–2

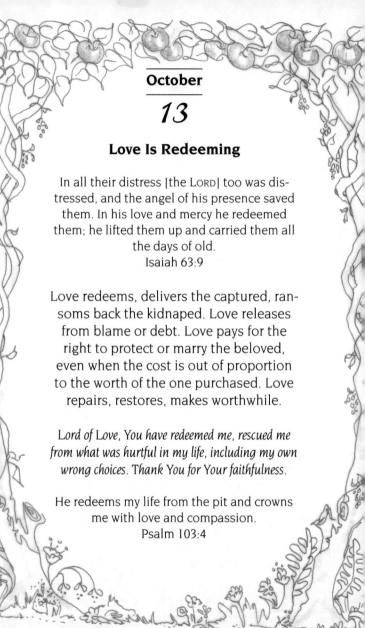

October

13

Love Is Redeeming

In all their distress [the LORD] too was distressed, and the angel of his presence saved them. In his love and mercy he redeemed them; he lifted them up and carried them all the days of old.
Isaiah 63:9

Love redeems, delivers the captured, ransoms back the kidnaped. Love releases from blame or debt. Love pays for the right to protect or marry the beloved, even when the cost is out of proportion to the worth of the one purchased. Love repairs, restores, makes worthwhile.

Lord of Love, You have redeemed me, rescued me from what was hurtful in my life, including my own wrong choices. Thank You for Your faithfulness.

He redeems my life from the pit and crowns me with love and compassion.
Psalm 103:4

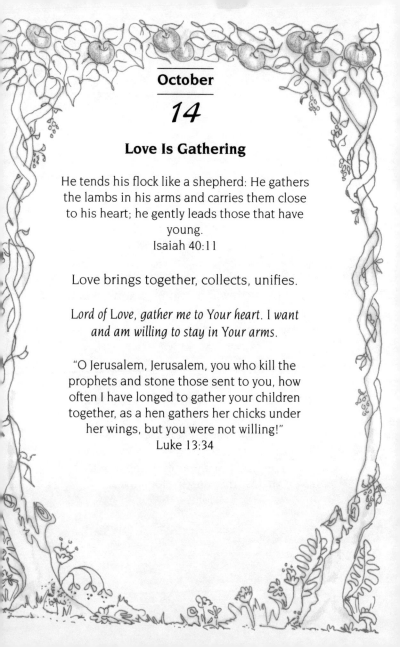

October

14

Love Is Gathering

He tends his flock like a shepherd: He gathers
the lambs in his arms and carries them close
to his heart; he gently leads those that have
young.
Isaiah 40:11

Love brings together, collects, unifies.

*Lord of Love, gather me to Your heart. I want
and am willing to stay in Your arms.*

"O Jerusalem, Jerusalem, you who kill the
prophets and stone those sent to you, how
often I have longed to gather your children
together, as a hen gathers her chicks under
her wings, but you were not willing!"
Luke 13:34

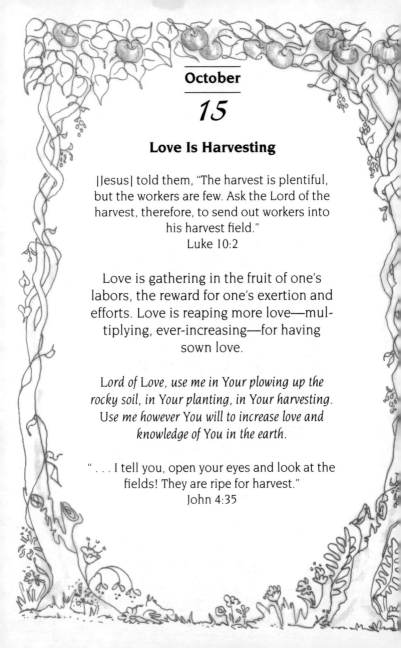

October

15

Love Is Harvesting

[Jesus] told them, "The harvest is plentiful,
but the workers are few. Ask the Lord of the
harvest, therefore, to send out workers into
his harvest field."
Luke 10:2

Love is gathering in the fruit of one's
labors, the reward for one's exertion and
efforts. Love is reaping more love—multiplying, ever-increasing—for having
sown love.

Lord of Love, use me in Your plowing up the
rocky soil, in Your planting, in Your harvesting.
Use me however You will to increase love and
knowledge of You in the earth.

" . . . I tell you, open your eyes and look at the
fields! They are ripe for harvest."
John 4:35

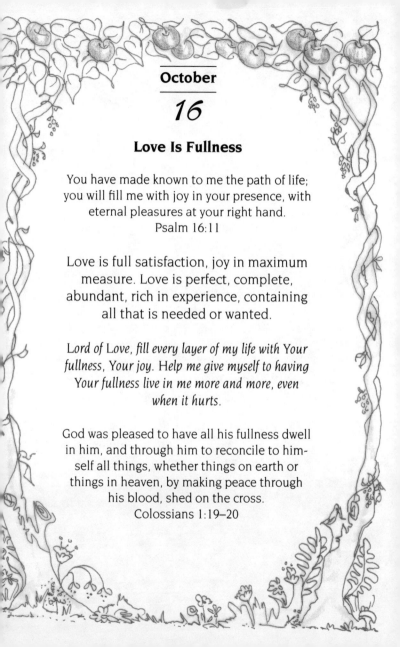

October

16

Love Is Fullness

You have made known to me the path of life;
you will fill me with joy in your presence, with
eternal pleasures at your right hand.
Psalm 16:11

Love is full satisfaction, joy in maximum
measure. Love is perfect, complete,
abundant, rich in experience, containing
all that is needed or wanted.

*Lord of Love, fill every layer of my life with Your
fullness, Your joy. Help me give myself to having
Your fullness live in me more and more, even
when it hurts.*

God was pleased to have all his fullness dwell
in him, and through him to reconcile to himself all things, whether things on earth or
things in heaven, by making peace through
his blood, shed on the cross.
Colossians 1:19–20

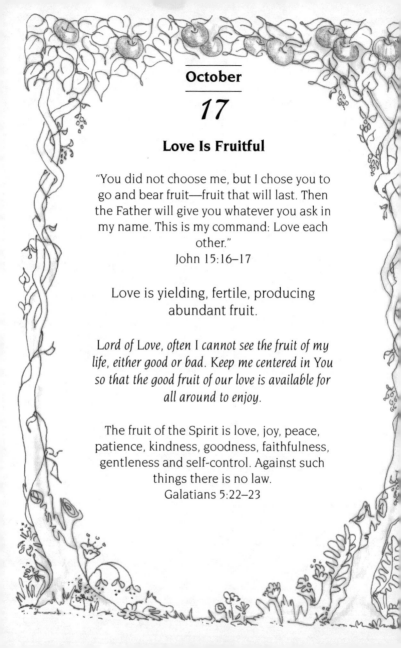

October

17

Love Is Fruitful

"You did not choose me, but I chose you to go and bear fruit—fruit that will last. Then the Father will give you whatever you ask in my name. This is my command: Love each other."
John 15:16–17

Love is yielding, fertile, producing abundant fruit.

Lord of Love, often I cannot see the fruit of my life, either good or bad. Keep me centered in You so that the good fruit of our love is available for all around to enjoy.

The fruit of the Spirit is love, joy, peace, patience, kindness, goodness, faithfulness, gentleness and self-control. Against such things there is no law.
Galatians 5:22–23

Love Is Satisfying

You open your hand and satisfy the desires of every living thing. The LORD is righteous in all his ways and loving toward all he has made.
Psalm 145:16–17

Love is being satisfied, fulfilled. Unconditional love is, for the thirsty, like drinking one's fill, soaking in an abundance of water.

Lord of Love, You know the needs and desires of my flesh, the hungers and thirsts of my soul, the longings of my spirit. Fill me with all Your goodness so that I am satisfying, pleasing to You.

May your fountain be blessed, and may you rejoice in the wife of your youth. A loving doe, a graceful deer—may her breasts satisfy you always, may you ever be captivated by her love.
Proverbs 5:18–19

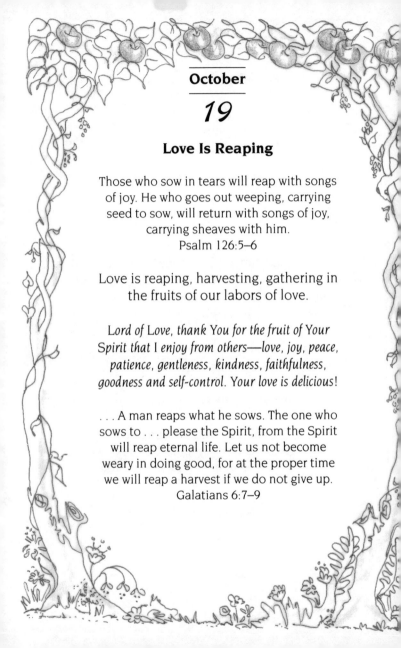

October

19

Love Is Reaping

Those who sow in tears will reap with songs
of joy. He who goes out weeping, carrying
seed to sow, will return with songs of joy,
carrying sheaves with him.
Psalm 126:5–6

Love is reaping, harvesting, gathering in
the fruits of our labors of love.

*Lord of Love, thank You for the fruit of Your
Spirit that I enjoy from others—love, joy, peace,
patience, gentleness, kindness, faithfulness,
goodness and self-control. Your love is delicious!*

. . . A man reaps what he sows. The one who
sows to . . . please the Spirit, from the Spirit
will reap eternal life. Let us not become
weary in doing good, for at the proper time
we will reap a harvest if we do not give up.
Galatians 6:7–9

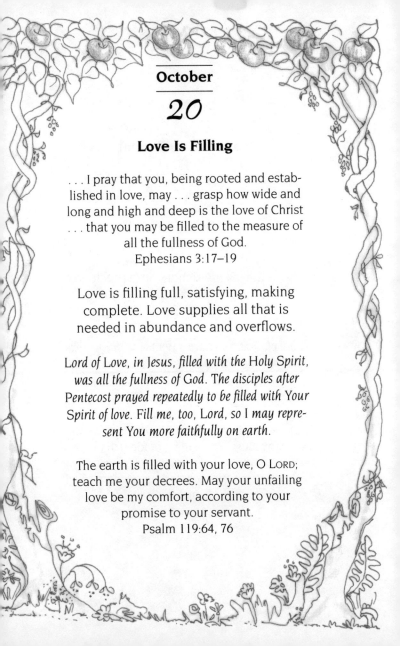

October

20

Love Is Filling

. . . I pray that you, being rooted and established in love, may . . . grasp how wide and
long and high and deep is the love of Christ
. . . that you may be filled to the measure of
all the fullness of God.
Ephesians 3:17–19

Love is filling full, satisfying, making
complete. Love supplies all that is
needed in abundance and overflows.

Lord of Love, in Jesus, filled with the Holy Spirit,
was all the fullness of God. The disciples after
Pentecost prayed repeatedly to be filled with Your
Spirit of love. Fill me, too, Lord, so I may repre-
sent You more faithfully on earth.

The earth is filled with your love, O LORD;
teach me your decrees. May your unfailing
love be my comfort, according to your
promise to your servant.
Psalm 119:64, 76

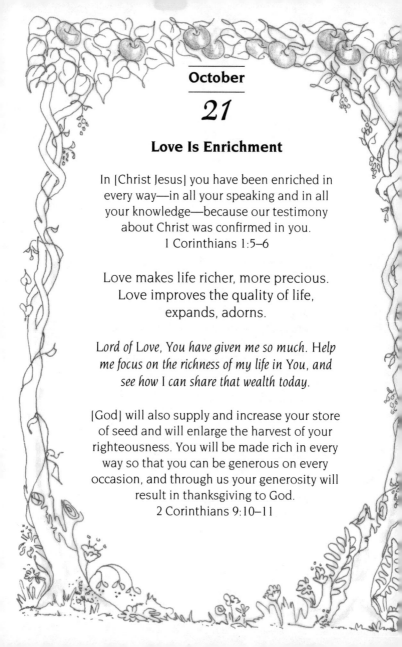

October

21

Love Is Enrichment

In [Christ Jesus] you have been enriched in
every way—in all your speaking and in all
your knowledge—because our testimony
about Christ was confirmed in you.
1 Corinthians 1:5–6

Love makes life richer, more precious.
Love improves the quality of life,
expands, adorns.

Lord of Love, You have given me so much. Help
me focus on the richness of my life in You, and
see how I can share that wealth today.

[God] will also supply and increase your store
of seed and will enlarge the harvest of your
righteousness. You will be made rich in every
way so that you can be generous on every
occasion, and through us your generosity will
result in thanksgiving to God.
2 Corinthians 9:10–11

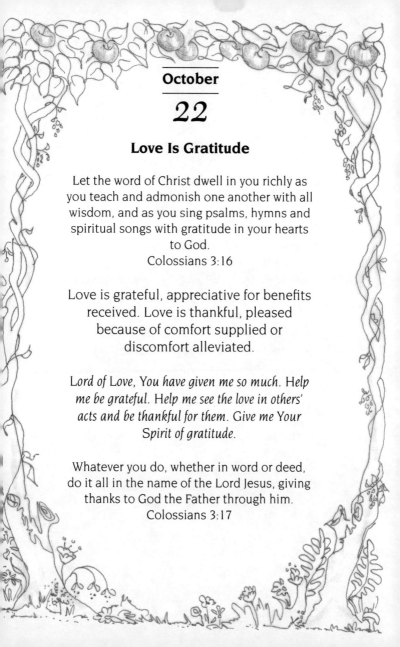

October

22

Love Is Gratitude

Let the word of Christ dwell in you richly as you teach and admonish one another with all wisdom, and as you sing psalms, hymns and spiritual songs with gratitude in your hearts to God.
Colossians 3:16

Love is grateful, appreciative for benefits received. Love is thankful, pleased because of comfort supplied or discomfort alleviated.

Lord of Love, You have given me so much. Help me be grateful. Help me see the love in others' acts and be thankful for them. Give me Your Spirit of gratitude.

Whatever you do, whether in word or deed, do it all in the name of the Lord Jesus, giving thanks to God the Father through him.
Colossians 3:17

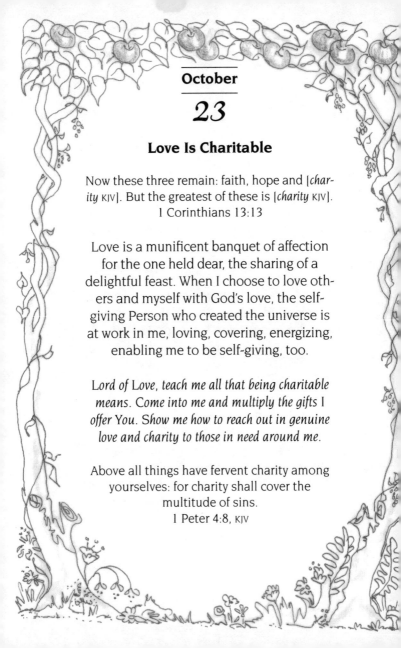

October

23

Love Is Charitable

Now these three remain: faith, hope and [*charity* KJV]. But the greatest of these is [*charity* KJV].
1 Corinthians 13:13

Love is a munificent banquet of affection for the one held dear, the sharing of a delightful feast. When I choose to love others and myself with God's love, the self-giving Person who created the universe is at work in me, loving, covering, energizing, enabling me to be self-giving, too.

Lord of Love, teach me all that being charitable means. Come into me and multiply the gifts I offer You. Show me how to reach out in genuine love and charity to those in need around me.

Above all things have fervent charity among yourselves: for charity shall cover the multitude of sins.
1 Peter 4:8, KJV

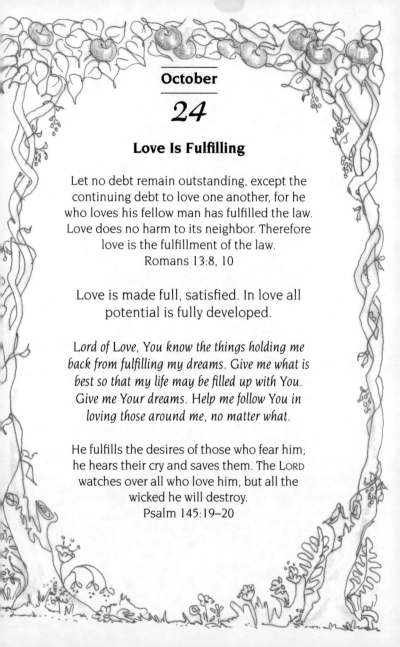

October

24

Love Is Fulfilling

Let no debt remain outstanding, except the
continuing debt to love one another, for he
who loves his fellow man has fulfilled the law.
Love does no harm to its neighbor. Therefore
love is the fulfillment of the law.
Romans 13:8, 10

Love is made full, satisfied. In love all
potential is fully developed.

*Lord of Love, You know the things holding me
back from fulfilling my dreams. Give me what is
best so that my life may be filled up with You.
Give me Your dreams. Help me follow You in
loving those around me, no matter what.*

He fulfills the desires of those who fear him;
he hears their cry and saves them. The LORD
watches over all who love him, but all the
wicked he will destroy.
Psalm 145:19–20

October

25

Love Is Keeping

Show the wonder of your great love, you who
save by your right hand those who take refuge
in you from their foes. Keep me as the apple
of your eye; hide me in the shadow of your
wings from the wicked who assail me. . . .
Psalm 17:7–9

Love is keeping, guarding, protecting,
preserving, saving.

*Lord of Love, You have kept me from much that
would have harmed me. Your love has been a
shield and strength through many trials. Thank
You for keeping me close to You.*

When I was a boy in my father's house . . . he
taught me and said, "Lay hold of my words
with all your heart; keep my commands and
you will live. Do not forsake wisdom, and she
will protect you; love her, and she will watch
over you."
Proverbs 4:3–4, 6

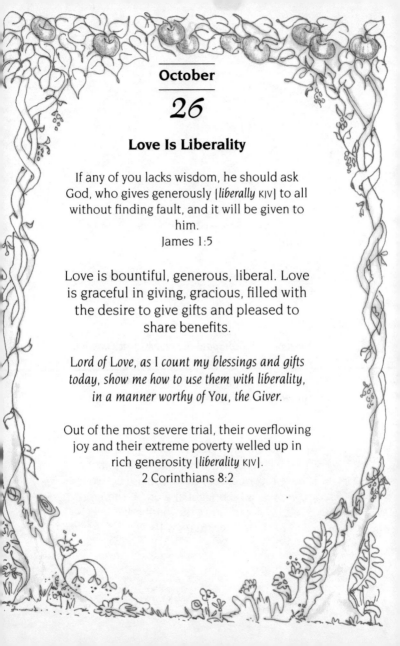

October

26

Love Is Liberality

If any of you lacks wisdom, he should ask God, who gives generously [*liberally* KJV] to all without finding fault, and it will be given to him.
James 1:5

Love is bountiful, generous, liberal. Love is graceful in giving, gracious, filled with the desire to give gifts and pleased to share benefits.

Lord of Love, as I count my blessings and gifts today, show me how to use them with liberality, in a manner worthy of You, the Giver.

Out of the most severe trial, their overflowing joy and their extreme poverty welled up in rich generosity [*liberality* KJV].
2 Corinthians 8:2

October

27

Love Is Priceless

How priceless is your unfailing love! Both
high and low among men find refuge in the
shadow of your wings. They feast on the
abundance of your house. . . .
Psalm 36:7–8

Love is beyond any price, invaluable, precious. Love is worthy of esteem in the
highest degree.

Lord of Love, You paid the highest price possible
for my life. You are worthy of highest praise. Help
me see You in the ordinary things and people in
my day, as well as in Your magnificent plan for
the universe.

Do you not know that your body is a temple
of the Holy Spirit, who is in you, whom you
have received from God? You are not your
own; you were bought at a price. Therefore
honor God with your body.
1 Corinthians 6:19–20

October

28

Love Is Ready

"Let us rejoice and be glad and give him
glory! For the wedding of the Lamb has come,
and his bride has made herself ready."
Revelation 19:7

Love is prepared mentally, physically and
spiritually for immediate use. Love is
spontaneously prompt, willing, inclined,
immediately available. Love is quick,
diligent, skillful.

*Lord of Love, in this age of instant everything,
You are available now, helping Your bride get
ready. Help me sort through my day, Lord, to see
what is essential and what is superfluous. Enable
me to be ready on time for Your coming.*

You are kind and forgiving [*ready to forgive* KJV],
O Lord, abounding in love to all who call to
you.
Psalm 86:5

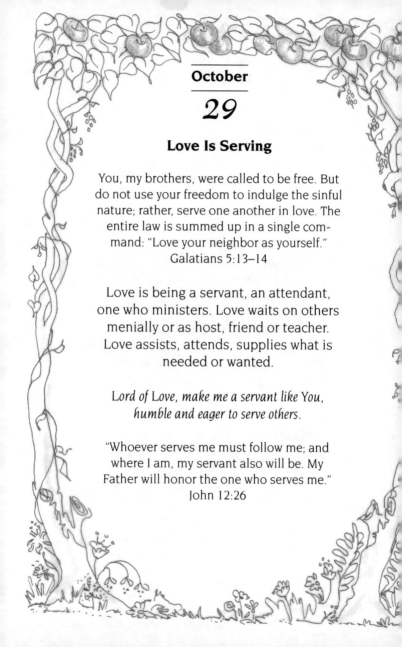

Love Is Serving

You, my brothers, were called to be free. But do not use your freedom to indulge the sinful nature; rather, serve one another in love. The entire law is summed up in a single command: "Love your neighbor as yourself." Galatians 5:13–14

Love is being a servant, an attendant, one who ministers. Love waits on others menially or as host, friend or teacher. Love assists, attends, supplies what is needed or wanted.

Lord of Love, make me a servant like You, humble and eager to serve others.

"Whoever serves me must follow me; and where I am, my servant also will be. My Father will honor the one who serves me." John 12:26

Love Is Fearless

Perfect love drives out fear, because fear has
to do with punishment. The man who fears is
not made perfect in love.
1 John 4:18b

Love fears neither man nor supernatural
forces because love is the central, eternal
force of the universe and cannot be overcome. Love is brave, courageous, secure
in its authority over every evil.

*Lord of Love, I know my love is not perfect
because in many situations I am afraid. Be
stronger in me, Perfect Love, and drive out
anxiety and fear. Help me reach out with Your
love to those who call themselves enemies.*

[Some Pharisees said to Jesus,] "Leave this
place. . . . Herod wants to kill you." He replied,
"Go tell that fox, 'I will drive out demons and
heal people today and tomorrow, and on the
third day I will reach my goal.'"
Luke 13:31–32

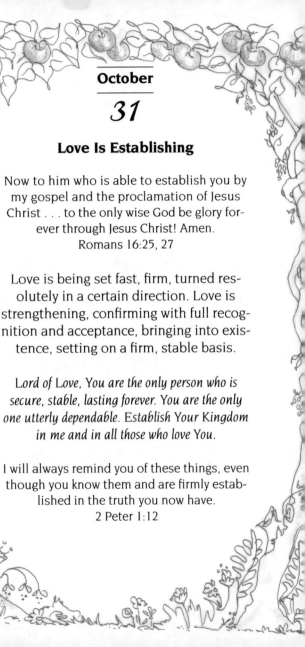

October

31

Love Is Establishing

Now to him who is able to establish you by
my gospel and the proclamation of Jesus
Christ . . . to the only wise God be glory forever through Jesus Christ! Amen.
Romans 16:25, 27

Love is being set fast, firm, turned res-
olutely in a certain direction. Love is
strengthening, confirming with full recognition and acceptance, bringing into exis-
tence, setting on a firm, stable basis.

*Lord of Love, You are the only person who is
secure, stable, lasting forever. You are the only
one utterly dependable. Establish Your Kingdom
in me and in all those who love You.*

I will always remind you of these things, even
though you know them and are firmly established in the truth you now have.
2 Peter 1:12

November
Love Is Thankful

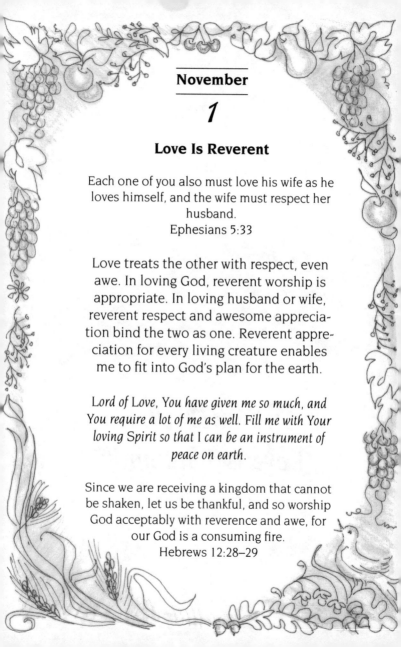

November

1

Love Is Reverent

Each one of you also must love his wife as he loves himself, and the wife must respect her husband.
Ephesians 5:33

Love treats the other with respect, even awe. In loving God, reverent worship is appropriate. In loving husband or wife, reverent respect and awesome appreciation bind the two as one. Reverent appreciation for every living creature enables me to fit into God's plan for the earth.

Lord of Love, You have given me so much, and You require a lot of me as well. Fill me with Your loving Spirit so that I can be an instrument of peace on earth.

Since we are receiving a kingdom that cannot be shaken, let us be thankful, and so worship God acceptably with reverence and awe, for our God is a consuming fire.
Hebrews 12:28–29

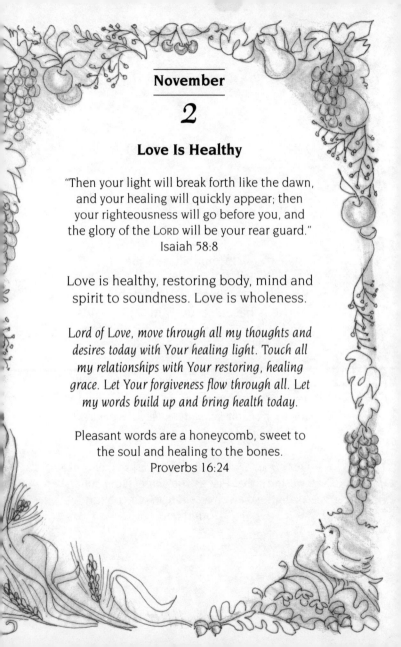

November

2

Love Is Healthy

"Then your light will break forth like the dawn,
and your healing will quickly appear; then
your righteousness will go before you, and
the glory of the LORD will be your rear guard."
Isaiah 58:8

Love is healthy, restoring body, mind and
spirit to soundness. Love is wholeness.

*Lord of Love, move through all my thoughts and
desires today with Your healing light. Touch all
my relationships with Your restoring, healing
grace. Let Your forgiveness flow through all. Let
my words build up and bring health today.*

Pleasant words are a honeycomb, sweet to
the soul and healing to the bones.
Proverbs 16:24

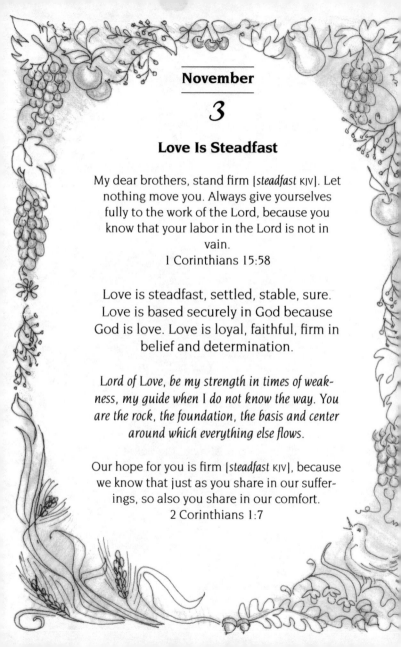

Love Is Steadfast

My dear brothers, stand firm [*steadfast* KJV]. Let nothing move you. Always give yourselves fully to the work of the Lord, because you know that your labor in the Lord is not in vain.

1 Corinthians 15:58

Love is steadfast, settled, stable, sure. Love is based securely in God because God is love. Love is loyal, faithful, firm in belief and determination.

Lord of Love, be my strength in times of weakness, my guide when I do not know the way. You are the rock, the foundation, the basis and center around which everything else flows.

Our hope for you is firm [*steadfast* KJV], because we know that just as you share in our sufferings, so also you share in our comfort.

2 Corinthians 1:7

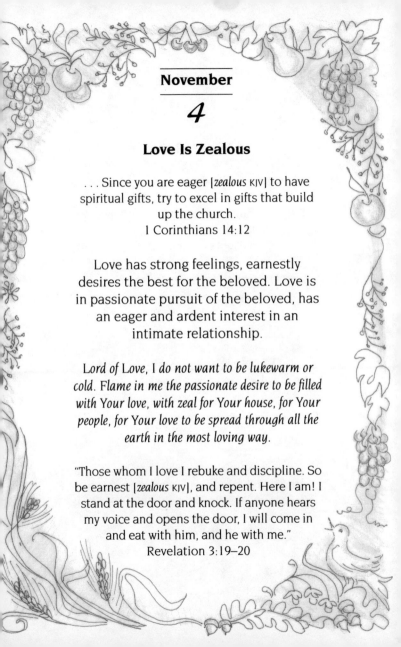

November

4

Love Is Zealous

. . . Since you are eager [*zealous* KJV] to have
spiritual gifts, try to excel in gifts that build
up the church.
1 Corinthians 14:12

Love has strong feelings, earnestly
desires the best for the beloved. Love is
in passionate pursuit of the beloved, has
an eager and ardent interest in an
intimate relationship.

*Lord of Love, I do not want to be lukewarm or
cold. Flame in me the passionate desire to be filled
with Your love, with zeal for Your house, for Your
people, for Your love to be spread through all the
earth in the most loving way.*

"Those whom I love I rebuke and discipline. So
be earnest [*zealous* KJV], and repent. Here I am! I
stand at the door and knock. If anyone hears
my voice and opens the door, I will come in
and eat with him, and he with me."
Revelation 3:19–20

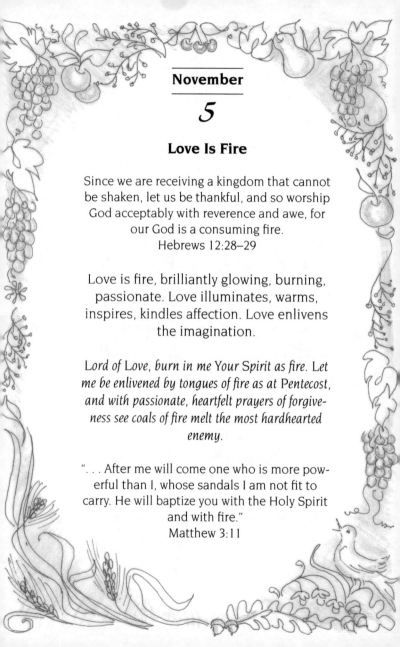

November

5

Love Is Fire

Since we are receiving a kingdom that cannot be shaken, let us be thankful, and so worship God acceptably with reverence and awe, for our God is a consuming fire.
Hebrews 12:28–29

Love is fire, brilliantly glowing, burning, passionate. Love illuminates, warms, inspires, kindles affection. Love enlivens the imagination.

Lord of Love, burn in me Your Spirit as fire. Let me be enlivened by tongues of fire as at Pentecost, and with passionate, heartfelt prayers of forgiveness see coals of fire melt the most hardhearted enemy.

". . . After me will come one who is more powerful than I, whose sandals I am not fit to carry. He will baptize you with the Holy Spirit and with fire."
Matthew 3:11

November

6

Love Is Light

Whoever loves his brother lives in the light,
and there is nothing in him to make him
stumble.
1 John 2:10

Love is light, shining with brightness,
illuminated. Love makes clear what is
true, radiates with brilliance.

*Lord of Love, where I stumble in darkness, take
my hand and bring me into Your light. Help me
share the light of Your love in a way that warms
and welcomes rather than burns.*

If we walk in the light, as he is in the light, we
have fellowship with one another, and the
blood of Jesus, his Son, purifies us from all
sin.
1 John 1:7

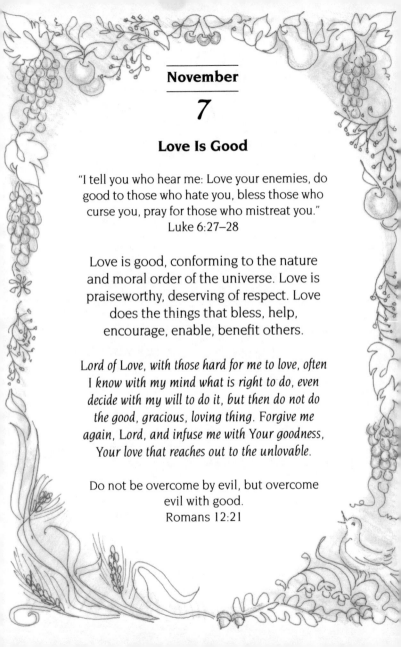

Love Is Good

"I tell you who hear me: Love your enemies, do good to those who hate you, bless those who curse you, pray for those who mistreat you."
Luke 6:27–28

Love is good, conforming to the nature and moral order of the universe. Love is praiseworthy, deserving of respect. Love does the things that bless, help, encourage, enable, benefit others.

Lord of Love, with those hard for me to love, often I know with my mind what is right to do, even decide with my will to do it, but then do not do the good, gracious, loving thing. Forgive me again, Lord, and infuse me with Your goodness, Your love that reaches out to the unlovable.

Do not be overcome by evil, but overcome evil with good.
Romans 12:21

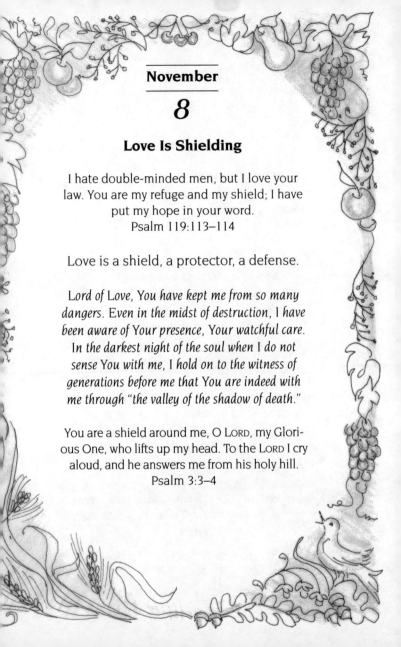

November

8

Love Is Shielding

I hate double-minded men, but I love your
law. You are my refuge and my shield; I have
put my hope in your word.
Psalm 119:113–114

Love is a shield, a protector, a defense.

*Lord of Love, You have kept me from so many
dangers. Even in the midst of destruction, I have
been aware of Your presence, Your watchful care.
In the darkest night of the soul when I do not
sense You with me, I hold on to the witness of
generations before me that You are indeed with
me through "the valley of the shadow of death."*

You are a shield around me, O LORD, my Glorious One, who lifts up my head. To the LORD I cry
aloud, and he answers me from his holy hill.
Psalm 3:3–4

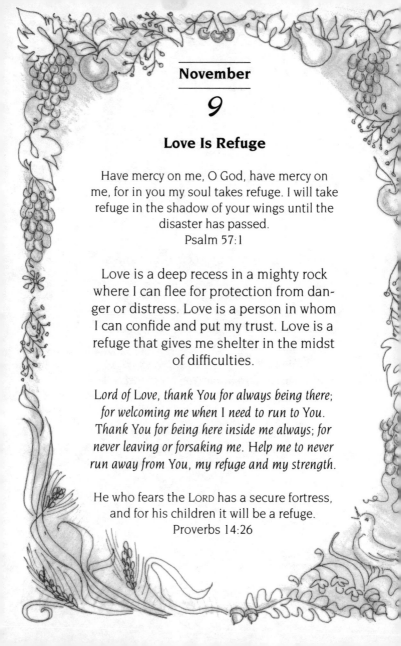

November

9

Love Is Refuge

Have mercy on me, O God, have mercy on me, for in you my soul takes refuge. I will take refuge in the shadow of your wings until the disaster has passed.
Psalm 57:1

Love is a deep recess in a mighty rock where I can flee for protection from danger or distress. Love is a person in whom I can confide and put my trust. Love is a refuge that gives me shelter in the midst of difficulties.

Lord of Love, thank You for always being there; for welcoming me when I need to run to You. Thank You for being here inside me always; for never leaving or forsaking me. Help me to never run away from You, my refuge and my strength.

He who fears the LORD has a secure fortress, and for his children it will be a refuge.
Proverbs 14:26

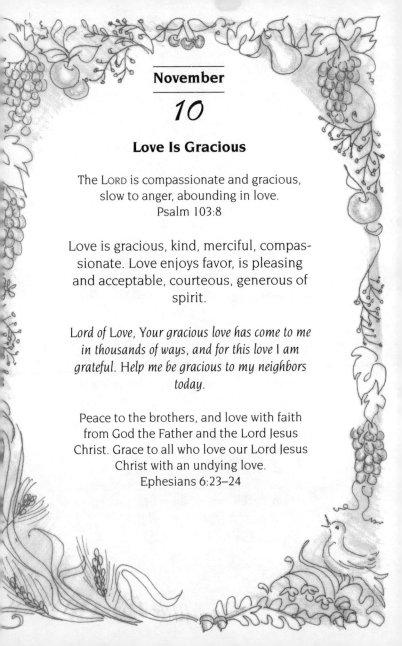

November

10

Love Is Gracious

The LORD is compassionate and gracious,
slow to anger, abounding in love.
Psalm 103:8

Love is gracious, kind, merciful, compassionate. Love enjoys favor, is pleasing
and acceptable, courteous, generous of
spirit.

*Lord of Love, Your gracious love has come to me
in thousands of ways, and for this love I am
grateful. Help me be gracious to my neighbors
today.*

Peace to the brothers, and love with faith
from God the Father and the Lord Jesus
Christ. Grace to all who love our Lord Jesus
Christ with an undying love.
Ephesians 6:23–24

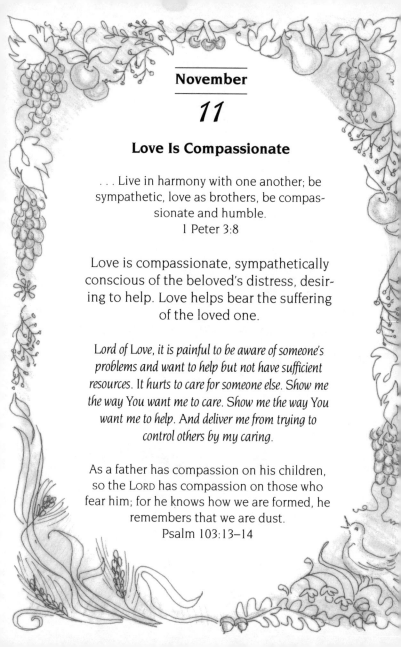

November

11

Love Is Compassionate

. . . Live in harmony with one another; be
sympathetic, love as brothers, be compassionate and humble.
1 Peter 3:8

Love is compassionate, sympathetically
conscious of the beloved's distress, desiring to help. Love helps bear the suffering
of the loved one.

*Lord of Love, it is painful to be aware of someone's
problems and want to help but not have sufficient
resources. It hurts to care for someone else. Show me
the way You want me to care. Show me the way You
want me to help. And deliver me from trying to
control others by my caring.*

As a father has compassion on his children,
so the LORD has compassion on those who
fear him; for he knows how we are formed, he
remembers that we are dust.
Psalm 103:13–14

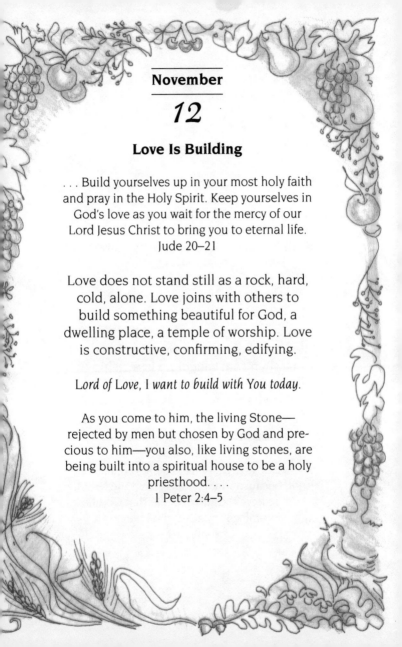

November

12

Love Is Building

. . . Build yourselves up in your most holy faith
and pray in the Holy Spirit. Keep yourselves in
God's love as you wait for the mercy of our
Lord Jesus Christ to bring you to eternal life.
Jude 20–21

Love does not stand still as a rock, hard,
cold, alone. Love joins with others to
build something beautiful for God, a
dwelling place, a temple of worship. Love
is constructive, confirming, edifying.

Lord of Love, I want to build with You today.

As you come to him, the living Stone—
rejected by men but chosen by God and precious to him—you also, like living stones, are
being built into a spiritual house to be a holy
priesthood. . . .
1 Peter 2:4–5

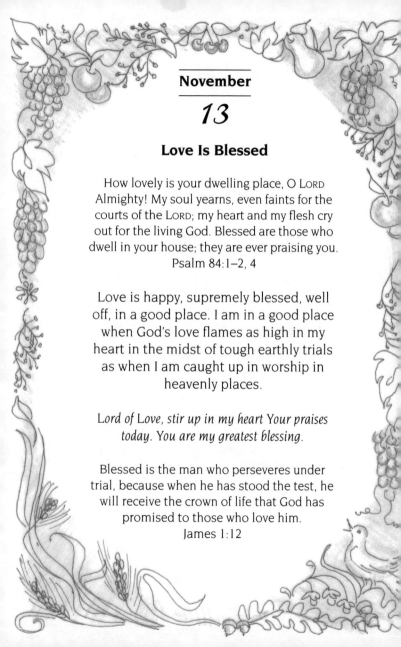

November

13

Love Is Blessed

How lovely is your dwelling place, O Lord Almighty! My soul yearns, even faints for the courts of the Lord; my heart and my flesh cry out for the living God. Blessed are those who dwell in your house; they are ever praising you.
Psalm 84:1–2, 4

Love is happy, supremely blessed, well off, in a good place. I am in a good place when God's love flames as high in my heart in the midst of tough earthly trials as when I am caught up in worship in heavenly places.

Lord of Love, stir up in my heart Your praises today. You are my greatest blessing.

Blessed is the man who perseveres under trial, because when he has stood the test, he will receive the crown of life that God has promised to those who love him.
James 1:12

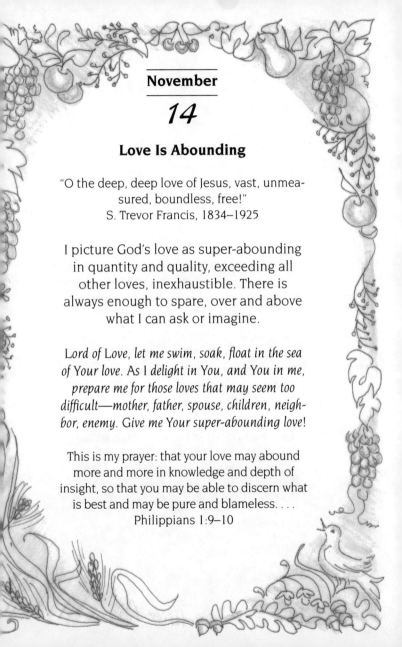

November

14

Love Is Abounding

"O the deep, deep love of Jesus, vast, unmeasured, boundless, free!"
S. Trevor Francis, 1834–1925

I picture God's love as super-abounding in quantity and quality, exceeding all other loves, inexhaustible. There is always enough to spare, over and above what I can ask or imagine.

Lord of Love, let me swim, soak, float in the sea of Your love. As I delight in You, and You in me, prepare me for those loves that may seem too difficult—mother, father, spouse, children, neighbor, enemy. Give me Your super-abounding love!

This is my prayer: that your love may abound more and more in knowledge and depth of insight, so that you may be able to discern what is best and may be pure and blameless. . . .
Philippians 1:9–10

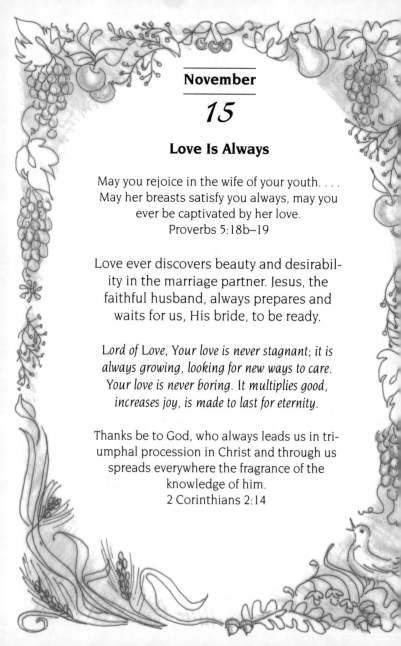

November

15

Love Is Always

May you rejoice in the wife of your youth. . . .
May her breasts satisfy you always, may you
ever be captivated by her love.
Proverbs 5:18b–19

Love ever discovers beauty and desirabil-
ity in the marriage partner. Jesus, the
faithful husband, always prepares and
waits for us, His bride, to be ready.

*Lord of Love, Your love is never stagnant; it is
always growing, looking for new ways to care.
Your love is never boring. It multiplies good,
increases joy, is made to last for eternity.*

Thanks be to God, who always leads us in triumphal procession in Christ and through us
spreads everywhere the fragrance of the
knowledge of him.
2 Corinthians 2:14

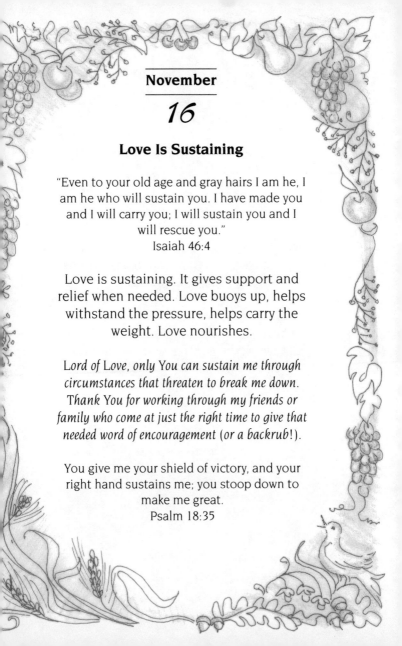

November

16

Love Is Sustaining

"Even to your old age and gray hairs I am he, I am he who will sustain you. I have made you and I will carry you; I will sustain you and I will rescue you."
Isaiah 46:4

Love is sustaining. It gives support and relief when needed. Love buoys up, helps withstand the pressure, helps carry the weight. Love nourishes.

Lord of Love, only You can sustain me through circumstances that threaten to break me down. Thank You for working through my friends or family who come at just the right time to give that needed word of encouragement (or a backrub!).

You give me your shield of victory, and your right hand sustains me; you stoop down to make me great.
Psalm 18:35

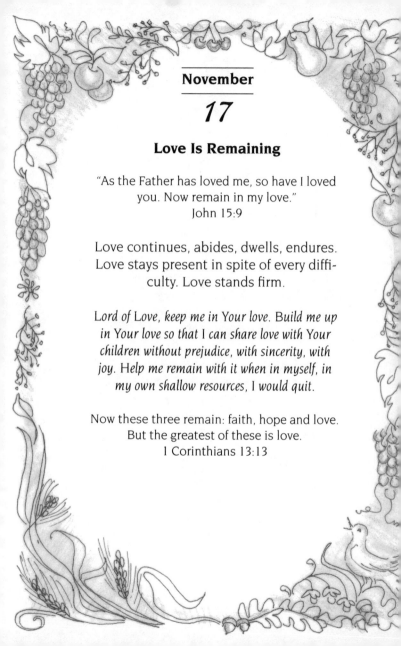

November

17

Love Is Remaining

"As the Father has loved me, so have I loved
you. Now remain in my love."
John 15:9

Love continues, abides, dwells, endures.
Love stays present in spite of every difficulty. Love stands firm.

*Lord of Love, keep me in Your love. Build me up
in Your love so that I can share love with Your
children without prejudice, with sincerity, with
joy. Help me remain with it when in myself, in
my own shallow resources, I would quit.*

Now these three remain: faith, hope and love.
But the greatest of these is love.
I Corinthians 13:13

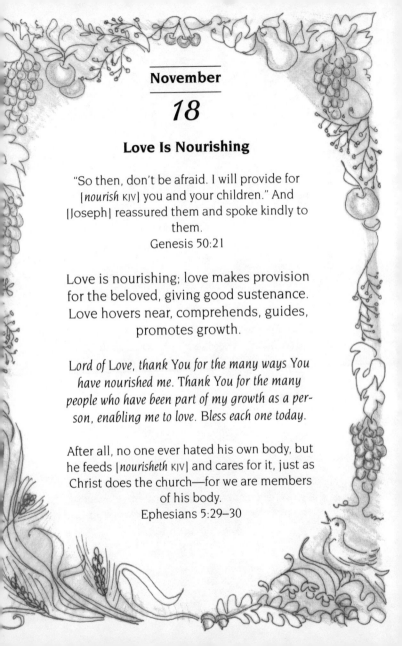

November

18

Love Is Nourishing

"So then, don't be afraid. I will provide for
[*nourish* KJV] you and your children." And
[Joseph] reassured them and spoke kindly to
them.
Genesis 50:21

Love is nourishing; love makes provision
for the beloved, giving good sustenance.
Love hovers near, comprehends, guides,
promotes growth.

*Lord of Love, thank You for the many ways You
have nourished me. Thank You for the many
people who have been part of my growth as a person, enabling me to love. Bless each one today.*

After all, no one ever hated his own body, but
he feeds [*nourisheth* KJV] and cares for it, just as
Christ does the church—for we are members
of his body.
Ephesians 5:29–30

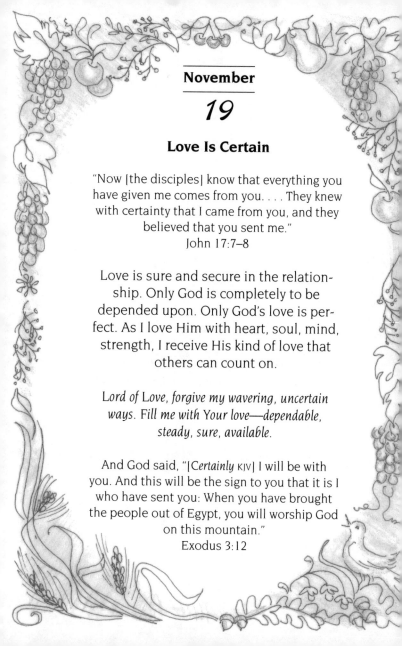

November

19

Love Is Certain

"Now [the disciples] know that everything you
have given me comes from you. . . . They knew
with certainty that I came from you, and they
believed that you sent me."
John 17:7–8

Love is sure and secure in the relationship. Only God is completely to be
depended upon. Only God's love is perfect. As I love Him with heart, soul, mind,
strength, I receive His kind of love that
others can count on.

*Lord of Love, forgive my wavering, uncertain
ways. Fill me with Your love—dependable,
steady, sure, available.*

And God said, "[*Certainly* KJV] I will be with
you. And this will be the sign to you that it is I
who have sent you: When you have brought
the people out of Egypt, you will worship God
on this mountain."
Exodus 3:12

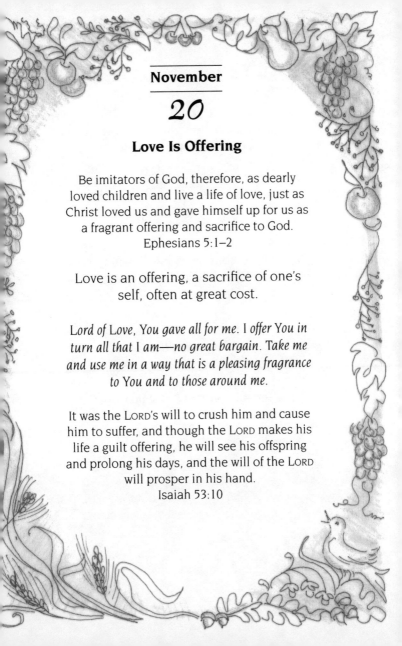

November

20

Love Is Offering

Be imitators of God, therefore, as dearly loved children and live a life of love, just as Christ loved us and gave himself up for us as a fragrant offering and sacrifice to God.
Ephesians 5:1–2

Love is an offering, a sacrifice of one's self, often at great cost.

Lord of Love, You gave all for me. I offer You in turn all that I am—no great bargain. Take me and use me in a way that is a pleasing fragrance to You and to those around me.

It was the LORD's will to crush him and cause him to suffer, and though the LORD makes his life a guilt offering, he will see his offspring and prolong his days, and the will of the LORD will prosper in his hand.
Isaiah 53:10

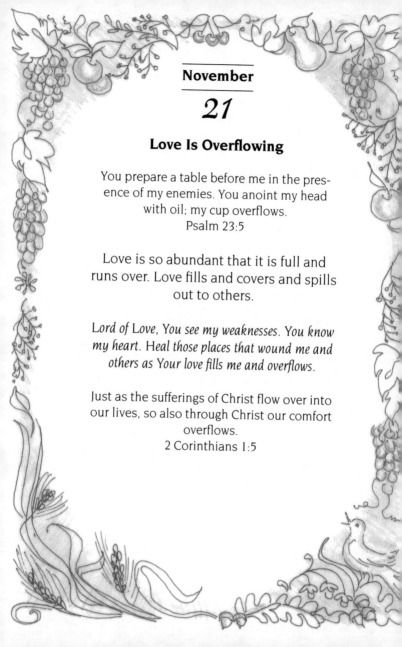

November

21

Love Is Overflowing

You prepare a table before me in the presence of my enemies. You anoint my head with oil; my cup overflows.
Psalm 23:5

Love is so abundant that it is full and runs over. Love fills and covers and spills out to others.

Lord of Love, You see my weaknesses. You know my heart. Heal those places that wound me and others as Your love fills me and overflows.

Just as the sufferings of Christ flow over into our lives, so also through Christ our comfort overflows.
2 Corinthians 1:5

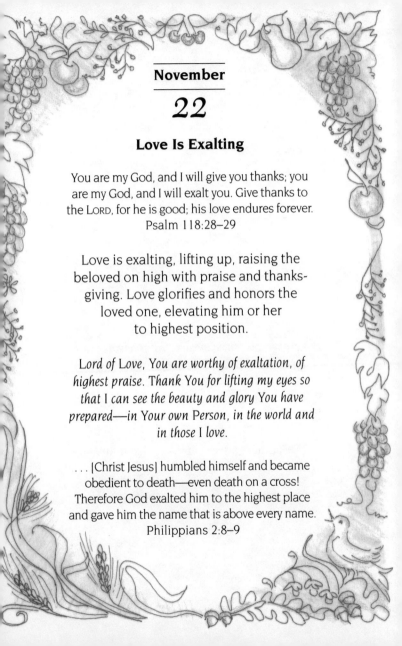

November

22

Love Is Exalting

You are my God, and I will give you thanks; you are my God, and I will exalt you. Give thanks to the LORD, for he is good; his love endures forever.
Psalm 118:28–29

Love is exalting, lifting up, raising the beloved on high with praise and thanksgiving. Love glorifies and honors the loved one, elevating him or her to highest position.

Lord of Love, You are worthy of exaltation, of highest praise. Thank You for lifting my eyes so that I can see the beauty and glory You have prepared—in Your own Person, in the world and in those I love.

. . . [Christ Jesus] humbled himself and became obedient to death—even death on a cross! Therefore God exalted him to the highest place and gave him the name that is above every name.
Philippians 2:8–9

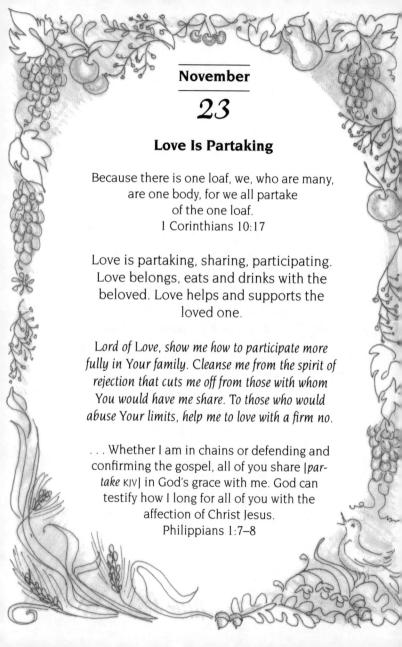

November

23

Love Is Partaking

Because there is one loaf, we, who are many,
are one body, for we all partake
of the one loaf.
1 Corinthians 10:17

Love is partaking, sharing, participating.
Love belongs, eats and drinks with the
beloved. Love helps and supports the
loved one.

*Lord of Love, show me how to participate more
fully in Your family. Cleanse me from the spirit of
rejection that cuts me off from those with whom
You would have me share. To those who would
abuse Your limits, help me to love with a firm no.*

. . . Whether I am in chains or defending and
confirming the gospel, all of you share [*partake* KJV] in God's grace with me. God can
testify how I long for all of you with the
affection of Christ Jesus.
Philippians 1:7–8

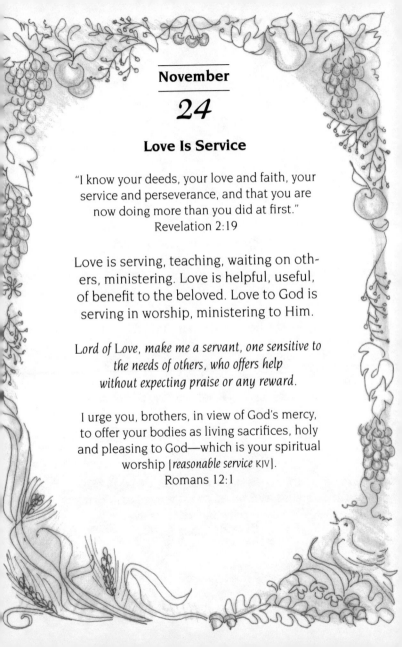

Love Is Service

"I know your deeds, your love and faith, your
service and perseverance, and that you are
now doing more than you did at first."
Revelation 2:19

Love is serving, teaching, waiting on others, ministering. Love is helpful, useful,
of benefit to the beloved. Love to God is
serving in worship, ministering to Him.

*Lord of Love, make me a servant, one sensitive to
the needs of others, who offers help
without expecting praise or any reward.*

I urge you, brothers, in view of God's mercy,
to offer your bodies as living sacrifices, holy
and pleasing to God—which is your spiritual
worship [*reasonable service* KJV].
Romans 12:1

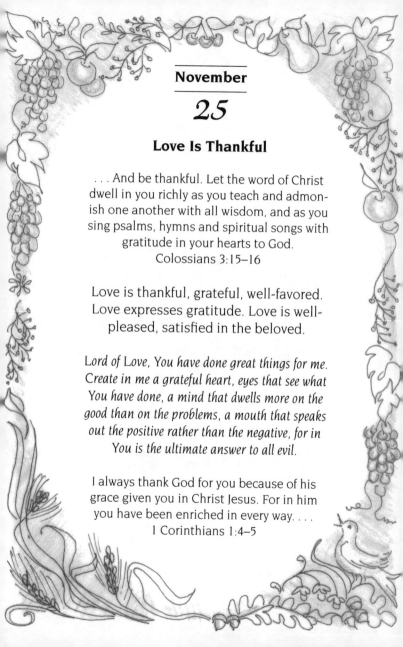

November

25

Love Is Thankful

. . . And be thankful. Let the word of Christ dwell in you richly as you teach and admonish one another with all wisdom, and as you sing psalms, hymns and spiritual songs with gratitude in your hearts to God.
Colossians 3:15–16

Love is thankful, grateful, well-favored. Love expresses gratitude. Love is well-pleased, satisfied in the beloved.

Lord of Love, You have done great things for me. Create in me a grateful heart, eyes that see what You have done, a mind that dwells more on the good than on the problems, a mouth that speaks out the positive rather than the negative, for in You is the ultimate answer to all evil.

I always thank God for you because of his grace given you in Christ Jesus. For in him you have been enriched in every way. . . .
1 Corinthians 1:4–5

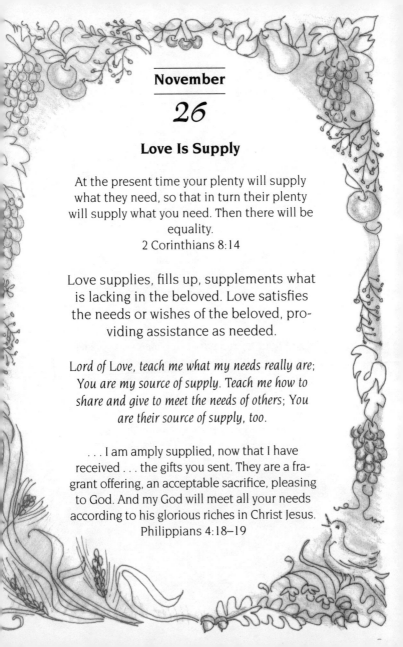

November

26

Love Is Supply

At the present time your plenty will supply what they need, so that in turn their plenty will supply what you need. Then there will be equality.
2 Corinthians 8:14

Love supplies, fills up, supplements what is lacking in the beloved. Love satisfies the needs or wishes of the beloved, providing assistance as needed.

Lord of Love, teach me what my needs really are; You are my source of supply. Teach me how to share and give to meet the needs of others; You are their source of supply, too.

. . . I am amply supplied, now that I have received . . . the gifts you sent. They are a fragrant offering, an acceptable sacrifice, pleasing to God. And my God will meet all your needs according to his glorious riches in Christ Jesus.
Philippians 4:18–19

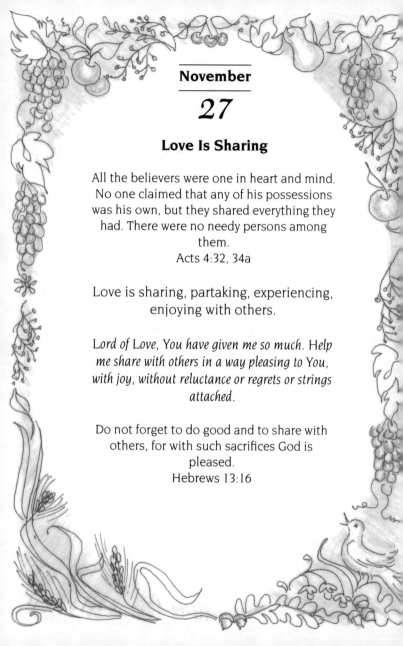

November

27

Love Is Sharing

All the believers were one in heart and mind. No one claimed that any of his possessions was his own, but they shared everything they had. There were no needy persons among them.
Acts 4:32, 34a

Love is sharing, partaking, experiencing, enjoying with others.

Lord of Love, You have given me so much. Help me share with others in a way pleasing to You, with joy, without reluctance or regrets or strings attached.

Do not forget to do good and to share with others, for with such sacrifices God is pleased.
Hebrews 13:16

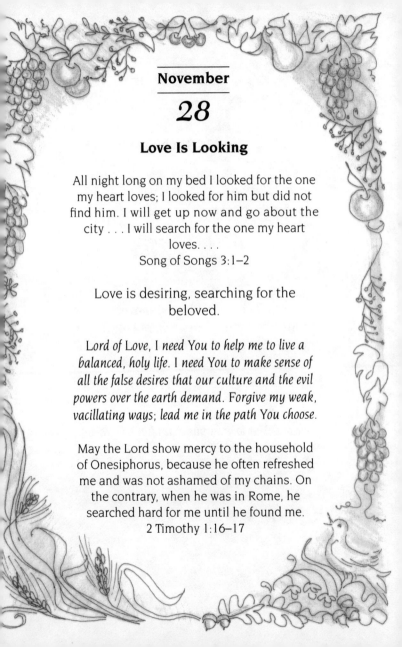

Love Is Looking

All night long on my bed I looked for the one
my heart loves; I looked for him but did not
find him. I will get up now and go about the
city . . . I will search for the one my heart
loves. . . .
Song of Songs 3:1–2

Love is desiring, searching for the
beloved.

*Lord of Love, I need You to help me to live a
balanced, holy life. I need You to make sense of
all the false desires that our culture and the evil
powers over the earth demand. Forgive my weak,
vacillating ways; lead me in the path You choose.*

May the Lord show mercy to the household
of Onesiphorus, because he often refreshed
me and was not ashamed of my chains. On
the contrary, when he was in Rome, he
searched hard for me until he found me.
2 Timothy 1:16–17

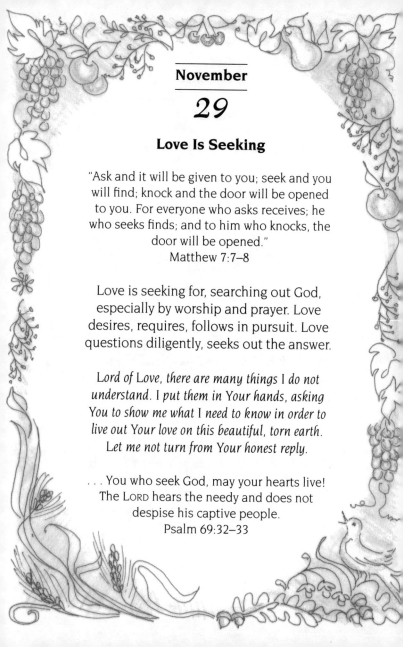

November

29

Love Is Seeking

"Ask and it will be given to you; seek and you
will find; knock and the door will be opened
to you. For everyone who asks receives; he
who seeks finds; and to him who knocks, the
door will be opened."
Matthew 7:7–8

Love is seeking for, searching out God,
especially by worship and prayer. Love
desires, requires, follows in pursuit. Love
questions diligently, seeks out the answer.

*Lord of Love, there are many things I do not
understand. I put them in Your hands, asking
You to show me what I need to know in order to
live out Your love on this beautiful, torn earth.
Let me not turn from Your honest reply.*

. . . You who seek God, may your hearts live!
The Lord hears the needy and does not
despise his captive people.
Psalm 69:32–33

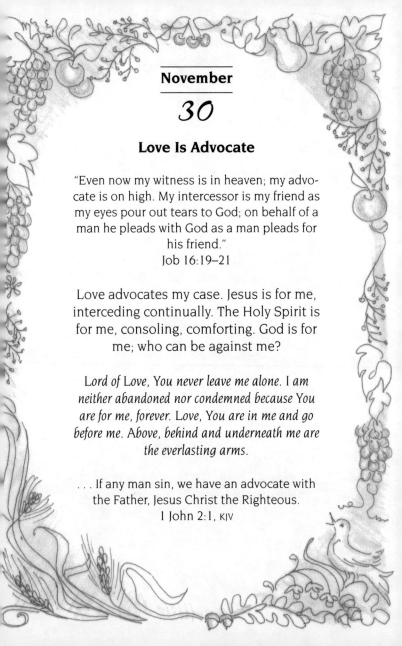

November

30

Love Is Advocate

"Even now my witness is in heaven; my advocate is on high. My intercessor is my friend as my eyes pour out tears to God; on behalf of a man he pleads with God as a man pleads for his friend."
Job 16:19–21

Love advocates my case. Jesus is for me, interceding continually. The Holy Spirit is for me, consoling, comforting. God is for me; who can be against me?

Lord of Love, You never leave me alone. I am neither abandoned nor condemned because You are for me, forever. Love, You are in me and go before me. Above, behind and underneath me are the everlasting arms.

. . . If any man sin, we have an advocate with the Father, Jesus Christ the Righteous.
1 John 2:1, KJV

December
Love Is Everlasting

December

1

Love Is Habitation

I love the house where you live, O LORD, the
place where your glory dwells.
Psalm 26:8

Love is a habitation: the lair of animals,
the home of a man and woman, the temple where God dwells. Love is a place of
retreat, a tent, residence, settlement,
dwelling place.

*Lord of Love, You have given me a place to stay
where I can withdraw from the pressures around me.
You have drawn people to me who want to share in
the goodness You have given. Please work in me the
balance of retreating and welcoming, being closed
and being open, conserving and sharing.*

You are . . . members of God's household. In
[Jesus] you too are being built together to
become a dwelling [*habitation* KJV] in which
God lives by his Spirit.
Ephesians 2:19, 22

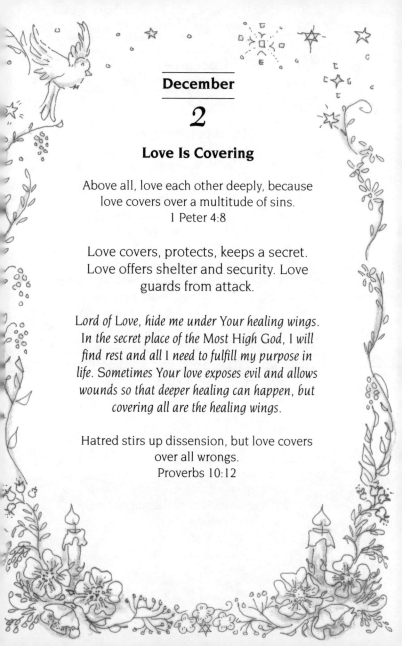

December

2

Love Is Covering

Above all, love each other deeply, because
love covers over a multitude of sins.
1 Peter 4:8

Love covers, protects, keeps a secret.
Love offers shelter and security. Love
guards from attack.

Lord of Love, hide me under Your healing wings.
In the secret place of the Most High God, I will
find rest and all I need to fulfill my purpose in
life. Sometimes Your love exposes evil and allows
wounds so that deeper healing can happen, but
covering all are the healing wings.

Hatred stirs up dissension, but love covers
over all wrongs.
Proverbs 10:12

December

3

Love Is Blessing

When he had led them out to the vicinity of
Bethany, he lifted up his hands and blessed
them. While he was blessing them, he left
them and was taken up into heaven. Then
they worshiped him and returned to
Jerusalem with great joy.
Luke 24:50–52

Love gives blessings, benedictions,
praise. Love desires prosperity for all;
speaks encouraging, uplifting words to
those who do not expect or deserve it,
especially to those antagonistic to all for
which love stands.

*Lord of Love, enable me to bless those who are
difficult to love. Help me do something special for
_____ today.*
[name]

Do not repay evil with evil or insult with
insult, but with blessing, because to this
you were called so that you may
inherit a blessing.
I Peter 3:9

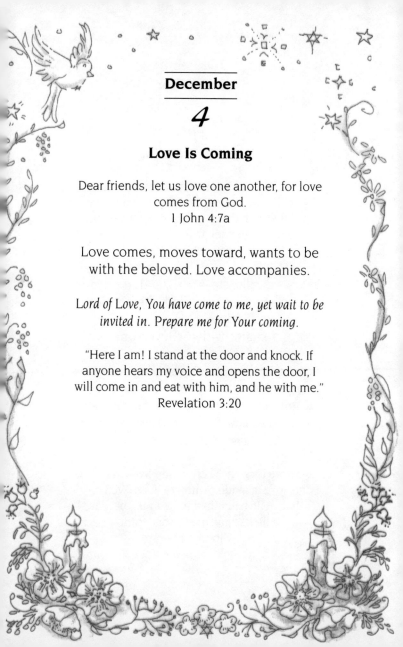

December

4

Love Is Coming

Dear friends, let us love one another, for love
comes from God.
1 John 4:7a

Love comes, moves toward, wants to be
with the beloved. Love accompanies.

*Lord of Love, You have come to me, yet wait to be
invited in. Prepare me for Your coming.*

"Here I am! I stand at the door and knock. If
anyone hears my voice and opens the door, I
will come in and eat with him, and he with me."
Revelation 3:20

December

5

Love Is Dwelling

I heard a loud voice from the throne saying,
"Now the dwelling of God is with men, and he
will live with them. They will be his people,
and God himself will be . . . their God."
Revelation 21:3

Love dwells, stays with, endures every
circumstance to be with the beloved.
Love stands with, is present with,
remains with the loved one.

*Lord of Love, You have said You will never leave
or forsake me. That gives me such a sense of
security, of being at home in You. In this unstable, uncertain world, be a dwelling place for me
and for all those I love.*

. . . If we love each other, God lives in us and
his love is made complete in us. We know
that we live in him and he in us, because
he has given us of his Spirit.
1 John 4:12–13

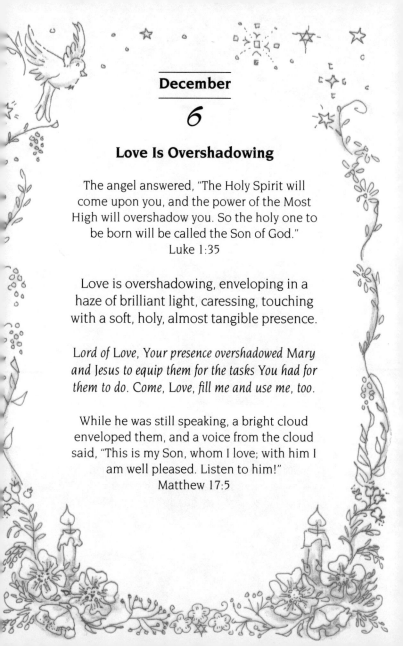

December

6

Love Is Overshadowing

The angel answered, "The Holy Spirit will come upon you, and the power of the Most High will overshadow you. So the holy one to be born will be called the Son of God."
Luke 1:35

Love is overshadowing, enveloping in a haze of brilliant light, caressing, touching with a soft, holy, almost tangible presence.

Lord of Love, Your presence overshadowed Mary and Jesus to equip them for the tasks You had for them to do. Come, Love, fill me and use me, too.

While he was still speaking, a bright cloud enveloped them, and a voice from the cloud said, "This is my Son, whom I love; with him I am well pleased. Listen to him!"
Matthew 17:5

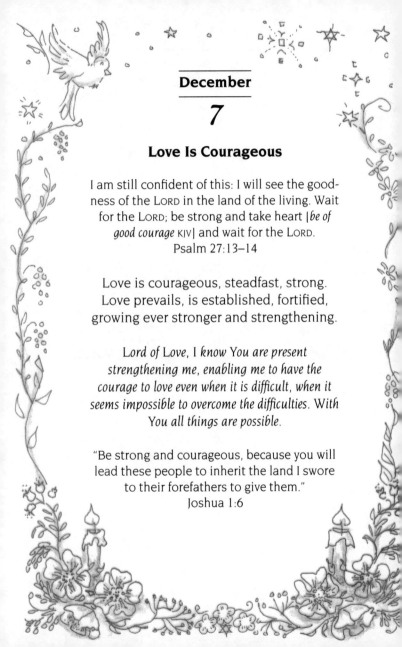

December

7

Love Is Courageous

I am still confident of this: I will see the goodness of the LORD in the land of the living. Wait
for the LORD; be strong and take heart [*be of
good courage* KJV] and wait for the LORD.
Psalm 27:13–14

Love is courageous, steadfast, strong.
Love prevails, is established, fortified,
growing ever stronger and strengthening.

*Lord of Love, I know You are present
strengthening me, enabling me to have the
courage to love even when it is difficult, when it
seems impossible to overcome the difficulties. With
You all things are possible.*

"Be strong and courageous, because you will
lead these people to inherit the land I swore
to their forefathers to give them."
Joshua 1:6

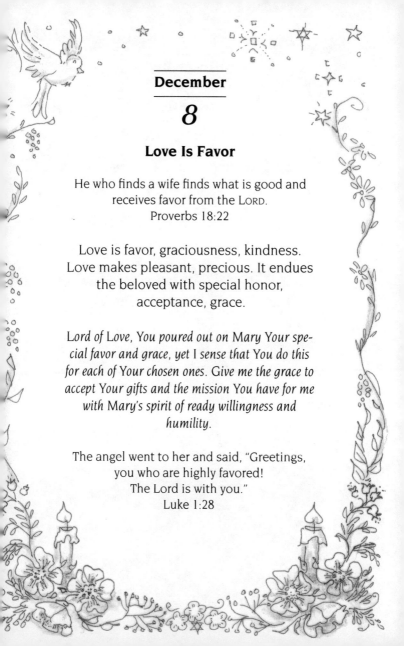

December

8

Love Is Favor

He who finds a wife finds what is good and
receives favor from the LORD.
Proverbs 18:22

Love is favor, graciousness, kindness.
Love makes pleasant, precious. It endues
the beloved with special honor,
acceptance, grace.

Lord of Love, You poured out on Mary Your spe-
cial favor and grace, yet I sense that You do this
for each of Your chosen ones. Give me the grace to
accept Your gifts and the mission You have for me
with Mary's spirit of ready willingness and
humility.

The angel went to her and said, "Greetings,
you who are highly favored!
The Lord is with you."
Luke 1:28

December

9

Love Is Pure

The goal of this command is love, which comes from a pure heart and a good conscience and a sincere faith.
1 Timothy 1:5

Love is pure, clean, clear, free of anything tainted. Love is marked by chastity. Love contains nothing that weakens, dilutes or pollutes its purity and profundity.

Lord of Love, I bring to You all my impurities and weaknesses and the pollution of my mind, emotions and spirit that comes from being a human in this imperfect world. I trust You to cleanse and free me to love with Your love.

Now that you have purified yourselves by obeying the truth so that you have sincere love for your brothers, love one another deeply, from the heart.
1 Peter 1:22

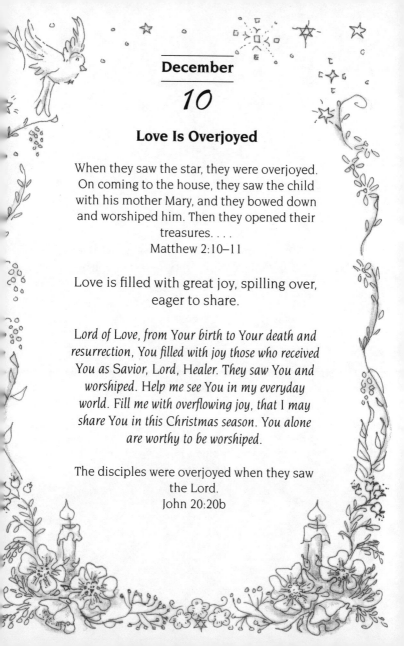

December

10

Love Is Overjoyed

When they saw the star, they were overjoyed.
On coming to the house, they saw the child
with his mother Mary, and they bowed down
and worshiped him. Then they opened their
treasures. . . .
Matthew 2:10–11

Love is filled with great joy, spilling over,
eager to share.

*Lord of Love, from Your birth to Your death and
resurrection, You filled with joy those who received
You as Savior, Lord, Healer. They saw You and
worshiped. Help me see You in my everyday
world. Fill me with overflowing joy, that I may
share You in this Christmas season. You alone
are worthy to be worshiped.*

The disciples were overjoyed when they saw
the Lord.
John 20:20b

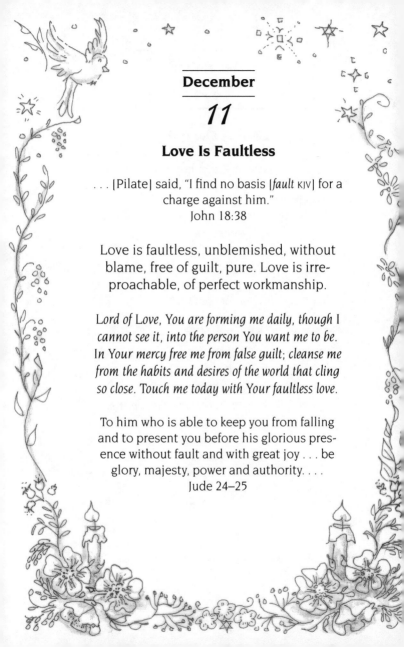

December

11

Love Is Faultless

. . . [Pilate] said, "I find no basis [*fault* KJV] for a
charge against him."
John 18:38

Love is faultless, unblemished, without
blame, free of guilt, pure. Love is irre-
proachable, of perfect workmanship.

Lord of Love, You are forming me daily, though I
cannot see it, into the person You want me to be.
In Your mercy free me from false guilt; cleanse me
from the habits and desires of the world that cling
so close. Touch me today with Your faultless love.

To him who is able to keep you from falling
and to present you before his glorious presence without fault and with great joy . . . be
glory, majesty, power and authority. . . .
Jude 24–25

December

12

Love Is Joy

The fruit of the Spirit is love, joy, peace,
patience, kindness, goodness, faithfulness,
gentleness and self-control. Against such
things there is no law.
Galatians 5:22–23

Love is cheerfulness, calm delight,
exceeding gladness. Love is the source or
cause of delight, bliss, happiness, great
pleasure.

*Lord of Love, Your joy is something supernatural
that the world's pleasures and my own striving
can never obtain. Your joy matures in me as a
fruit as I am rooted in You. Grow joy in me today
so that those around me can taste and see that
You are love and that You are good.*

"You will grieve, but your grief will turn to joy.
Until now you have not asked for anything
in my name. Ask and you will receive,
and your joy will be complete."
John 16:20b, 24

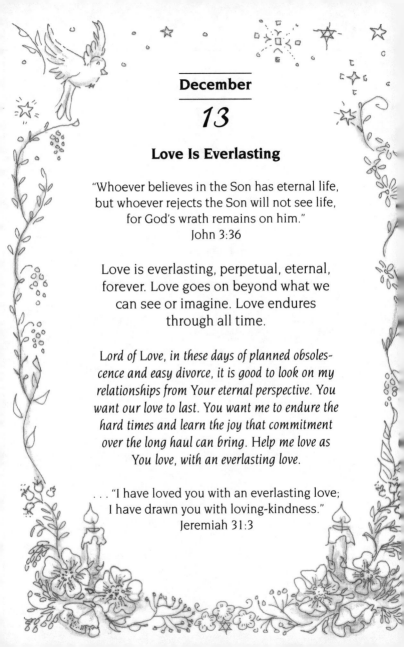

December

13

Love Is Everlasting

"Whoever believes in the Son has eternal life,
but whoever rejects the Son will not see life,
for God's wrath remains on him."
John 3:36

Love is everlasting, perpetual, eternal,
forever. Love goes on beyond what we
can see or imagine. Love endures
through all time.

*Lord of Love, in these days of planned obsoles-
cence and easy divorce, it is good to look on my
relationships from Your eternal perspective. You
want our love to last. You want me to endure the
hard times and learn the joy that commitment
over the long haul can bring. Help me love as
You love, with an everlasting love.*

. . . "I have loved you with an everlasting love;
I have drawn you with loving-kindness."
Jeremiah 31:3

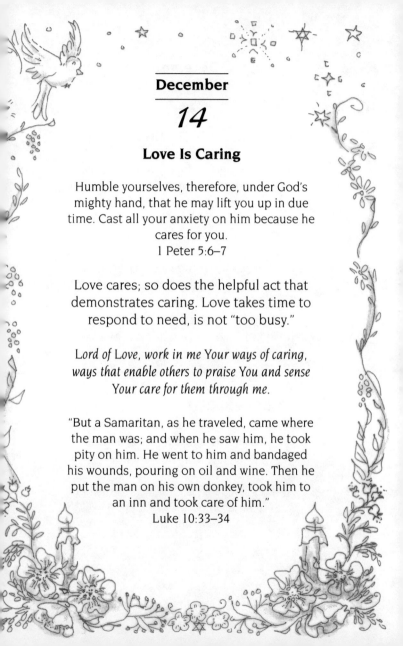

December

14

Love Is Caring

Humble yourselves, therefore, under God's
mighty hand, that he may lift you up in due
time. Cast all your anxiety on him because he
cares for you.
1 Peter 5:6–7

Love cares; so does the helpful act that
demonstrates caring. Love takes time to
respond to need, is not "too busy."

*Lord of Love, work in me Your ways of caring,
ways that enable others to praise You and sense
Your care for them through me.*

"But a Samaritan, as he traveled, came where
the man was; and when he saw him, he took
pity on him. He went to him and bandaged
his wounds, pouring on oil and wine. Then he
put the man on his own donkey, took him to
an inn and took care of him."
Luke 10:33–34

December

15

Love Is Brotherly

We love because he first loved us. If anyone says, "I love God," yet hates his brother, he is a liar. . . . Whoever loves God must also love his brother.
1 John 4:19–21

Love is not vague and only spiritual. Love is kindness visibly expressed toward those in the family of faith, extended to the family of God's creation. Many of these family members are unlovable at times; so am I. But it is through love that we are changed.

Lord of Love, surge in me a new way of seeing my brother's or sister's faults. Help me see the good You have given him or her. Thank You for Your family, and that I am a part.

Whoever loves his brother lives in the light, and there is nothing in him to make him stumble.
1 John 2:10

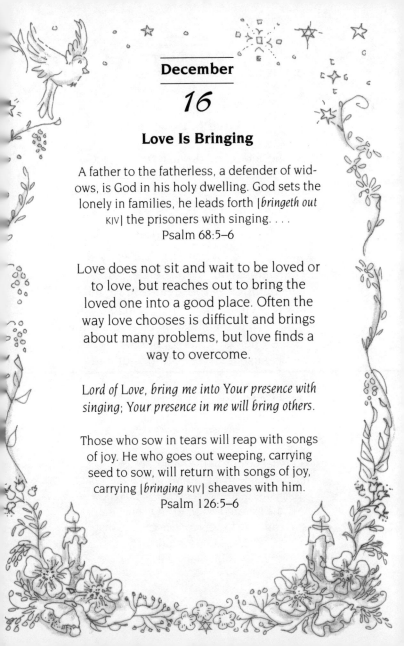

December

16

Love Is Bringing

A father to the fatherless, a defender of widows, is God in his holy dwelling. God sets the lonely in families, he leads forth |*bringeth out* KJV| the prisoners with singing. . . .
Psalm 68:5–6

Love does not sit and wait to be loved or to love, but reaches out to bring the loved one into a good place. Often the way love chooses is difficult and brings about many problems, but love finds a way to overcome.

Lord of Love, bring me into Your presence with singing; Your presence in me will bring others.

Those who sow in tears will reap with songs of joy. He who goes out weeping, carrying seed to sow, will return with songs of joy, carrying |*bringing* KJV| sheaves with him.
Psalm 126:5–6

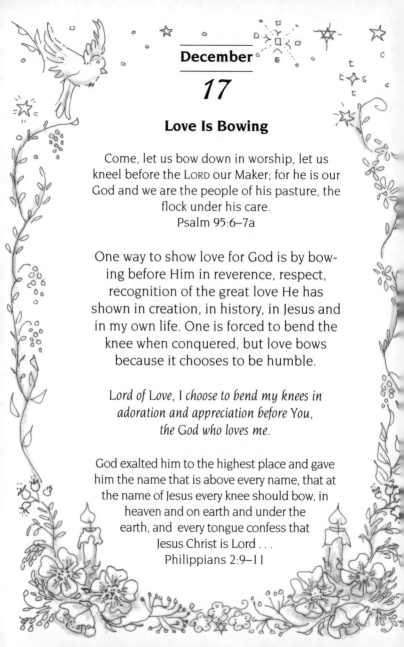

Love Is Bowing

Come, let us bow down in worship, let us
kneel before the LORD our Maker; for he is our
God and we are the people of his pasture, the
flock under his care.
Psalm 95:6–7a

One way to show love for God is by bow-
ing before Him in reverence, respect,
recognition of the great love He has
shown in creation, in history, in Jesus and
in my own life. One is forced to bend the
knee when conquered, but love bows
because it chooses to be humble.

*Lord of Love, I choose to bend my knees in
adoration and appreciation before You,
the God who loves me.*

God exalted him to the highest place and gave
him the name that is above every name, that at
the name of Jesus every knee should bow, in
heaven and on earth and under the
earth, and every tongue confess that
Jesus Christ is Lord . . .
Philippians 2:9–11

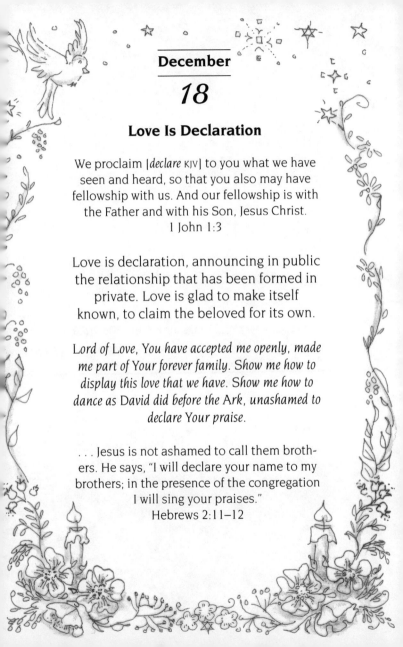

Love Is Declaration

We proclaim [*declare* KJV] to you what we have seen and heard, so that you also may have fellowship with us. And our fellowship is with the Father and with his Son, Jesus Christ.
1 John 1:3

Love is declaration, announcing in public the relationship that has been formed in private. Love is glad to make itself known, to claim the beloved for its own.

Lord of Love, You have accepted me openly, made me part of Your forever family. Show me how to display this love that we have. Show me how to dance as David did before the Ark, unashamed to declare Your praise.

. . . Jesus is not ashamed to call them brothers. He says, "I will declare your name to my brothers; in the presence of the congregation I will sing your praises."
Hebrews 2:11–12

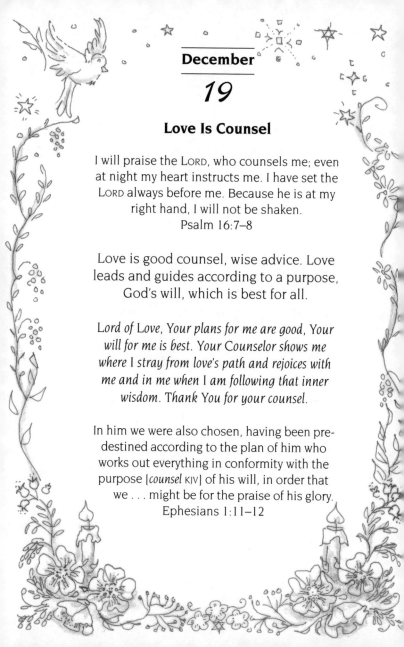

Love Is Counsel

I will praise the Lord, who counsels me; even
at night my heart instructs me. I have set the
Lord always before me. Because he is at my
right hand, I will not be shaken.
Psalm 16:7–8

Love is good counsel, wise advice. Love
leads and guides according to a purpose,
God's will, which is best for all.

*Lord of Love, Your plans for me are good, Your
will for me is best. Your Counselor shows me
where I stray from love's path and rejoices with
me and in me when I am following that inner
wisdom. Thank You for your counsel.*

In him we were also chosen, having been predestined according to the plan of him who
works out everything in conformity with the
purpose [*counsel* KJV] of his will, in order that
we . . . might be for the praise of his glory.
Ephesians 1:11–12

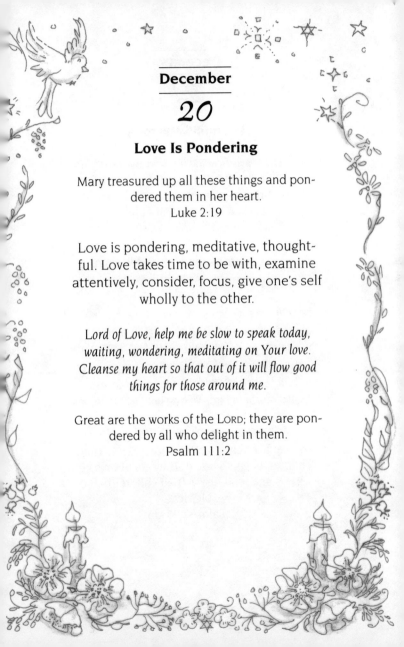

December

20

Love Is Pondering

Mary treasured up all these things and pondered them in her heart.
Luke 2:19

Love is pondering, meditative, thoughtful. Love takes time to be with, examine attentively, consider, focus, give one's self wholly to the other.

Lord of Love, help me be slow to speak today, waiting, wondering, meditating on Your love. Cleanse my heart so that out of it will flow good things for those around me.

Great are the works of the Lord; they are pondered by all who delight in them.
Psalm 111:2

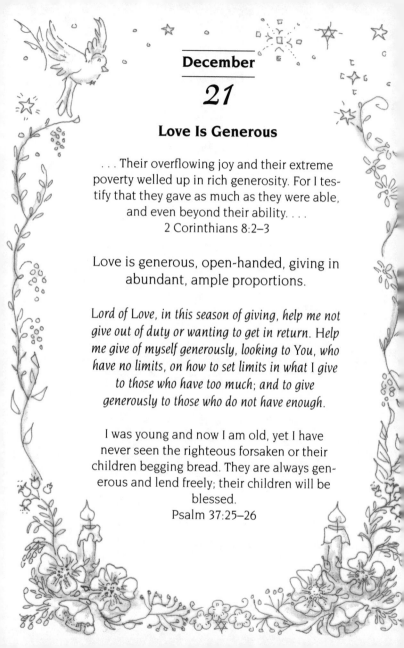

December

21

Love Is Generous

. . . Their overflowing joy and their extreme poverty welled up in rich generosity. For I testify that they gave as much as they were able, and even beyond their ability. . . .
2 Corinthians 8:2–3

Love is generous, open-handed, giving in abundant, ample proportions.

Lord of Love, in this season of giving, help me not give out of duty or wanting to get in return. Help me give of myself generously, looking to You, who have no limits, on how to set limits in what I give to those who have too much; and to give generously to those who do not have enough.

I was young and now I am old, yet I have never seen the righteous forsaken or their children begging bread. They are always generous and lend freely; their children will be blessed.
Psalm 37:25–26

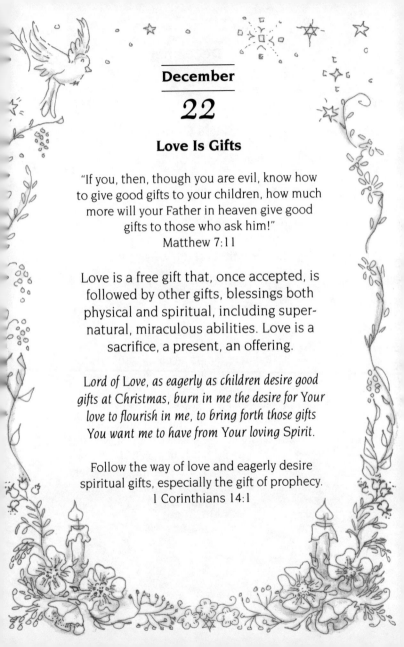

December

22

Love Is Gifts

"If you, then, though you are evil, know how
to give good gifts to your children, how much
more will your Father in heaven give good
gifts to those who ask him!"
Matthew 7:11

Love is a free gift that, once accepted, is
followed by other gifts, blessings both
physical and spiritual, including supernatural, miraculous abilities. Love is a
sacrifice, a present, an offering.

*Lord of Love, as eagerly as children desire good
gifts at Christmas, burn in me the desire for Your
love to flourish in me, to bring forth those gifts
You want me to have from Your loving Spirit.*

Follow the way of love and eagerly desire
spiritual gifts, especially the gift of prophecy.
1 Corinthians 14:1

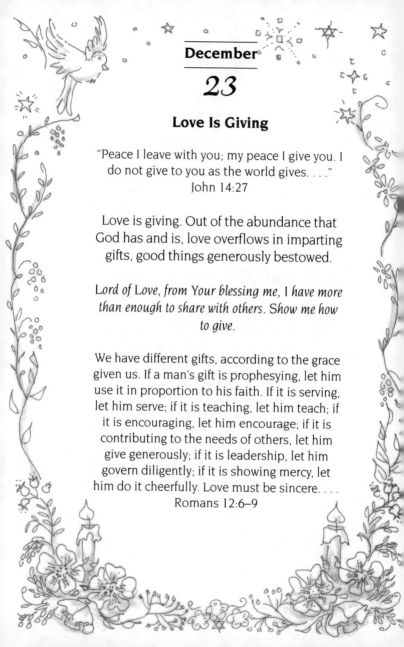

December

23

Love Is Giving

"Peace I leave with you; my peace I give you. I
do not give to you as the world gives. . . ."
John 14:27

Love is giving. Out of the abundance that
God has and is, love overflows in imparting
gifts, good things generously bestowed.

*Lord of Love, from Your blessing me, I have more
than enough to share with others. Show me how
to give.*

We have different gifts, according to the grace
given us. If a man's gift is prophesying, let him
use it in proportion to his faith. If it is serving,
let him serve; if it is teaching, let him teach; if
it is encouraging, let him encourage; if it is
contributing to the needs of others, let him
give generously; if it is leadership, let him
govern diligently; if it is showing mercy, let
him do it cheerfully. Love must be sincere. . . .
Romans 12:6–9

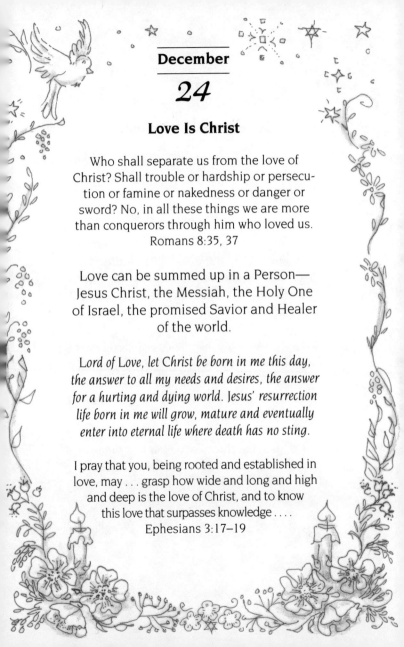

December

24

Love Is Christ

Who shall separate us from the love of
Christ? Shall trouble or hardship or persecution or famine or nakedness or danger or
sword? No, in all these things we are more
than conquerors through him who loved us.
Romans 8:35, 37

Love can be summed up in a Person—
Jesus Christ, the Messiah, the Holy One
of Israel, the promised Savior and Healer
of the world.

Lord of Love, let Christ be born in me this day,
the answer to all my needs and desires, the answer
for a hurting and dying world. Jesus' resurrection
life born in me will grow, mature and eventually
enter into eternal life where death has no sting.

I pray that you, being rooted and established in
love, may . . . grasp how wide and long and high
and deep is the love of Christ, and to know
this love that surpasses knowledge . . . .
Ephesians 3:17–19

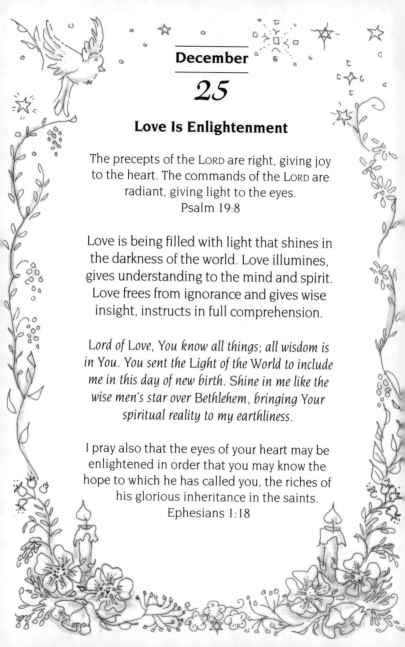

December

25

Love Is Enlightenment

The precepts of the LORD are right, giving joy
to the heart. The commands of the LORD are
radiant, giving light to the eyes.
Psalm 19:8

Love is being filled with light that shines in
the darkness of the world. Love illumines,
gives understanding to the mind and spirit.
Love frees from ignorance and gives wise
insight, instructs in full comprehension.

*Lord of Love, You know all things; all wisdom is
in You. You sent the Light of the World to include
me in this day of new birth. Shine in me like the
wise men's star over Bethlehem, bringing Your
spiritual reality to my earthliness.*

I pray also that the eyes of your heart may be
enlightened in order that you may know the
hope to which he has called you, the riches of
his glorious inheritance in the saints.
Ephesians 1:18

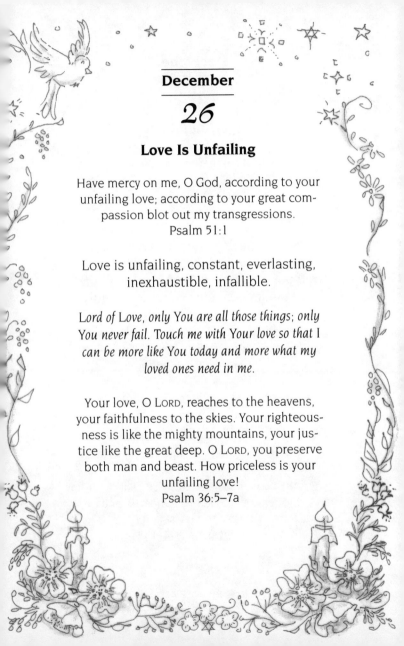

December

26

Love Is Unfailing

Have mercy on me, O God, according to your unfailing love; according to your great compassion blot out my transgressions.
Psalm 51:1

Love is unfailing, constant, everlasting, inexhaustible, infallible.

Lord of Love, only You are all those things; only You never fail. Touch me with Your love so that I can be more like You today and more what my loved ones need in me.

Your love, O LORD, reaches to the heavens, your faithfulness to the skies. Your righteousness is like the mighty mountains, your justice like the great deep. O LORD, you preserve both man and beast. How priceless is your unfailing love!
Psalm 36:5–7a

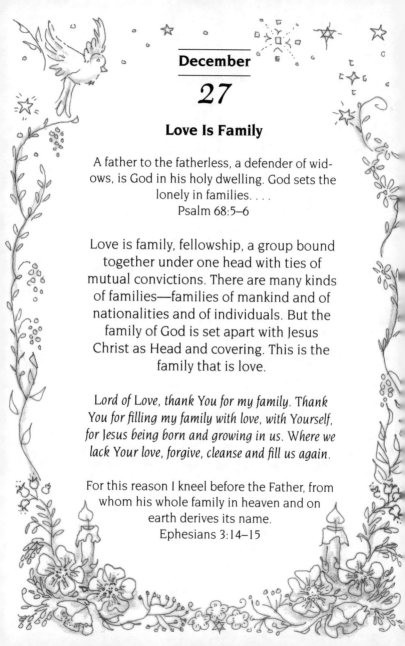

December

27

Love Is Family

A father to the fatherless, a defender of widows, is God in his holy dwelling. God sets the lonely in families. . . .
Psalm 68:5–6

Love is family, fellowship, a group bound together under one head with ties of mutual convictions. There are many kinds of families—families of mankind and of nationalities and of individuals. But the family of God is set apart with Jesus Christ as Head and covering. This is the family that is love.

Lord of Love, thank You for my family. Thank You for filling my family with love, with Yourself, for Jesus being born and growing in us. Where we lack Your love, forgive, cleanse and fill us again.

For this reason I kneel before the Father, from whom his whole family in heaven and on earth derives its name.
Ephesians 3:14–15

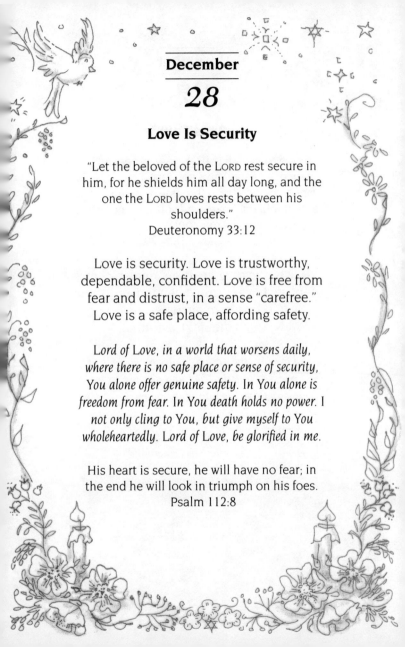

December

28

Love Is Security

"Let the beloved of the LORD rest secure in him, for he shields him all day long, and the one the LORD loves rests between his shoulders."
Deuteronomy 33:12

Love is security. Love is trustworthy, dependable, confident. Love is free from fear and distrust, in a sense "carefree." Love is a safe place, affording safety.

Lord of Love, in a world that worsens daily, where there is no safe place or sense of security, You alone offer genuine safety. In You alone is freedom from fear. In You death holds no power. I not only cling to You, but give myself to You wholeheartedly. Lord of Love, be glorified in me.

His heart is secure, he will have no fear; in the end he will look in triumph on his foes.
Psalm 112:8

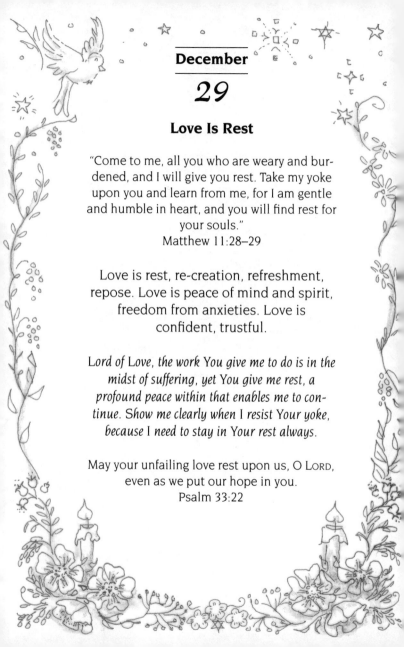

December

29

Love Is Rest

"Come to me, all you who are weary and burdened, and I will give you rest. Take my yoke upon you and learn from me, for I am gentle and humble in heart, and you will find rest for your souls."
Matthew 11:28–29

Love is rest, re-creation, refreshment, repose. Love is peace of mind and spirit, freedom from anxieties. Love is confident, trustful.

Lord of Love, the work You give me to do is in the midst of suffering, yet You give me rest, a profound peace within that enables me to continue. Show me clearly when I resist Your yoke, because I need to stay in Your rest always.

May your unfailing love rest upon us, O LORD, even as we put our hope in you.
Psalm 33:22

Love Is Content

Keep your lives free from the love of money
and be content with what you have, because
God has said, "Never will I leave you; never
will I forsake you."
Hebrews 13:5

Love is content, satisfied, free from worry
and cares.

*Lord of Love, You have given me so much. You
have filled me with holy longings and wrestlings,
hungers that can be satisfied only in You. Fill me
with praise. Strain away my desire for material
things; make me a good steward of what You
have given. Content me with Your love.*

I know what it is to be in need, and I know
what it is to have plenty. I have learned the
secret of being content in any and every situation, whether well fed or hungry, whether
living in plenty or in want.
Philippians 4:12

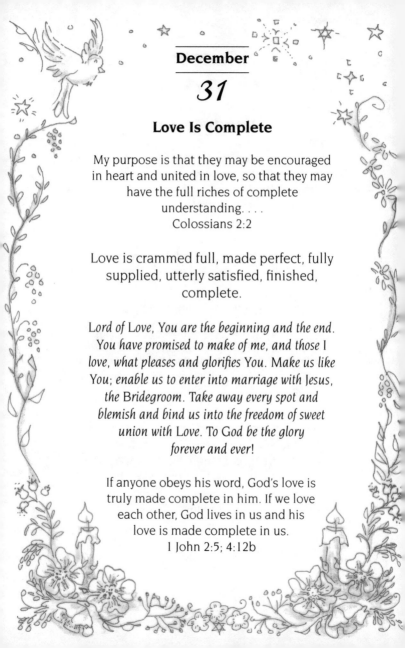

December

31

Love Is Complete

My purpose is that they may be encouraged
in heart and united in love, so that they may
have the full riches of complete
understanding. . . .
Colossians 2:2

Love is crammed full, made perfect, fully
supplied, utterly satisfied, finished,
complete.

*Lord of Love, You are the beginning and the end.
You have promised to make of me, and those I
love, what pleases and glorifies You. Make us like
You; enable us to enter into marriage with Jesus,
the Bridegroom. Take away every spot and
blemish and bind us into the freedom of sweet
union with Love. To God be the glory
forever and ever!*

If anyone obeys his word, God's love is
truly made complete in him. If we love
each other, God lives in us and his
love is made complete in us.
1 John 2:5; 4:12b

Index

Love Is . . .

400

401

402